Joe Celko's
Data, Measurements and Standards in SQL

The Morgan Kaufmann Series in Data Management Systems (Selected Titles)

Joe Celko's Data, Measurements and Standards in SQL
Joe Celko

Information Modeling and Relational Databases, 2nd Edition
Terry Halpin, Tony Morgan

Joe Celko's Thinking in Sets
Joe Celko

Business Metadata
Bill Inmon, Bonnie O'Neil, Lowell Fryman

Unleashing Web 2.0
Gottfried Vossen, Stephan Hagemann

Enterprise Knowledge Management
David Loshin

Business Process Change, 2nd Edition
Paul Harmon

IT Manager's Handbook, 2nd Edition
Bill Holtsnider & Brian Jaffe

Joe Celko's Puzzles and Answers, 2nd Edition
Joe Celko

Making Shoes for the Cobbler's Children
Charles Betz

Joe Celko's Analytics and OLAP in SQL
Joe Celko

Data Preparation for Data Mining Using SAS
Mamdouh Refaat

Querying XML: XQuery, XPath, and SQL/XML in Context
Jim Melton and Stephen Buxton

Data Mining: Concepts and Techniques, 2nd Edition
Jiawei Han and Micheline Kamber

Database Modeling and Design: Logical Design, 4th Edition
Toby J, Teorey, Sam S. Lightstone, Thomas P. Nadeau

Foundations of Multidimensional and Metric Data Structures
Hanan Samet

Joe Celko's SQL for Smarties: Advanced SQL Programming, 3rd Edition
Joe Celko

Moving Objects Databases
Ralf Hartmut Güting and Markus Schneider

Joe Celko's SQL Programming Style
Joe Celko

Data Mining, Second Edition: Concepts and Techniques
Ian Witten and Eibe Frank

Fuzzy Modeling and Genetic Algorithms for Data Mining and Exploration
Earl Cox

Data Modeling Essentials, 3rd Edition
Graeme C. Simsion and Graham C. Witt

Location-Based Services
Jochen Schiller and Agnès Voisard

Database Modeling with Microsoft® Visio for Enterprise Architects
Terry Halpin, Ken Evans, Patrick Hallock, Bill Maclean

Designing Data-Intensive Web Applications
Stephano Ceri, Piero Fraternali, Aldo Bongio, Marco Brambilla, Sara Comai, Maristella Matera

Mining the Web: Discovering Knowledge from Hypertext Data
Soumen Chakrabarti

Advanced SQL: 1999—Understanding Object-Relational and Other Advanced Features
Jim Melton

Database Tuning: Principles, Experiments, and Troubleshooting Techniques
Dennis Shasha, Philippe Bonnet

SQL:1999—Understanding Relational Language Components
Jim Melton, Alan R. Simon

Information Visualization in Data Mining and Knowledge Discovery
Edited by Usama Fayyad, Georges G. Grinstein, Andreas Wierse

Transactional Information Systems
Gerhard Weikum and Gottfried Vossen

Spatial Databases
Philippe Rigaux, Michel Scholl, and Agnes Voisard

Managing Reference Data in Enterprise Database
Malcolm Chisholm

Understanding SQL and Java Together
Jim Melton and Andrew Eisenberg

Database: Principles, Programming, and Performance, 2nd Edition
Patrick and Elizabeth O'Neil

The Object Data Standar
Edited by R. G. G. Cattell, Douglas Barry

Data on the Web: From Relations to Semistructured Data and XML
Serge Abiteboul, Peter Buneman, Dan Suciu

Data Mining: Practical Machine Learning Tools and Techniques with Java Implementations
Ian Witten, Eibe Frank

Joe Celko's Data and Databases: Concepts in Practice
Joe Celko

Developing Time-Oriented Database Applications in SQL
Richard T. Snodgrass

Web Farming for the Data Warehouse
Richard D. Hackathorn

Management of Heterogeneous and Autonomous Database Systems
Edited by Ahmed Elmagarmid, Marek Rusinkiewicz, Amit Sheth

Object-Relational DBMSs: 2nd Edition
Michael Stonebraker and Paul Brown,with Dorothy Moore

Universal Database Management: A Guide to Object/Relational Technology
Cynthia Maro Saracco

Readings in Database Systems, 3rd Edition
Edited by Michael Stonebraker, Joseph M. Hellerstein

Understanding SQL's Stored Procedures: A Complete Guide to SQL/PSM
Jim Melton

Principles of Multimedia Database Systems
V. S. Subrahmanian

Principles of Database Query Processing for Advanced Applications
Clement T. Yu, Weiyi Meng

Advanced Database Systems
Carlo Zaniolo, Stefano Ceri, Christos Faloutsos, Richard T. Snodgrass, V. S. Subrahmanian, Roberto Zicari

Principles of Transaction Processing, 2nd Edition
Philip A. Bernstein, Eric Newcomer

Using the New DB2: IBMs Object-Relational Database System
Don Chamberlin

Distributed Algorithms
Nancy A. Lynch

Active Database Systems: Triggers and Rules For Advanced Database Processing
Edited by Jennifer Widom, Stefano Ceri

Migrating Legacy Systems: Gateways, Interfaces, & the Incremental Approach
Michael L. Brodie, Michael Stonebraker

Atomic Transactions
Nancy Lynch, Michael Merritt, William Weihl, Alan Fekete

Query Processing for Advanced Database Systems
Edited by Johann Christoph Freytag, David Maier, Gottfried Vossen

Transaction Processing
Jim Gray, Andreas Reuter

Database Transaction Models for Advanced Applications
Edited by Ahmed K. Elmagarmid

A Guide to Developing Client/Server SQL Applications
Setrag Khoshafian, Arvola Chan, Anna Wong, Harry K. T. Wong

Joe Celko's
Data, Measurements and Standards in SQL

Joe Celko

AMSTERDAM • BOSTON • HEIDELBERG • LONDON
NEW YORK • OXFORD • PARIS • SAN DIEGO
SAN FRANCISCO • SINGAPORE • SYDNEY • TOKYO

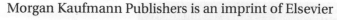

ELSEVIER

Morgan Kaufmann Publishers is an imprint of Elsevier

Morgan Kaufmann Publishers is an imprint of Elsevier.
30 Corporate Drive, Suite 400, Burlington, MA 01803, USA
This book is printed on acid-free paper.

Library of Congress Cataloging-in-Publication Data
Celko, Joe.
    Joe Celko's data, measurements, and standards in SQL/Joe Celko.
        p. cm.—(The Morgan Kaufmann series in data management systems)
    ISBN 978-0-12-374722-8
  1. SQL (Computer program language) 2. Database management. I. Title. II. Title: Data, measurements, and standards in SQL.

    QA76.73.S67C4324   2010
    005.74—dc22

                                                            2009030587

British Library Cataloguing-in-Publication Data
A catalogue record for this book is available from the British Library.

Printed in the United States of America

09 10 11 12 13 14 15 16   5 4 3 2 1

Contents

Introduction

As I sit here typing this introduction, I am looking at a copy of *The North American Arithmetic, Part Third, for Advanced Scholars,* by Frederick Emerson. It was written in 1834.

It has chapters on the money, weights, and measures in use in Europe and America at that time. The English still had pence, shillings, and farthings. The countries and city-states on the continent had a local currency instead of a Euro. Troy, Avoirdupois, and Apothecary weights were mentioned as standards in Europe.

But after that, there were English ells, French ells, and Flemish ells for measuring cloth—all of them different. There were separate liquid measures for wine and beer. Cities had local measures, so "100 lbs" in Trieste was 123.6 pounds Avoirdupois and 74.77 pounds Avoirdupois in Rome. The good news was that the new metric system in France seemed to be catching on and becoming more popular. How, do you suppose?

All of these differences were handled by Gaugers in each city. These were usually government tax employees who kept a set of dip sticks (or gauges) to measure liquids in barrels, weights for balance scales, baskets for dry goods, and so forth. The term survives today in the oil refinery business for people who test oil in storage tanks. They also calibrated the local merchant's tools to assure fair trade within their jurisdiction. The seal cast on the front of a wine carafe is a leftover of a Gauger's official seal, which would have been stamped into a piece of lead.

Remember that all of this was a long time before computers and electronic data exchange. Think about the manual records needed. You can imagine what effect this had on commerce, since it made accurate data almost impossible to keep and exchange.

The bad news is that this "local measurement" mentality has not died in the 21st century. Ignorance of international and industry standards and a "cowboy coder" mind-set led programmers to code first and think never. Instead of looking for an ISO or industry-specific standard for something, the "cowboy coder" gallops in and writes a list or uses a proprietary auto-numbering feature in his current SQL product to give him an encoding for an attribute.

Programmers still spend time and effort avoiding the use of common units of measure and industry standards. It can actually become quite silly.

In a posting on the Microsoft SQL Server Programming newsgroup, an MVP ("Most Valuable Programmer"—an award given by Microsoft in their product categories) posted a complaint that passing temporal data that will work across regional settings doesn't work in the ANSI Standard! His example was two values on a machine configured to Microsoft's U.K. formats instead of to ISO standards, thus:

```
CAST('2007-04-01' AS DATETIME) - ISO/ANSI SQL format
versus
CAST('2007-04-01T00:00:00' AS DATETIME) - set to UK format
```

To quote: "Here in the UK in cloudy Harpenden the default connection settings give these results …":

```
'2007-01-04 00:00:00.000'
versus
'2007-04-01 00:00:00.000'
```

The use of a T is an alternative ANSI standard, which makes a timestamp into a single unbroken string (this can be useful in some systems). But the "T" is not part of SQL's subset of the ISO-8601 standard (this might be changed by the time you read this book). But the ordering of year-month-day is in all ISO-8601 standards—and it makes sense for sorting!

I have run into this problem with a system that collected data from the United States and the United Kingdom. You would be surprised how long you can screw up the database before you catch the error.

The poster ranted (imagine strong British accent): "At what point will this guy [Celko] stop telling us duff information and bashing people for not following best practice and standards when he himself knows there's a problem yet refuses to yield to the correct best practice?"

It was very hard to tell him that Harpenden, UK, is not the center of the world, whether it is cloudy or not! Even Greenwich Time is no longer the standard. The best practices are to store time in UTC and use the TIMEZONE options in SQL to get local lawful time in the applications. It is all there in the standards.

COMMON UNITS EVOLVE TO STANDARDS

There is a common pattern in moving to standards, which is easy to see in physical goods. Since beer is one of my favorite physical goods, consider this history.

Units of measurement become standardized and replace local measurements.
But we do not have standard sizes yet. For example, after a few hundred

years, we get rid of pints, firkins, and a host of local units with strange names to use liters for our beer. But every pub still has a different size glass.

Enterprises working in the same area agree on standard sizes for common use. For example, the pubs all get together in one town and agree that a glass of beer is 0.50 liters; in other town, they decide that a "fair pour" as it is called in the bar trade, should be 0.75 liters (nice place to visit).

National standards emerge, usually by law based on the need for taxation. Continuing my example, the government decided to pass a beer tax based on the glass, so we need a National Fair Pour Standard.

International standards emerge, usually by agreement based on the need for trade and data exchange.

Notice that the glassmaker has a strong influence with his offerings to the bar trade. One trade affects another. Let me give a specific example. Before the 1800s, machine screws were made by individual machine shops in the United States. The common units of measure were inches for the physical dimensions such as length, pitch, and diameter and degrees for the angle of the thread. But that did not mean that the screws were interchangeable or even used the same names for various sizes. It was very much a cottage industry.

Some national standards did eventually arise within industries inside the United States, but it was not until World War II that American, Canadian, and British manufacturers decided to standardize their inch-based sizes for the war effort. The Unified Thread Standard was adopted by the Screw Thread Standardization Committees of Canada, the United Kingdom, and the United States on November 18, 1949, in Washington, DC, with the hope that they would be adopted universally.

It did not work out that way. Europe and much of the rest of the world turned to the ISO metric screw thread system. Today, globalization has forced the United Kingdom and the United States to use this same system. The best example is that the ISO metric screw thread is now the standard for the automotive industry and that very few parts use any inch-based sizes, regardless of where they are made. The United States used to completely dominate the auto industry but lost out for various reasons. A major factor is that ISO machinery is engineered to the millimeter while the U.S. auto industry was working at 1/32 of an inch. An "ISO automobile" is simply more precise and accurate than an "Imperial automobile" because of the measurements used. This was not a problem with the Model T, but it is a disaster with a modern vehicle.

WHAT DOES THIS HAVE TO DO WITH DATABASES?

Today, the database designer is finding himself in the position of the Gauger from the Middle Ages and Renaissance, only his role is greatly expanded.

We have to share and move data, rather than physical goods, from one enterprise to another accurately. The enterprise is not in the next village but anywhere on Earth. We all have to "speak a common language" with the rest of the world.

We still deal with a lot of physical measurements, but we don't use dip sticks to convert "London firkins" to "Harpenden fuddles" anymore. We need a bit more math and have rules about accuracy and computations.

The good news is that we have the Internet, ISO, the EU, ANSI, DIN, JIS, and scores of other organizations that do nothing but help us with standards. These days, many of those standards come with a description of how they are represented in a database. They come with Web sites so that we can download and update our systems for little or nothing. They are easy to find—God bless Google!

And if we don't like them, these same organizations have mechanisms for submitting comments and proposals. It the old days, you had to appeal to the king to become the royal barrel maker, bottle blower, or whatever.

The purpose of this book is to turn a new database designer in a 21st-century Gauger. He is going to need some new skills, in particular:

Knowledge of standards
How to migrate as standards evolve
How to create and use a data dictionary
How to maintain data integrity
How to maintain data quality

In *MAD* magazine #33, Donald E. Knuth wrote a parody of the metric system while in high school, long before he became one of the greatest computer scientists of all time. The title was "Potrzebie System of Weights and Measures," and it was illustrated by Wally Wood (see next page for the image).

Potrzebie is a Polish noun ("potrzeba" translates as "a need") that *MAD* magazine used as a nonsense word in their articles and cartoons.

While Dr. Knuth was being funny, the number of database designers who invent elaborate measurement and encoding schemes when standards exist is not so funny.

THE POTRZEBIE SYSTEM
OF WEIGHTS AND MEASURES

THE POTRZEBIE SYSTEM

This new system of measuring, which is destined to become the measuring system of the future, has decided improvements over the other systems now in use. It is based upon measurements taken 6-9-12 at the Physics Lab. of Milwaukee Lutheran High School, in Milwaukee, Wis., when the thickness of MAD Magazine #26 was determined to be 2.26334851-7438173216473 mm. This length is the basis for the entire system, and is called one potrzebie of length.

The Potrzebie has also been standardized at 3515.-3502 wave lengths of the red line in the spectrum of cadmium. A partial table of the Potrzebie System, the measuring system of the future, is given below .

LENGTH

1 potrzebie = thickness of MAD #26
.000001 p = 1 farshimmelt potrzebie (fp)
1000 fp = 1 millipotrzebie (mp)
10 mp = 1 centipotrzebie (cp)
10 cp = 1 decipotrzebie (dp)

10 dp = 1 potrzebie (p)
10 p = 1 dekapotrzebie (Dp)
10 Dp = 1 hectopotrzebie (Hp)
10 Hp = 1 kilopotrzebie (Kp)
1000 Kp = 1 furshlugginer potrzebie (Fp)

VOLUME

1 cubic dekapotrzebie = 1 ngogn (n)
.000001 n = 1 farshimmelt ngogn (fn)
1000 fn = 1 millingogn (mn)
10 mn = 1 centingogn (cn)
10 cn = 1 decingogn (dn)

10 dn = 1 ngogn (n)
10 n = 1 dekangogn (Dn)
10 Dn = 1 hectongogn (Hn)
10 Hn — 1 kilongogn (Kn)
1000 Kn = 1 furshlugginer ngogn (Fn)

MASS

1 ngogn of halavah* = 1 blintz (b)
.000001 b = 1 farshimmelt blintz (b)
1000 fb = 1 milliblintz (mb)
10 mb = 1 centiblintz (c)
10 cb = 1 deciblintz (db)

10 db = 1 blintz (b)
10 b = 1 dekablintz (Db)
10 Db = 1 hectoblintz (Hb)
10 Hb = 1 kiloblintz (Kb)
1000 Kb = 1 furshlugginer blintz (Fb)

*Halavah is a form of pie, and it has a specific gravity of 3.1416 and a specific heat of .31416.

PICTURES BY WALLACE WOOD

36

Let's get started. The first part of this book is the preliminaries and basics of measurements, data, and standards. The second part is the particulars for standards that should be useful for a working SQL programmer.

Please send any corrections, additions, suggestions, improvements, or alternative solutions to me or to the publisher.

Morgan Kaufmann Publishers
30 Corporate Dr #400
Burlington, MA 01803

History, Standards, and Designing Data

The first of this book discusses the principles of designing data encoding schemes and some of the history of standardization. This second part will give examples of actual standards used in a variety of industries.

In the first six chapters, I look at the foundations from the view point of a database designer who needs some understanding of the how and why.

I find it odd that database designers are very physical about their data and do not work with many abstractions. They were never taught the theory of scales and measurements. They have only a minimal knowledge of validation, verification, and risk of error as a part of the data.

Check digit algorithms are taught as single "programming tricks" in undergraduate computer science classes rather than a mathematical discipline.

To the best of my knowledge, I am the only person who teaches Data Encoding Schemes in an orderly fashion.

The failure of cowboy coders to use standards leads to problems. The homegrown encoding schemes have to be maintained internally. A standard is maintained for you. It is usually maintained by an organization devoted to that standard and with subject area experts who you could not hire.

The days of isolated databases are long gone. You can exchange data with other organizations or buy it from companies when it is standardized. Would you rather buy census data on magnetic tapes or conduct the census yourself?

You can read data and understand it because you know the units of measure.

Scales and Measurements

"In physical science the first essential step in the direction of learning any subject is to find principles of numerical reckoning and practicable methods for measuring some quality connected with it. I often say that when you can measure what you are speaking about, and express it in numbers, you know something about it; but when you cannot measure it, when you cannot express it in numbers, your knowledge is of a meager and unsatisfactory kind; it may be the beginning of knowledge, but you have scarcely in your thoughts advanced to the state of Science, whatever the matter may be."

PLA, Vol. 1, Electrical Units of Measurement, 1883-05-03

Before you can put data into a database, you actually need to think about how it will be represented and manipulated. Most programmers have never heard of measurement theory or thought about the best way to represent their data. They either use whatever was there before or invent their own schemes on the fly. Most of the time, the data is put into the database in the units in which it was collected without regard to even a quick validation. It is assumed the input is in an appropriate unit, with appropriate scale and precision. In short, application programmers and users are perfect. This tendency to believe the computer, no matter how absurd the data, is called the "Garbage In, *Gospel* out" principle in IT folklore.

This unwillingness to do validation and verification is probably the major reason for the lack of data quality.

1.1. MEASUREMENT THEORY

"Measure all that is measurable and attempt to make measurable that which is not yet so."

—Galileo (1564–1642)

Measurement theory is a branch of applied mathematics that is useful in data analysis and database design. Measurements are not the same as the attribute being measured. Measurement is not just assigning numbers to things or their attributes so much as it is finding a property in things that can be expressed in numbers or other computable symbols. This structure is the scale used to take the measurement; the numbers or symbols represent units of measure.

Strange as it might seem, measurement theory came from psychology, not mathematics, statistics, or computer science. S. S. Stevens originated the idea of levels of measurement and classification of scales in 1946 for psychology testing. This is more recent than you would have thought. Scales are classified into types by the properties they do or do not have. The properties with which we are concerned are the following.

1. There is a natural origin point on the scale. This is sometimes called a zero, but it does not literally have to be a numeric zero. For example, if the measurement is the distance between objects, the natural zero is zero meters—you cannot get any closer than that. If the measurement is the temperature of objects, the natural zero is absolute zero—nothing can get any colder. However, consider time; it goes from an eternal past into an eternal future, so you cannot find a natural origin for it.

2. Meaningful operations can be performed on the units. It makes sense to add weights together to get a new weight. Adding temperatures has to consider mass. Dates can be subtracted to give a duration in days. However, adding names or shoe sizes together is absurd.

3. There is a natural ordering to the units. It makes sense to speak about events occurring before or after one another in time or a physical object being heavier, longer, or hotter than another object.

But the alphabetical order imposed on a list of names is arbitrary, not natural—a foreign language, with different names for the same objects, would impose another alphabetical ordering. And that assumes the other language even had an alphabet for an ordering; Chinese, for example, does not.

4. There is a natural metric function on the units. A metric function has nothing to do with the "metric system" of measurements, which is more properly called SI, for "Systemé International d'units" in French. Metric functions have the following three properties:

   a. The metric between an object and itself is the natural origin of the scale. We can write this in a notation as M(a, a) = 0.

   b. The order of the objects in the metric function does not matter. Again in the semimathematical notation, M(a, b) = M(b, a).

   c. There is a natural additive function that obeys the rule that M(a, b) + M(b, c) >= M(a, c), which is also known as the triangular inequality.

This notation is meant to be more general than just arithmetic. The "zero" in the first property is the origin of the scale, not just a numeric zero. The third property, defined with a "plus" and a "greater than or equal" sign, is a symbolic way of expressing general ordering relationships. The "greater than or equal" sign refers to a natural ordering on the attribute being measured. The "plus" sign refers to a meaningful operation in regard to that ordering, not just arithmetic addition.

The special case of the third property, where the "greater than or equal to" is always "greater than," is very desirable to people because it means that they can use numbers for units and do simple arithmetic with the scales. This is called a strong metric property. For example, human perceptions of sound and light intensity follow a cube root law—that is, if you double the intensity of light, the perception of the intensity increases by only 20% (Stevens 1957). The actual formula is "Physical intensity to the 0.3 power equals perceived intensity" in English. Knowing this, designers of stereo equipment use controls that work on a logarithmic scale internally but that show evenly spaced marks on the control panel of the amplifier.

It is possible to have a scale that has any combination of the metric properties. For example, instead of measuring the distance between two places in meters, you can measure it in units of effort. This is the old Chinese system, which had uphill and downhill units of distance, so you could estimate the time required to make a journey on foot.

Does this system of distances have the property that $M(a, a) = 0$? Yes; it takes no effort to get to where you are already located. Does it have the property that $M(a, b) = M(b, a)$? No; it takes less effort to go downhill than to go uphill. Does it have the property that $M(a, b) + M(b, c) >= M(a, c)$? Yes with the direction considered; the amount of effort needed to go directly to a place will always be less than the effort of making another stop along the way.

As you can see, these properties can be more intuitive than mathematical. Obviously, we like the more mathematical side of this model because it fits into a database, but you have to be aware of the intuitive side.

1.1.1. Range, Granularity, and Your Instruments

"The only man who behaves sensibly is my tailor; he takes my measurements anew every time he sees me, while all the rest go on with their old measurements and expect me to fit them."

—George Bernard Shaw

Range and granularity are properties of the way the measurements are made. Since we have to store data in a database within certain limits, they are very important to a database designer. The type of scales is unrelated to whether you use discrete or continuous variables. While measurements in a database are always discrete due to finite precision, attributes can be conceptually either discrete or continuous regardless of measurement level. Temperature is usually regarded as a continuous attribute, so temperature

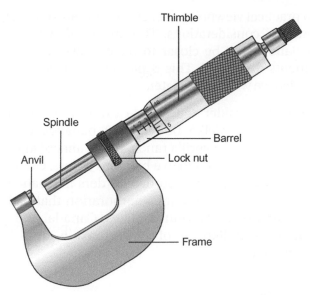

■ **FIGURE 1-1:** Micrometer (http://www.design-technology.org/micrometer.jpg).

measurement to the nearest degree Celsius is a ratio-level measurement of a continuous attribute.

However, quantum mechanics holds that the universe is fundamentally discrete, so temperature may actually be a discrete attribute. In ordinal scales for continuous attributes, ties are impossible (or have probability zero). In ordinal scales for discrete attributes, ties are possible. Nominal scales usually apply to discrete attributes. Nominal scales for continuous attributes can be modeled but are rarely used.

Aside from these philosophical considerations, there is the practical aspect of the instrument used for the measurement. A radio telescope, surveyor's transit, meter stick, and a micrometer are tools that measure distance. Nobody would claim that they are interchangeable. I can use a measuring tape to fit furniture in my house but not to make a mechanical wristwatch or to measure the distance to the moon.

From a purely scientific viewpoint, measurements should be reduced to the least precise instrument's readings. This means that you can be certain that the final results of calculations can be justified.

From a practical viewpoint, measurements are often adjusted by statistical considerations. This means that final results of calculations will be closer to reality—assuming that the adjustments were valid. This is particularly true for missing data, which we will discuss later.

But for now consider the simple example of a database showing that Joe Celko bought 500 bananas this week. Unless I just started a gorilla ranch, this is absurd and probably ought to be adjusted to five bananas or less. On the other hand, if the Dairy Queen Company orders five bananas this week, this is absurd. They are a corporation that had about 6000 restaurants in the United States, Canada, and 20 foreign countries in 2007, all of which make a lot of banana splits every day.

1.1.2. Range

A scale also has other properties that are of interest to someone building a database. First, scales have a range—what are the highest and lowest values that can appear on the scale? It is possible to have a finite or an infinite limit on either the lower or the upper bound. Overflow and underflow errors are the result of range violations inside the database hardware.

Database designers do not have infinite storage, so we have to pick a subrange to use in the database when we have no upper or lower bound. For example, very few computer calendar routines will handle geological time periods. But then very few companies have bills that have been outstanding for that long, either, so we do not mind a range of less than 100 years. Oops! There are contracts and leases that are good for decades, centuries, or eternity. The range depends on the situation.

1.1.3. Granularity, Accuracy, and Precision

Look at a ruler and a micrometer. They both measure length, using the same scale, but there is a difference. A micrometer is more precise because it has a finer granularity of units. Granularity is a static property of the scale itself—how many notches there are on your ruler. In Europe, all industrial drawings are done in millimeters; the United States has been most commonly using 1/32 of an inch. Granularity is also related to tolerance, which we will discuss later.

Accuracy is how close the measurement comes to the actual value. Precision is a measure of how repeatable a measurement is. The instrument is what gives you the measurement.

Both depend on granularity, but they are not the same things. Human nature says that a number impresses according to the square of the number of decimal places. Hence, some people will use a computer system to express things to as many decimal places as possible, even when it makes no sense. For example, civil engineering in the United States uses decimal feet for road design. Nobody can build a road any more precisely than that, but you will see civil engineering students turning in work that is expressed in 1/1000 of a foot. You don't use a micrometer to pour asphalt!

A database often does not give the user a choice of precision for many calculations. In fact, the SQL standards leave the number of decimal places in the results of many arithmetic operations to be defined by the SQL implementation. If the end user want more or fewer places than the defaults, they have to do explicit casting and rounding. Even then, there can be hardware limitations.

The ideas are easier to explain with rifle targets, which are scales to measure the ability of a shooter to put bullets in the center of a target. The rifle is the instrument, with the target as the output display. A bigger target has a wider range than a smaller target. A target with more rings has a higher granularity. If my projectile is a .22 caliber bullet for a competition match target, the target will be small and have closer rings. My instrument will be a highly accurate rifle designed for Olympic-style target shooting.

If my projectile is a large caliber bullet for military combat, the target will be large, with wider rings. My instrument will be a mass-produced military rifle.

At the extreme, if I am firing artillery shells, getting within 10 meters of the center of the target has the same effect as hitting it dead center. My instrument is a rather large piece of field artillery.

Once you start shooting, a group of shots that are closer together is more precise because the shots were more repeatable. A shot group that is closer to the center is more accurate because the shots were closer to the goal. Notice that precision and accuracy are not the same thing! If I have a good gun whose sights are off, I can get a very tight cluster that is not near the bull's eye. If I have a poorly made gun whose sights are good, I can get a very wide cluster that is centered on the bull's eye.

1.2. DEFINING A MEASUREMENT

It is important to have a definition of a unit of measure that can be tested in some way. There are, generally speaking, two ways of testing a unit. We can have a trusted *process* to calibrate the instrument or we can have a single trusted *standard* available.

A simple example of a trusted process is measuring how hot a wok is by flicking droplets of water on the surface. When the water forms beads that skim on the surface, then the wok is ready for peanut cooking oil. If the wok is too cold, the water makes a puddle at the center and then boils. If the wok is too hot, the water vaporizes without making beads and will burn the oil. This method is surprisingly accurate.

In the database world, the most common test is simply to ask the source of the data for the value. Automobiles have a VIN number physically etched into the glass and metal of the vehicle. Most people are very sure about their gender. And so forth.

A simple example of a trusted source is the use of any standardized unit of measure. For most common units of measure, we are willing to assume that we will not find serious errors in secondary sources. That is, very few people go to NIST (National Institute for Science and Technology, née National Bureau of Standards) laboratories to calibrate their rulers and weights. We are willing to believe that the rulers and scales we buy commercially are accurate enough and have passed a NIST test for commercial use.

However, today we sometimes do have an available single trusted source for some encodings. It is easy to log on to the Web site of almost every national postal service on Earth and get their postal codes and abbreviations. We assume that the values in another database maintained by the source are accurate because that source is the creator of the data.

1.3. TOLERANCE

Tolerance is usually thought to be a manufacturing and engineering term. We speak of parts being manufactured to a certain tolerance, such as a part being made to "±0.01 mm" tolerance. But tolerance is a more general concept.

Tolerance is a measure of how much error or inaccuracy can we stand in a measurement. For example, ask for someone's credit score from the three major U.S. credit bureaus (Experian, Equifax, and TransUnion). Each company uses a different scale—Equifax's ScorePower, Experian's PLUS score, and TransUnion's credit score—but they also sell the VantageScore credit score. This measurement went into effect in 2006 and assigns a letter grade based on a number from a formula:

A: 901–990
B: 801–900
C: 701–800
D: 601–700
F: 501–600

All three bureaus use the same formula to calculate the VantageScore, however, there are still discrepancies between the VantageScores. This is a result of the different input data that the three bureaus use.

You would expect the scores to be within a certain tolerance of each other for the same person—that is, that they would all report the same letter grade in the majority of cases.

There would be a certain statistical error on the borderlines of the letter grades.

When one credit bureau has a score greatly different from the other two, you tend to think that bureau either knows something the others don't know, or it lacks information the other two have (i.e., Joe Celko just won the lottery or Joe Celko is going to prison).

If all three scores are out of tolerance and have been repeatedly out of tolerance over time, then there is a problem. Either we have a serious data quality problem or criminal activity involving identity theft.

1.3.1. Scale Conversion Errors

The VantageScore was a result of trying to come up with a usable, common scale instead of having three different formulas with different results. Conversions from one credit bureau's score to another's were full of errors. While credit bureaus claimed to measure the same attribute, they disagreed on the basic factors and calculations. Is a low-debt ratio more important than years of constant employment? Is home ownership more important than savings? Even if you could precisely weigh all these factors, would the score still hold in a different economy?

Even precise physical measurements on different scales have conversion errors. We have had "spacecraft" failures caused by metric and imperial unit conversion problems. My favorite was the 2004 incident at Tokyo Disneyland's Space Mountain amusement ride. An axle broke on a "spacecraft" (roller-coaster car) and it derailed, without injury to anyone. The cause was determined to be a part being the wrong size due to a conversion of the master plans in 1995 from imperial units to SI units. In 2002, new axles were mistakenly ordered using the pre-1995 imperial specifications instead of the current SI specifications. Apparently size does matter, even if it's only a 0.86 mm difference.

1.4. VALIDATION

Validation means that the measurement is a valid measurement on its scale. It does not mean that the *value* is correct but that the *syntax* is good. For database designers, this means that we need to have a constraint that makes sure we have a valid scalar value in all the columns. How we do this in SQL is a whole section by itself.

1.5. VERIFICATION

If a column is not valid, then we don't have to bother with verification. You do not need to bother looking for any event to happen on "2009-02-31," because that date does not exist. Verification assumes that the value is syntactically valid but might not be the actual value or a possible value.

We prefer a trusted external source to verify the data. Many times, this source is a governmental agency with some legal power, but not always. Industry groups and certain non-profits have the same function without full legal power. Tradition can also play a part.

The least preferred, but often used, verification is individual judgment. Meat inspection and grading is done by professionals who have a lot of discretion in the values they assign, but they have the final decision.

This has been the case for millennia. You can find a reference to "honest weights and measures" in a cuneiform tablet in the Istanbul Museum (about 300 years before the Code of Hammurabi) in 2050 BCE. The rules were enforced by King Ur-Nammu of Sumeria at that time. Before that, the standardized Egyptian cubit used to build Khufu's pyramid goes back to 2750 BCE. It was more accurate than many of the measurements that were used in medieval Europe. The usual penalty for violations was death or torture, which is a little hard to put into a CHECK() constraint.

1.5.1. Erroneous Values

An erroneous value is valid and possible, but it does not reflect the truth. Do not attribute this problem to malice or criminal intent. For example, I might lie about my weight on a medical form because of vanity or ignorance. Or my bathroom scale might be wrong and I reported that wrong data in good faith. This is the hardest error to find, since the trusted source (bathroom scale) might not be able to tell you the current situation (busted force transducer).

1.5.2. Phony Values

A phony value is valid in its syntax but does not reflect the truth. For example, I can create a VIN for an automobile that was not actually manufactured or use a VIN from an automobile that has been destroyed. Again, do not attribute this problem to malice or criminal intent. In the publishing industry, the ISBN for a book is often issued before the book is actually in production or even written, in the case of series books. If the publisher cancels the book or goes out of business altogether, then that ISBN is clearly not used. But you might find the ISBN listed in the publisher's advance order catalog.

1.5.3. Degree of Trust versus Risk of Error

Charles Babbage, the father of the modern computer, said that the cost of data verification is inseparable from the cost of collecting it. Trust comes in degrees and it comes at some cost. Some verification sources are more trustworthy than others and they will *generally* cost more. The scale that measures the degree of trust can be precise or a bit vague. A precise source is often defined by law or by a single authority (e.g., the latest catalog determines the part numbers and product specifications for all current orders from Company X).

When I go to an ATM, the machine assumes that if I can input the four-digit PIN code within three attempts, I should be allowed to use the account. The ATM is providing verification at a certain level of trust.

When I go to the supermarket, they will cash my check if the photograph on my current local driver's license and the name on it match my general appearance (ugly bald white guy) and the name on the check.

For other activities, I require a current driver's license, a current passport, a notarized birth certificate, and perhaps some combination of official documents like that. In short, verification has to come from multiple sources. This gives a much stronger degree of trust than the supermarket uses.

In the prison system, every time inmates are moved around a new "ten card"—the fingerprint card with all ten fingers on it—is made, compared against official records and signed off by separate corrections officers at the origin and destination points of the trip. In a court of law, a DNA test is used to establish the identity of a person. This is the strongest degree of trust we currently have.

The cost we will spend on verification is directly related to the risk we expect an error to cost. The use of DNA is currently reserved for matters of life and death—literally. A DNA test is too slow and costly to be built into an ATM machine, even if people were willing to give a blood sample to such a device every time they made a withdrawal. The risk exposure with an ATM card is the daily withdrawal limit, usually a few hundred dollars in the United States.

When the risk increases, we become willing to pay more to verify data. A practical example of that was the experiment by Kroger grocery stores to use a fingerprint for check cashing in 2001 (http://archive.newsmax.com/archives/articles/2001/3/30/172528.shtml). Biometric Access Corporation tested a point-of-sale finger-scanning device at four Kroger stores in Houston, Texas. The experiment used the device for payroll check cashing, not for actual sales.

As of 2008, there is talk of having a "smart card" or embedded chip with a full medical history and a DNA profile on it for soldiers. The idea is that a field hospital could take the card history and the unconscious soldier, match them, and begin treatments.

Chapter

2

Validation

Validation is the property of a data element to be shown to be syntactically correct by simple inspection. The major methods are:

1. Table look-up
2. Check digits and other mathematical computations
3. Patterns and regular expressions

The application program can perform a relatively simple operation and spot invalid inputs. The back end (the database engine) must also do the same simple calculation on the columns in a database, just in case someone gets data directly into the tables with a tool or other application. While this sounds like a "belt and suspenders (braces, galluses)" approach, you can write the database side code to favor clean data for performance. Even without front end edits in the application programs and other software tools, most input is clean anyway, so the trade-off of a little execution time for the certainty of clean data is worth the extra nanoseconds.

Charles Babbage, the father of the computer, observed in the mid-1800s that an inseparable part of the cost of obtaining data is the cost of verifying its accuracy. The best situation is to exclude bad data on entry so that it is never in the system.

That implies that the data can verify itself in some way at entry time without having to go to the database. Statistics classifies errors as either Type I or Type II. A Type I error rejects a truth and a Type II error accepts a falsehood. In a database, a Type I error would be a failure to get valid data into the schema. This is usually a physical failure of some kind and the hardware tells you your transaction failed.

But a Type II error is harder to detect. Some of these errors do require that the data get to the database to be checked against other internal data ("Mr. Celko, your checking account is overdrawn!") or even checked against external data ("Mr. Celko, there is a warrant for your arrest!").

But most of the time, the Type II error is a keying error that can be detected at input time. F. J. Damerau (1964) reported that four common input errors caused 80% of total spelling errors:

1. A single missing character
2. A single extra character
3. A single erroneous character
4. Pairwise-transposed characters

The single missing, extra, or erroneous character explained 60% to 95% of all errors in his sample of 12,000 errors; pairwise transposes ("ba" for "ab") accounted for 10% to 20% of the total.

The first three categories can be expanded to more than a single character, but the single-character cases are by far the most common. In the last category, pairwise transposes are far more common than jump transposes (transposes of pairs with one or more characters between them, as when "abc" becomes "cba"). This is because we use keyboards for data entry and your fingers can get ahead of each other.

If a human is doing the data entry from verbal input, you might wish to include a special case for phonetic errors, which are language-dependent (e.g., thirty [30] and thirteen [13] sound similar in English). Verhoeff (1969) gave more details in his study, *Error-Detecting Decimal Codes*.

2.1. LOOK-UP TABLES

When you have a limited set of allowed values, you have two options for implementation. You can use a CHECK() constraint or the REFERENCES clause. The CHECK(value IN (,list.))

constraint is best used when the list is stable and short. The REFERENCES clause is best used with the list is long and/or dynamic.

Did you notice that those heuristics were vague? The term "short/long" loosely means that the list will fit into main storage so it can be checked instantly. But the amount of main storage is a physical measurement. What was a lot of storage in 2000 becomes a giveaway video game in 2010.

Likewise, "static" and "dynamic" are relative. For example, the two-letter state abbreviation codes in the United States are stable—no state is likely to leave the Union or to be added. But stock keeping units (SKU) codes might be very dynamic in a fashion-oriented industry ("Purple vinyl miniskirts are ever so last year, darling!").

The advantage of a look-up table accessed via a REFERENCES clause over a CHECK() list is that a look-up table:

1. Can have constraints on it. This means it can have elaborate CHECK() constraints on the columns and reference other tables in the schema in complex ways, include temporal ranges, use VIEWs, and so on.

2. Can be loaded with data from external sources more easily. Every SQL product has an ETL (bulk data loading) tool. New encodings are easily added with an INSERT INTO statement, whereas a CHECK() constraint requires an ALTER statement that will lock the database and require system-level admin privileges.

Changes in the dynamic look-up table have to be monitored. The dynamic look-up table might need a temporal data element (Purple vinyl miniskirts were a valid SKU from "2011-01-01" to "2011-02-01" while the fad lasted).

Another advantage of look-up tables is that they can be multicolumn. This lets you validate combinations of data by using multicolumn FOREIGN KEY constraints. This is easier to show with code than to explain in text:

```
CREATE TABLE Customers
(cust_nbr INTEGER NOT NULL PRIMARY KEY,
 ..
```

```
foo_code INTEGER NOT NULL,
bar_code INTEGER NOT NULL,
CONSTRAINT legal_foo_bar_combo
 FOREIGN KEY (foo, bar)
 REFERENCES ValidFoobars (foo, bar),
 ..);
```

2.1.1. Auxiliary Tables for Noncomputed Data

We do not always know what values we want to add to a look-up table. Very often, we need to do some data mining in our historical data to discover rules we did not know as a formal, computable rule.

If you watch the Food Channel on cable television or if you just like Memphis-style barbeque, you know the name "Corky's" as an advertiser. The chain was started in 1984 in Memphis by Don Pelts and has grown by franchise at a steady rate ever since. They sell a small menu of 25 items by mail order or from their Web site (http://www.corkysbbq.com) and ship the merchandise in special boxes, sometimes using dry ice. Most of the year, their staff can handle the orders. But at Christmastime, they have the problem of success.

Their packing operation consists of two lines. At the start of the line, someone pulls a box of the right size and puts the pick list in it. As it goes down the line, packers put in the items, and when it gets to the end of the line, it is ready for shipment. This is a standard business operation in lots of industries. Their people know what boxes to use for the standard gift packs and can pretty accurately judge any odd-sized orders.

At Christmastime, however, mail-order business is so good that they have to get outside temporary help. The temporary help does not have the experience to judge the box sizes by looking at a pick list. If a box that is too small starts down the line, it will jam up things at some point. The supervisor has to get it off the line and repack the order by hand. If a box that is too large goes down the line, it is a waste of money and creates extra shipping costs.

Mark Tutt (of Mark Solutions, LLC) has been consulting with Corky's for years and set up a new order system for them on a Sybase platform. One of the goals of the new system is to print the pick list and shipping labels with all of the calculations done, including what box size the order requires.

Following the rule that you do not reinvent the wheel, Mr. Tutt went to the newsgroups to find out if anyone had a solution already. The suggestions tended to be along the lines of getting the weights and shapes of the items and using a "3D Tetris" program to figure out the box size and packing.

Programmers seem to love to face every new problem as if nobody has ever done it before and nobody will ever do it again. The "Code first, research later!" mentality is hard to overcome.

The answer was not in complicated 3-D math, but in the past 4 or 5 years of orders in the database. Human beings with years of experience had been packing orders and leaving a record of their work to be mined. Obviously, the standard gift packs are easy to spot. But most of the orders tend to be something that had occurred before, too. Here were the answers, if anyone bothered to dig them out.

First, Mr. Tutt found all of the unique configurations in the orders, how often they occurred, and the boxes used to pack them. If the same configuration had two or more boxes, then you should go with the smaller size. As it turned out, there were about 4995 unique configurations in the custom orders, which covered about 99.5% of the cases.

Next, this table of configurations was put into a stored procedure that did a slightly modified exact relational division to obtain the box size required. In the 0.5% of the orders that were not found, the box size was put into a custom packing job stack for an experienced employee to handle. If new products were added or old ones removed, the table could be regenerated overnight from the most recent data.

2.2. CHECK DIGITS

You can find a discussion of check digits at http://www. academic.marist.edu/mwa/idsn.htm. The basic idea is that by making an encoded value a little longer, you can validate it at input time. You still need to verify (and by implication, validate) data in the database.

2.2.1. Error Detection versus Error Correction

The distinction between error-detecting and error-correcting codes is worth mentioning. The error-detecting code will find that an encoding is wrong, but gives no help in finding the error itself. An error-correcting code will try to repair the problem. Error-correcting schemes for binary numbers play an important part in highly reliable computers but require several extra digits on each computer word to work. If you would like to do research on error-correction codes some of the algorithms are:

- Hamming codes
- Fire codes
- Bose-Chandhuri-Hocquenghem (BCH) codes
- Reed-Solomon (RS) codes
- Goppa codes

On the other hand, error detection can be done with only one extra character, usually a digit, on the end of the encoding.

2.2.2. Check Digit Algorithms

The most common check digit procedures come in a few broad classes. One class takes the individual digits, multiplies them by a constant value (called a weight) for each position, sums the results, divides the sum by another constant, and uses the remainder as the check digit. These are called weighted-sum algorithms.

Another approach is to use functions based on group theory, a branch of abstract algebra; these are called algebraic algorithms. A discussion of group theory is a little too complex to take up here, so I will do a little hand-waving when I get to the mathematics. Finally, you can use look-up tables for check digit functions that cannot be easily calculated.

The look-up tables can be almost anything, including functions that are tuned for the data in a particular application.

2.2.2.1. *Weighted-Sum Algorithms*

Weighted-sum algorithms are probably the most common class of check digit. They have the advantage of being easy to compute by hand, since they require no tables or complex arithmetic, so they were first used in manual systems.

To calculate a weighted-sum check digit:

1. Multiply each of the digits in the encoding by a weight. A weight is a positive integer value.

2. Add the products of the above multiplication to get a sum, s.

3. Take that sum (s) and apply a function to it. The function is usually `MOD(s,n)` where (n is a prime number and n $<=$ 10), but it can be more complicated. An exception in this step is to allow the letter "X" (Roman numeral 10) as the result of a `MOD(s,11)` function. This is a very strong check digit and was used in the old International Standard Book Number (ISBN).

4. The check digit is concatenated to the encoding, usually on the right end of the string. There are a few schemes that place the check digit inside the string.

This is one of the most popular check digit procedures. It is easy to implement in hardware or software. It will detect most of the single-character and pairwise-transpose errors. However, it is not perfect.

Consider the Bank routing check digit , whose weights are 3, 7, and 1, repeated as needed from left to right with a `MOD(s, 10)` function. This is used in the United States on personal checks, where the bank processing numbers have eight information digits. Look at the lower left-hand corner of your checkbook, at the magnetic ink character recognition (MICR) numbers for your bank's code. The formula uses the check digit itself in the formula, so that the result should be a constant zero for correct numbers. Otherwise, you could use "10-`MOD(total, 10)` = check digit" for your formula.

This scheme fails when the digits of a pairwise transpose differ by 5. For example, imagine that we wanted to validate the number 1621, but we typed 6121 instead, swapping the first two digits.

Since $(6 - 1) = 5$, this algorithm cannot detect the problem. Here is the arithmetic:

```
  1 * 3 =  3
+ 6 * 7 = 42
+ 2 * 1 =  2
+ 1 * 3 =  3

==================
   total   50

MOD(50, 10) = 0

  6 * 3 = 18
+ 1 * 7 =  7
+ 2 * 1 =  2
+ 1 * 3 =  3

==================
   total   30

MOD(30, 10) = 0
```

A better scheme is the IBM Check Digit, also known as "Luhn's Algorithm", whose weights alternate between 1 and f(x), where f(x) is defined by the look-up table given here or by the formula `f(x) = IF (x < 9) THEN MOD((x + x), 9) ELSE 9 END IF`; where x is the position of the digit in the code.

```
f(1) = 2
f(2) = 4
f(3) = 6
f(4) = 8
f(5) = 1
f(6) = 3
f(7) = 5
f(8) = 7
f(9) = 9
```

```
CREATE TABLE Weights
(digit_position INTEGER NOT NULL PRIMARY KEY,
  wgt INTEGER NOT NULL);
```

Using the look-up table is usually faster than doing the arithmetic because it is small and can take advantage of indexing and parallel processing. Obviously, the look-up table needs to have as many rows as digits in the encoding.

```
SELECT foo_code,
       MOD(SUM(CAST(SUBSTRING(foo_code FROM seq
FOR 1)
                   AS INTEGER) * W.wgt), 10) AS
       check_digit
  FROM Weights AS W,
       Foobar AS F,
       Sequence AS S
 WHERE S.seq <= 4 -- length of encoding -1
   AND W.digit_position = S.seq
   GROUP BY foo_code;
```

The Sequence table is a standard SQL programming technique used to replace loops with declarative code. It has a primary key, an INTEGER named "seq", of all integers from 1 to (n), where (n) is large enough to handle the particular programming problem.

DB2 has a special optimization that detects Star schemas by looking for a large fact table that references many smaller dimension tables. This works nicely with this kind of query.

Another popular version of the weighted-sum check digit is the Bull codes, which use the sum of two alternating sums, each with a modulus less than 10. The modulus pair has to be relatively prime numbers. The most popular pairs, in order of increasing error detection ability, are (4, 5), (4, 7), (3, 7), (3, 5), (5, 6), and (3, 8).

For example, using the pair (4, 5) and modulus 7, we could check the code 2345-1 with these calculations:

```
((2*4) + (3*5) + (4*4) = (5*5)) = 64 MOD 7 = 1
```

2.2.2.2. *Power-Sum Check Digits*
The weights can be defined as variable powers of a fixed base number and a modulus can then be applied to get the remainder. Prime numbers are the best modulus, but 10 is very common. The most common schemes use a base of 2 or 3 with a modulus of 7, 10, or 11. The combination of 2 and 11 with a separate symbol for a remainder of 10 is one of these types of check digit. For example, we could check the code 2350 with these calculations:

```
(2^2) + (2^3) + (2^5) = 44
MOD (44, 11) = 0
```

You can prove that any pair of weights, a and b, for which it is true that b = a + 2n and n is an integer, suffer from the fault that they do not detect transpose errors that differ by five.

```
Let x = digit
    y = following digit
    y = x + 5
Let a = weight of x
    b = weight of y
    b = a + 2n

Compute the check digit for
a*x + b*y
= a*x + (a + 2n) * (x + 5)
= a*x + a*x + 5*a + 2*n*x + 10*n
= 2*a*x + 5*a + 2*n*x + 10*n

Compute the check digit for
a*y + b*x =
= a*(x + 5) + (a + 2*n)*x =
= a*x + 5*a + a*x + 2*n*x =
= 2*a*x + 5*a + 2*n*x
```

The difference between the two is (10*n); thus they have the same remainder when divided by 10.

2.2.2.3. Luhn Algorithm

The Luhn algorithm, or IBM Check Digit, is also known as "double-add-double" check digit or "mod ten" method. It was patented by IBM scientist Hans Peter Luhn in 1960 and is widely used today.

Double the value of alternate digits beginning with the first right-hand digit (low order).

Add the individual digits comprising the products obtained in step one to each of the unaffected digits in the original number.

Subtract the total obtained in step two from the next higher number ending in 0. This in the equivalent of calculating the "tens complement" of the low order digit (unit digit) of the total. If the total obtained in step two is a number ending in zero (30, 40, etc.), the check digit is 0.

For example:

Account number without check digit: 4992 73 9871

```
 4 9 9 2 7 3 9 8 7 1
*1 *2 *1 *2 *1 *2 *1 *2 *1 *2
----------------------------
4 18 9 4 7 6 9 16 7 2

4 + 1 + 8 + 9 + 4 + 7 + 6 + 9 + 1 + 6 + 7 + 2 = 64
70 - 64 = 6
```

The account number with the check digit is 4992-73-9871-6. The weakness is that it fails on a transposition of "09" to "90" in the input.

A look-up table for this is very short:

```
CREATE TABLE Luhn
(digit INTEGER NOT NULL PRIMARY KEY,
 twice INTEGER NOT NULL);

INSERT INTO Luhn
VALUES (0, 0), (1, 2), (2, 4), (3, 6), (4, 8),
       (5, 1), (6, 3), (7, 5), (8, 7), (9, 9);

SELECT F.foo_code,
       MOD (SUM(CASE WHEN MOD(seq, 2) = 0
                     THEN L.twice
                     ELSE L.digit END), 10)
       AS checkdigit
  FROM Foobar AS F, Sequence AS S, Luhn AS L
 WHERE L.digit = SUBSTRING(foo_code FROM seq FOR 1)
   AND S.seq < CHARLENGTH(foo_code)
GROUP BY F.foo_code;
```

2.2.2.4. Dihedral Five Check Digit

A very good, but somewhat complicated, scheme was proposed by J. Verhoeff in a tract from the Mathematical Centre in Amsterdam, Netherlands (Verhoeff 1969). It is based on the properties of multiplication in an algebraic structure known as the Dihedral Five Group.

Though some of the calculations could be done with arithmetic formulas, the easiest and fastest way is to build lookup tables for functions. The look-up tables involved are a multiplication look-up table, an inverse look-up table, and a permutation table. Using look-up tables makes the programs look larger, but the superior ability of this scheme to detect errors more than makes up for the very slight increase in size.

This is the multiplication table for the dihedral five group. The important thing to notice is that D_5 multiplication (shown by d(j, k)) does not always commute—for example, d(8, 9) = 4 and d(9, 8) = 1. This property is what lets it detect transposition errors that other methods miss. The following look-up tables are taken from the Wikipedia entry (http://www.en.wikipedia.org/wiki/Verhoeff_algorithm).

Multiplication in the dihedral group D_5.

d(j,k)		k									
		0	1	2	3	4	5	6	7	8	9
	0	0	1	2	3	4	5	6	7	8	9
	1	1	2	3	4	0	6	7	8	9	5
	2	2	3	4	0	1	7	8	9	5	6
	3	3	4	0	1	2	8	9	5	6	7
j	4	4	0	1	2	3	9	5	6	7	8
	5	5	9	8	7	6	0	4	3	2	1
	6	6	5	9	8	7	1	0	4	3	2
	7	7	6	5	9	8	2	1	0	4	3
	8	8	7	6	5	9	3	2	1	0	4
	9	9	8	7	6	5	4	3	2	1	0

This is a permutation based on the position of a digit in the input string. The positions of the digits are counted from right to left, starting with zero. This repeats after eight rows. When you do this with a table, you will find it is easier to simply fill the table with repeated rows for all the positions in your encoding. This will save you a MOD(i, 8) function and let the optimizer work with the indexing on the PRIMARY KEY column.

Permutation repeats after eight rows (the row for pos = 8 is identical to the row for pos = 0, etc.).

p(pos,num)		num									
		0	1	2	3	4	5	6	7	8	9
pos	0	0	1	2	3	4	5	6	7	8	9
	1	1	5	7	6	2	8	3	0	9	4
	2	5	8	0	3	7	9	6	1	4	2
	3	8	9	1	6	0	4	3	5	2	7
	4	9	4	5	3	1	2	6	8	7	0
	5	4	2	8	6	5	7	3	9	0	1
	6	2	7	9	3	8	0	6	4	1	5
	7	7	0	4	6	9	1	3	2	5	8

The third table is the multiplicative inverse (i.e., d(k, inv (j)) = 0.

j	0	1	2	3	4	5	6	7	8	9
inv(j)	0	4	3	2	1	5	6	7	8	9

Using an example from the Wikipedia article, given the encoding 1428570, validate the check digit.

> Compute P(digit, position number) from the second table. Remember that we count from right to left, starting at zero.

```
p(0, 0) = 0
p(7, 1) = 0
p(5, 2) = 9
p(8, 3) = 2
p(2, 4) = 5
p(4, 5) = 5
p(1, 6) = 7
```

> Add these digits together using the d() operator in order:

```
d(d(d(d(d(d(0, 0), 9), 2), 5), 5), 7) = 0
```

When the final cumulative sum is 0, we have a valid check digit. The idea is that position zero is assigned the inverse of the cumulative dihedral five total of positions 1 to (n); this assures that the sum of all the positions will be zero.

2.3. DECLARATIONS, NOT FUNCTIONS, NOT PROCEDURES

After having learned all of these algorithms, you should not use them in procedural code in your schema; if you want to use these and other algorithms in procedural code, then go to http:// www.codeproject.com/KB/cpp/CheckDigit.aspx for routiens already written in C. Convert them to constraints instead. This is an example of thinking in sets and not procedures. In a posting on http://www.swug.org, a regular contributor posted a Transact-SQL function that calculates the checksum digit of a standard, 13-digit barcode. The rules are simple:

Sum each digit in an odd position to get S1.
Sum each digit in an even position to get S2.

The formula is ABS(MOD(S1-S2), 10) for the barcode checksum digit. Here is the author's suggested function code translated from T-SQL in Standard SQL/PSM:

```
CREATE FUNCTION BarcodeCheckSum(IN my_barcode
  CHAR(12))
RETURNS INTEGER
LANGUAGE SQL
DETERMINISTIC
 BEGIN
 DECLARE barcode_checker INTEGER;
 DECLARE idx INTEGER;
 DECLARE sgn INTEGER;
 SET barcode_checker = 0;
-- check if given barcode is numeric
 IF IsNumeric(my_barcode) = 0
 THEN RETURN-1;
 END IF;
-- check barcode length
 IF CHAR_LENGTH(TRIM(BOTH ' ' FROM my_barcode)) <> 12
 THEN RETURN-2;
 END IF;
-- compute barcode checksum algorithm
```

```
   SET idx = 1;
   WHILE idx <= 12
   DO -- Calculate sign of digit
   IF MOD(idx, 2) = 0
   THEN SET sgn =-1;
   ELSE SET sgn = + 1;
   END IF;

   SET barcode_checker = barcode_checker +
     CAST(SUBSTRING(my_barcode FROM idx FOR 1) AS
       INTEGER)
           *sgn;
   SET idx = idx + 1;
   END WHILE;

   -- check digit
   RETURN ABS(MOD(barcode_checker, 10));
 END;
```

Let's see how it works:

```
barcode_checkSum('283723281122')
= ABS (MOD(2-8 + 3-7 + 2-3 + 2-8 + 1-1
  +2 -2), 10))
= ABS (MOD(-6-4-1-6 + 0+0), 10)
= ABS (MOD(-17, 10))
= ABS(-7) = 7
```

Okay, where to begin? Notice the creation of unneeded local variables, the assumption of an IsNumeric() function taken from the T-SQL dialect, and the fact that the check digit is supposed to be a character in the barcode and not an integer separated from the barcode. We have three IF statements and a WHILE loop in the code. This is about as procedural as you can get.

In fairness, SQL/PSM does not handle errors by returning negative numbers, but I don't want to get into a lesson on the mechanism used, which is quite different from the one used in T-SQL dialect.

Why use all that procedural code? Most of it can be replaced by declarative expressions. Let's start with the usual Sequence auxiliary table in place of the loop, nest function calls, and use CASE expressions to remove IF statements.

The rough pseudo-formula for conversion is:

1. A procedural loop becomes a sequence set:

```
FOR seq FROM 1 TO n DO f(x);
    => SELECT seq FROM Sequence WHERE seq <= n;
```

2. A procedural selection becomes a CASE expression:

```
IF.. THEN .. ELSE
   => CASE WHEN.. THEN .. ELSE.. END;
```

3. A series of assignments and function calls become a single nested set of function calls:

```
DECLARE x <type>;
SET x = f(y, ..);
SET y = g(x);
..;
 => f(g(x), ..)
```

Here is a translation of those guidelines into a first shot at a rewrite:

```
CREATE FUNCTION Barcode_CheckSum(IN my_barcode
CHAR(12))
RETURNS INTEGER
BEGIN
 IF barcode NOT SIMILAR TO '[^[:DIGIT:]+]'
 THEN RETURN -1; --error condition
 ELSE RETURN
 (SELECT ABS(SUM((CAST (SUBSTRING(barcode
            FROM S.seq FOR 1) AS INTEGER)
   *CASE MOD(S.seq, 2) WHEN 0 THEN 1 ELSE -1 END)))
   FROM Sequence AS S
  WHERE S.seq <= 12);
END IF;
END;
```

The SIMILAR TO regular expression predicate is a cute trick worth mentioning. It is a double negative that assures the input string is all digits in all 12 positions. Remember that an oversized string will not fit into the parameter and will give you an overflow error, while a short string will be padded with blanks.

But wait! We can do better:

```
CREATE FUNCTION Barcode_CheckSum(IN my_barcode
 CHAR(12))
RETURNS INTEGER
RETURN
 (SELECT ABS(SUM((CAST (SUBSTRING(barcode
                       FROM S.seq FOR 1) AS INTEGER)
   *CASE MOD(S.seq, 2)WHEN 0 THEN 1 ELSE -1 END)))
   FROM Sequence AS S
  WHERE S.seq <= 12
    AND barcode NOT SIMILAR TO '[^[:DIGIT:]+]';
```

This will return a NULL if there is an improper barcode. It is only one SQL statement, so we are doing pretty well. There are some minor tweaks, like this:

```
CREATE FUNCTION Barcode_CheckSum(IN my_barcode
CHAR(12))
RETURNS INTEGER
RETURN
 (SELECT ABS(SUM(CAST(SUBSTRING(barcode
        FROM Weights.seq FOR 1) AS INTEGER)
        *Weights.wgt))
   FROM (VALUES (CAST(1 AS INTEGER), CAST(-1 AS
   INTEGER)),
(2, +1), (3, -1), (4, +1), (5, -1),
   (6, +1), (7, -1), (8, +1), (9, -1), (10, +1),
   (11, -1), (12, +1)) AS Weights(seq, wgt)
  WHERE barcode NOT SIMILAR TO '[^[:DIGIT:]+]');
```

Another cute trick in Standard SQL is to construct a table constant with a VALUES() expression. The first row in the table expression establishes the data types of the columns by explicit casting.

What is the best solution? The real answer is none of the above. The point of this exercise is to come up with a set-oriented, declarative answer. We have been writing functions to check a condition. What we want is a CHECK() constraint for the barcode. Try this instead.

```
CREATE TABLE Products
(..
 barcode CHAR(13) NOT NULL
 CONSTRAINT all_numeric_checkdigit
  CHECK (barcode NOT SIMILAR TO '[^[:DIGIT:]+]')
 CONSTRAINT valid_checkdigit
  CHECK ((SELECT ABS(SUM(CAST(SUBSTRING(barcode
             FROM Weights.seq FOR 1) AS INTEGER)
                *Weights.wgt))
           FROM (VALUES (CAST(1 AS INTEGER),
             CAST(-1 AS INTEGER)),
  (2, +1), (3, -1), (4, +1), (5, -1),
        (6, +1), (7, -1), (8, +1), (9, -1), (10, +1),
        (11, -1), (12, +1)) AS weights(seq, wgt)
 = CAST(SUBSTRING(barcode FROM 13 FOR 1) AS INTEGER)),
 ..);
```

This will keep bad data out of the schema. The reason for splitting the code into two constraints is to provide better error messages. That is how we think in SQL. Avoid procedural code in favor of declarative code.

2.4. PATTERNS AND REGULAR EXPRESSIONS

SQL is a data retrieval language, and not a string processing language. The first string-matching function in SQL was the LIKE predicate, which is simple enough to be fast when used in a search.

The LIKE predicate is a string pattern-matching test with the syntax

```
<like predicate> ::=
    <match value> [NOT] LIKE <pattern>
        [ESCAPE <escape character>]

<match value> ::= <character value expression>
<pattern> ::= <character value expression>
<escape character> ::= <character value expression>
```

The expression M NOT LIKE P is equivalent to NOT (M LIKE P), which follows the usual syntax pattern in SQL. There are two wildcards allowed in the <pattern> string. They are the "%" and "_" characters. The "_" character represents a single arbitrary character; the "%" character represents an arbitrary substring, possibly of length 0. Notice that there is no way to represent 0 or one arbitrary character. This is not the case in many text-search languages, and can lead to problems or very complex predicates.

Any other character in the <pattern> represents that character itself. This means that SQL patterns are case sensitive, but many vendors allow you to set case sensitivity on or off at the database system level.

The <escape character> is used in the <pattern> to specify that the character that follows it is to be interpreted as a literal rather than a wildcard. This means that the escape character is followed by the escape character itself, an "_," or a "%." Old C programmers are used to this convention, where the language defines the escape character as "\," so this is a good choice for SQL programmers, too.

2.4.1. Tricks with Patterns

The "_" character tests much faster than the "%" character. The reason is obvious: The parser that compares a string to the pattern needs only one operation to match an underscore before it can move to the next character, but it has to do some look-ahead parsing to resolve a percentage sign. The wildcards can be inserted in the middle or beginning of a pattern. Thus, "B%K" will match "BOOK," "BLOCK," and "BK," but it will not match "BLOCKS."

The parser would scan each letter and classify it as a wildcard match or an exact match. In the case of "BLOCKS", the initial "B" would be an exact match and the parser would continue; "L", "O", and "C" have to be wildcard matches, since they don't appear in the pattern string; "K" cannot be classified until we read the last letter. The last letter is "S," so the match fails.

For example, given a column declared to be seven characters long, and a LIKE predicate looking for names that start with "Mac", you would usually write:

```
SELECT last_name, first_name, ..
  FROM People
 WHERE (last_name LIKE 'Mac%');
but this might actually run faster:
```

```
SELECT last_name, first_name, ..
  FROM People
 WHERE (last_name LIKE 'Mac_ ')
    OR (last_name LIKE 'Mac__ ')
    OR (last_name LIKE 'Mac___ ')
    OR (last_name LIKE 'Mac____'); -- length of
       the column
```

The trailing blanks are also characters that are matched exactly.

Putting a "%" at the front of a pattern is very time-consuming. For example, you might try to find all names that end in "son" with the query:

```
SELECT last_name, first_name, ..
  FROM People
 WHERE (last_name LIKE '%son');
```

The use of underscores instead will make a real difference in most SQL implementations for this query, because most of them parse from left to right.

```
SELECT last_name, first_name, ..
  FROM People
 WHERE (last_name LIKE '_son ')
    OR (last_name LIKE '__son ')
    OR (last_name LIKE '___son ')
    OR (last_name LIKE '____son'); -- length of
       the column
```

Remember that the "_" character requires a matching character and the "%" character does not. Thus, the query

```
SELECT last_name, first_name, ..
  FROM People
 WHERE (last_name LIKE 'John_%');
```

and the query

```
SELECT last_name, first_name, ..
  FROM People
 WHERE (last_name LIKE 'John%');
```

are subtly different. Both will match to "Johnson" and "Johns," but the first will not accept "John" as a match. This is how you get a "one-or-more-characters" pattern match in SQL.

Remember that the <pattern> as well as the <match value> can be constructed with concatenation operators, SUBSTRING(), and other string functions. For example, let's find people whose first names are part of their last names with the query:

```
SELECT last_name, first_name, ..
  FROM People
 WHERE (last_name LIKE '%' || first_name || '%');
```

which will show us people like "John Johnson," "Anders Andersen," and "Bob McBoblin." This query will also run very slowly. However, this is case sensitive and would not work for names such as "Jon Anjon," so you might want to modify the statement to:

```
SELECT last_name, first_name, ..
  FROM People
 WHERE (UPPER(last_name) LIKE '%' || UPPER(first_
   name) || '%';
```

Usually encoding schemes are not case sensitive, favor uppercase letters, and have strong patterns. A strong pattern is a fixed-length string with alpha, numeric, and special characters allowed only in certain positions.

2.4.2. Results with NULL Values and Empty Strings

As you would expect, a NULL in the predicate returns an UNKNOWN result. The NULL can be the escape character, pattern, or match value.

If M and P are both character strings of length zero, M LIKE P defaults to TRUE. If one or both are longer than zero characters, you use the regular rules to test the predicate.

2.4.3. LIKE Is Not Equality

A very important point that is often missed is that two strings can be equal but not LIKE in SQL. The test of equality first pads the shorter of the two strings with rightmost blanks, then matches the characters in each, one for one. Thus "Smith" and "Smith " (with three trailing blanks) are equal. However, the LIKE predicate does no padding, so "Smith" LIKE "Smith " tests FALSE because there is nothing to match to the blanks.

A good trick to getting around these problems is to use the TRIM() function to remove unwanted blanks from the strings within either or both of the two arguments.

2.4.4. Avoiding the LIKE Predicate with a Join

Beginners often want to write something similar to "<string> IN LIKE (<pattern list>)" rather than a string of OR-ed LIKE predicates. That syntax is illegal, but you can get the same results with a table of patterns and a join.

```
CREATE TABLE Patterns
(template VARCHAR(10) NOT NULL PRIMARY KEY);

INSERT INTO Patterns
VALUES ('Celko%'),
       ('Chelko%'),
       ('Cilko%'),
       ('Selko%),
       ('Silko%');

SELECT A1.last_name
  FROM Patterns AS P1, Authors AS A1
 WHERE A1.last_name LIKE P1.template;
```

This idea can be generalized to find strings that differ from a pattern by one position and without actually using a LIKE predicate. First, assume that we have a table of sequential numbers and these following tables with sample data.

the match patterns

```
CREATE TABLE MatchList (pattern CHAR(9) NOT NULL
 PRIMARY KEY);
INSERT INTO MatchList VALUES ('_========');
INSERT INTO MatchList VALUES ('=_=======');
INSERT INTO MatchList VALUES ('==_======');
INSERT INTO MatchList VALUES ('===_=====');
INSERT INTO MatchList VALUES ('====_====');
```

```
INSERT INTO MatchList VALUES ('=====_===');
INSERT INTO MatchList VALUES ('======_==');
INSERT INTO MatchList VALUES ('=======_=');
INSERT INTO MatchList VALUES ('========_');
```

—the strings to be matched or near-matched

```
CREATE TABLE Target (nbr CHAR(9) NOT NULL
  PRIMARY KEY);
INSERT INTO Target VALUES ('123456089'),
  ('543434344');
```

—the strings to be searched for those matches

```
CREATE TABLE Source (nbr CHAR(9) NOT NULL
  PRIMARY KEY);
INSERT INTO Source
VALUES ('123456089'),('123056789'),('123456780'),
       ('123456789'),('023456789'),('023456780');
```

We are using an equal sign in the match patterns as a signal to replace it with the appropriate character in the source string to see if they match but to skip over the underscore.

```
SELECT DISTINCT TR1.nbr
  FROM Sequence AS SE1, Source AS SR1,
       MatchList AS ML1, Target AS TR1
 WHERE NOT EXISTS
       (SELECT *
          FROM Sequence AS SE1, Source AS SR2,
               MatchList AS ML2, Target AS TR2
         WHERE SUBSTRING (ML2.pattern FROM seq FOR
           1) = '='
           AND SUBSTRING (SR2.nbr FROM seq FOR 1)
               <>SUBSTRING (TR2.nbr FROM seq FOR 1)
           AND SR2.nbr = SR1.nbr
           AND TR2.nbr = TR1.nbr
           AND ML2.pattern = ML1.pattern
           AND SE1.seq BETWEEN 1 AND (CHARLENGTH
             (TR2.nbr) -1));
```

This code was written by Jonathan Blitz.

2.4.5. CASE Expressions and LIKE Predicates

The CASE expression in Standard SQL lets the programmer use the LIKE predicate in some interesting ways. The simplest example is counting the number of times a particular string appears inside another string. Assume that text_col is CHAR(25) and we want the count of a particular string, "term", within it.

```
SELECT text_col,
       CASE
       WHEN text_col LIKE '%term%term%term%term%ter
         m%term%'
       THEN 6
       WHEN text_col LIKE '%term%term%term%term%t
         erm%'
       THEN 5
       WHEN text_col LIKE '%term%term%term%term%'
       THEN 4
       WHEN text_col LIKE '%term%term%term%'
       THEN 3
       WHEN text_col LIKE '%term%term%'
       THEN 2
       WHEN text_col LIKE '%term%'
       THEN 1
       ELSE 0 END AS term_tally
  FROM Foobar
 WHERE text_col LIKE '%term%';
```

This depends on the fact that a CASE expression executes the WHEN clauses in order of their appearance. We know that a substring can appear at most six times because of the length of text_col.

Another use of the CASE is to adjust the pattern within the LIKE predicate.

```
name LIKE CASE
     WHEN language = 'English'
     THEN 'Red%'
     WHEN language = 'French'
     THEN 'Rouge%'
     ELSE 'R%' END
```

2.4.6. Similar to Predicates

As you can see, the `LIKE` predicate is pretty weak, especially if you have used a version of `grep()`, a utility program from the UNIX operating system. The name is short for "general regular expression parser" and before you ask, a regular expression is a class of formal languages. If you are a computer science major, you have seen them; otherwise, don't worry about it. The bad news is that there are several versions of `grep()` in the UNIX community: `egrep()`, `fgrep()`, `xgrep()`, and a dozen or so others.

The SQL-99 standard added a regular expression predicate of the form "`<string expression> SIMILAR TO <pattern>`," which is based on the POSIX version of `grep()` found in ISO/IEC 9945.

The special symbols in a pattern are:

| means alternation (either of two alternatives)
*means repetition of the previous item zero or more times
+ means repetition of the previous item one or more times
() may be used to group items into a single unit
[...] specifies a match to any of the characters inside the brackets.

There are abbreviations for lists of commonly used character subsets, taken from POSIX.

[:ALPHA:] match any alphabetic character, regardless of case.
[:UPPER:] match any upper case alphabetic character
[:LOWER:] match any lower case alphabetic character
[:DIGIT:] match any numeric digit
[:ALNUM:] match any numeric digit or alphabetic character

Examples:

1. The letters "foo" or "bar" followed by any string

```
Foobar SIMILAR TO '(foo|bar)%'
```

2. The "SER #" followed by one or more digits

```
serial_nbr SIMILAR TO 'SER #[:DIGIT:]+'
```

You should still read your product manual for details, but most grep() functions accept other special symbols for more general searching than the SIMILAR TO predicate.

. any character (same as the SQL underscore)
^ start of line (not used in an SQL string)
$ end of line (not used in an SQL string)
\ The next character is a literal and not a special symbol; this is called an ESCAPE in SQL.
[^] match anything but the characters inside the brackets, after the caret

Regular expressions have a lot of nice properties but they can be expensive to process. If you can do the job with a LIKE instead of a SIMILAR TO predicate, that is a faster and more portable choice.

2.4.7. Tricks with Strings

This is a list of miscellaneous tricks that you might not think about when using strings.

2.4.7.1. String Character Content

A weird way of providing an edit mask for a varying character column is to see if it has only digits in it. Ken Sheridan proposed this on the ACCESS forum of CompuServe in October 1999. If the first character is not a zero, then you can check that the VARCHAR(n) string is all digits with:

```
CAST (LOG10 (CAST (test_column AS INTEGER) AS
   INTEGER) = n
```

If the first (n) characters are not all digits then it will not return (n). If they are all digits, but the (n + 1) character is also a digit it will return (n + 1), and so forth. If there are nondigit characters in the string, then the innermost CAST() function will fail to convert the test_column into a number.

If you do have to worry about leading zeros or blanks, then concatenate "1" to the front of the string.

Another trick is to think in terms of whole strings and not in a "character at a time" mind-set. So how can you tell if a string is all alphabetic, partly alphabetic, or completely non-alphabetic without scanning each character? The answer from the folks at Ocelot software is surprisingly easy:

```
CREATE TABLE Foobar
(no_alpha VARCHAR(6) NOT NULL
          CHECK (UPPER(no_alpha) = LOWER(no_
             alpha)),
some_alpha VARCHAR(6) NOT NULL
          CHECK (UPPER(some_alpha) <> LOWER(some_
             alpha)),
all_alpha VARCHAR(6) NOT NULL
          CHECK (UPPER(all_alpha) <> LOWER(all_
             alpha)
                AND LOWER (all_alpha)
                    BETWEEN 'aaaaaa' AND
                       'zzzzzz'),
...);
```

Letters have different upper and lowercase values, but other characters do not. This lets us edit a column for no alphabetic characters, some alphabetic characters, and all alphabetic characters.

2.4.7.2. Searching versus Declaring a String

You need to be very accurate when you declare a string column in your DDL, but after doing that, you can slack off a bit when you search on those columns in your DML. For example, most credit card numbers are made up of four groups of four digits, and each group has some validation rule, thus:

```
CREATE TABLE CreditCards
(card_nbr CHAR(17) NOT NULL PRIMARY KEY
 CONSTRAINT valid_card_nbr_format
   CHECK (card_nbr SIMILAR TO
          '[:DIGIT:][:DIGIT:][:DIGIT:][:DIGIT:]-
[:DIGIT:] [:DIGIT:][:DIGIT:][:DIGIT:]-[:DIGIT:]
```

```
[:DIGIT:] [:DIGIT:][:DIGIT:]-[:DIGIT:][:DIGIT:]
[:DIGIT:] [:DIGIT:]'),
 CONSTRAINT valid_bank_nbr
   CHECK (SUBSTRING (card_nbr FROM 1 FOR 4)
            IN ('2349', '2345', ..),
 ..);
```

Since we are sure that the credit card number is stored correctly, we can search for it with a simple LIKE predicate. For example, to find all the cards that 1234 in the third group, you can use this.

```
SELECT card_nbr
  FROM CreditCards
  WHERE card_nbr LIKE '____-____-1234-____';
```

Or even

```
SELECT card_nbr
  FROM CreditCards
  WHERE card_nbr LIKE '_____1234_____';
```

The SIMILAR TO predicate will build an internal finite state machine to parse the pattern, while the underscores in the LIKE can be optimized so that it can run in parallel down the whole column.

2.4.7.3. *Creating an Index on a String*
Many string encoding techniques have the same prefix because we read from left to right and tend to put the codes for the largest category to the left. For example, the first group of digits in the credit card numbers is the issuing bank. The syntax might look like this:

```
CREATE INDEX acct_searching
    ON CreditCards
   WITH REVERSE(card_nbr); -- not Standard SQL
```

If your SQL has the ability to define a function in an index, you can reverse or rearrange the string to give faster access. This is very vendor-dependent, but often the query must explicitly use the same function as the index.

An alternative is to store the rearranged value in the base table and show the actual value in a view. When the view is invoked, the rearranged value will be used for the query without the users knowing it.

2.4.8. Regular Expression Web Sites

There are a number of Web sites with regular expressions to validate various common encoding schemes.

A starting point is http://www.regular-expressions.info/email.html, but you will need to do a Web search for whatever is current.

You may or may not be able to use each pattern in your particular SQL, but you can probably convert then to your dialect. There are examples and links at http://www.regular-expressions.info/email.html for you to use. But how easy/fast do you want the regular expression to be versus its accuracy?

As an example of a trade-off between regular expression complexity and exactness, consider \b\d{1,3}\.\d{1,3}\.\d{1,3}\.\d{1,3}\b, which will match any IP address just fine, but will also match 999.999.999.999 as if it were a valid IP address. Whether this is a problem depends on the files or data you intend to apply the regular expression to. To restrict all four numbers in the IP address to 0 thru 255, you can use this complex expression:

```
'\b(25[0-5]|2[0-4][0-9]|[01]?[0-9][0-9]?)\.(25[0-5]
|2[0-4][0-9]|[01]?[0-9][0-9]?)\.(25[0-5]|2[0-4]
[0-9]|[01]?[0-9][0-9]?)\.(25[0-5]|2[0-4][0-9]
|[01]?[0-9][0-9]?)\b'
```

Another alternative is to use four TINYINTs, whose range is 0 to 255, to model the IP address. You might find that to be much easier.

2.5. NONDATABASE VALIDATION

The front end application can easily do most basic data validations. It is pretty easy to reject a form with missing elements, or one that has a date of February 31. But even when the applications have such validations, you have to repeat them in the database constraints. It is too easy for someone with direct access to the tables via a query tool to circumvent data integrity.

If you know that the data is mostly clean, you can design the database constraints to look for good data first. This is especially true when the constraint uses a CASE expression since the WHEN clauses are invoked in order.

It is not always possible to immediately validate data. You need to go to an external source and request that information ("Joe Celko says he has an 'A' credit rating, but we want to confirm that with a credit bureau"). This requires a conditional validation status of some kind. It might be code in the data element or separate column(s) that track the validation process.

Keeping the application program rules and the database constraints in synch is difficult, but vital. If you can set a library of procedures in your application development environment, then the job is easier. A good way to do this is to set up a file with valid and invalid data, then load each row into a test harness for the validation procedure and into a test harness for the table constraint. The declarative (database) code should reject the same data as the procedural code. But the application code can accept more data than the database because it cannot do database level validations ("Joe Celko is over his credit limit") or external validations ("Joe Celko is wanted for murder").

Validation is not an optional feature; it is a vital part of any database, but it is more than just a database problem. It is often a good idea to assign degrees of trust at various points in a system. The classic example is a loan application approval. The initial application starts at middle level of trust based on the unconfirmed data. The loan's worthiness moves up (or down) as more information is verified. It is a whole process and not just a schema design.

Data Encoding Schemes

You do not put data directly into a database. You convert it into an encoding scheme first and then put the encoding into the rows of the tables. Words have to be written in an alphabet and belong to a language or a limited vocabulary; measurements are expressed as numbers. We are so used to seeing words and numbers that we no longer think of them as encoding schemes. We also often fail to distinguish among the possible ways to identify (and therefore to encode) an entity or property. Do we encode the person receiving medical services or the policy that is paying for them? That might depend on whether the database is for the doctor or for the insurance company. Do we encode the first title of a song, the alternate title, or both? Or should we include the music itself in a multimedia database? And should it be as an image of the sheet music or as an audio recording?

Nobody teaches people how to design these encoding schemes, so they are all too often done on the fly. Where standardized encoding schemes exist, the schemes are often ignored in favor of some AD hoc scheme. Beginning programmers have the attitude that encoding schemes do not really matter because the computer will take care of it, so they do not have to spend time designing encoding schemes. This attitude has probably gotten worse with SQL than it was before. The new database designer thinks that an ALTER statement can fix any bad things done at the start of the project.

Yes, the computer can take care of a lot of problems. But the data entry and validation programs become very complex and hard to maintain. Database queries that have to follow the same convoluted encodings will cost both computer time and money. And a human being still has to use the code at some point. Bad encoding schemes give rise to errors in data entry and misreading of outputs.

3.1. BAD ENCODING SCHEMES

To use an actual example, the automobile tag system for a certain southern state started as a punch-card system written in COBOL. Many readers are too young to remember punch-card machines.

A punch card is a stiff piece of paper in which a character is represented as one or more rectangular holes made in 1 of 80 vertical columns on the card. Contiguous groups of columns make up fixed-length fields of data. The keypunch machine has a typewriter-like keyboard; it automatically feeds cards into the punch as fast as a human being can type. The position, length, and alphabetic or numeric shift for each field on the card can be set by a control card in the keypunch machine to save the operator keystrokes. This is a very fixed format and a very fast input method, and making changes to a program once it is in place is very hard.

The automobile license plate system had a single card column for a single-position numeric code to indicate the type

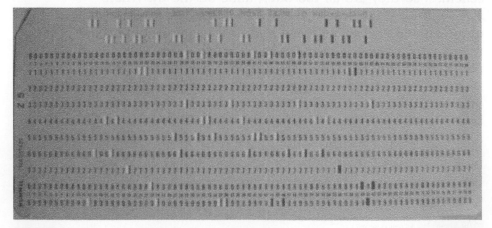

■ **FIGURE 3-1:** Eighty-column IBM punch card.

of plate: private car, chauffeured car, taxi, truck, public bus, and so forth. As time went on, more plate types were added for veterans of assorted wars, for university alumni, and for whatever other pressure group happened to have the political power to pass a bill allocating it a special automobile license plate or "vanity plate."

Soon there were more than 10 types, so a single digit could not represent them. There was room on the punch card to change the length of the field to two digits. But COBOL uses fixed-length fields, so changing the card layout would require changes in the programs and in the keypunch procedures.

The first new automobile license plate types were handled by letting the data-entry clerk press a punctuation-mark key instead of changing from numeric lock to manual shift mode. Once that kludge was made, it was followed for each new code thereafter, until the scheme looked like everything on the upper row of keys on a typewriter.

Unfortunately, different makes and models of keypunch machines have different punctuation marks in the same keyboard position, so each deck of cards had to have a special program to convert its punches to the original model IBM 026 keypunch codes before the master file could be updated. This practice continued even after all of the original machines had been retired to used-equipment heaven.

The edit programs could not check for a simple numeric range to validate input but had to use a small look-up routine with over 20 values in it. That does not sound like much until you realize that the system had to handle over 3 million records in the first quarter of the year. The error rate was quite high, and each batch needed to know which machine had punched the cards before it could use a look-up table.

If the encoding scheme had been designed with two digits (00 to 99) at the beginning, all of these problems would have been avoided. If I were to put this system into a database today, using video terminals for data entry, the tag type could be INTEGER and it could hold as many tag types as I would ever need. This is part of the legacy database problem. SQL has abstract data types, while file systems were tied to physical implementations.

The second example was reported in *Information Systems Week* in 1987. The first sentence told the whole story: "The chaos and rampant error rates in New York City's new Welfare Management System appear to be due to a tremendous increase in the number of codes it requires in data entry and the subsequent difficulty for users in learning to use it." The rest of the article explains how the new system attempted to merge several old existing systems. In the merger, the error rates increased from 2% to over 20% because the encoding schemes used could not be matched up and consolidated. Some of the non-technical details were covered in the New York Time that year (see http://www.nytimes.com/1987/12/26/nyregion/computers-continue-to-delay-welfare-payments-in-new-york.html?scp=1&sq=New%20York%20City%E2%80%99s%20new%20Welfare%20Management%20System%201987&st=cse&pagewanted=2)

How do you know a bad encoding scheme when you see one? One bad feature is the failure to allow for growth. Talk to anyone who has had to reconfigure a fixed-length record system to allow for the change from the old ZIP codes to the current ZIP + 4 codes in their address data. SQL does not have this as a physical problem, but it can show up as a logical problem.

Another bad property is ambiguous encodings in the scheme. Perhaps the funniest example of this problem was the Italian telephone system's attempt at a "time of day" service. They used a special three-digit number, which was meant to work like the 411 information number or the 911 emergency phone number in the United States. But the three digits they picked were also those of a telephone exchange in Milan, so nobody could call into that exchange without getting the time signal before they completed their call.

Ambiguity happens more often than you would think, but the form that it usually takes is that of a "miscellaneous" code that is too general. Very different cases are then encoded as identical and the queries produce incorrect or misleading information.

A bad encoding scheme lacks codes for missing, unknown, not applicable, or miscellaneous values. The classic story is the man who bought a prestige auto tag reading "NONE" and got thousands of traffic tickets as a result. The police had no special provision for a missing tag on the tickets, so when a car had no tag, they wrote "none" in the field for the tag number on the citation form. The database simply matched his name and address to every unpaid missing tag in Los Angeles.

Before you say that the NULL in SQL is a quick solution to this problem, think about how NULL is ignored in many SQL functions. The SQL query "SELECT tag_nbr, SUM(fine_amt) FROM Tickets GROUP BY tag_nbr;" will give the total fines on each car. But it also puts all the missing tags into one group (i.e., one car), although we want to see each one as a separate case, since it is very unlikely that there is only one untagged car in all of California.

There are also differences among "missing," "unknown,""not applicable," "miscellaneous," and erroneous values. They are subtle but important. For example, the International Classification of Disease (ICD) uses 999.999 for miscellaneous illness. It means that we have diagnosed the patient, know that he has an illness, and cannot classify it; this is a very scary condition for the patient. But this is not quite the same thing as a missing disease code (just admitted, might not even be sick), an inapplicable disease code (pregnancy complications in a male), an unknown disease code (sick and awaiting lab results), or an error in the data collection process (the patient's temperature is recorded as 100 degrees Celsius, not Fahrenheit).

3.2. ENCODING SCHEME TYPES

The following is my classification system for encoding schemes and my suggestions for using each of them. You will find some of these same ideas in library science and other fields, but I have never seen anyone else attempt a classification system for data processing.

3.2.1. Enumeration Encoding

Enumeration encoding arranges the attribute values in some order and assigns a number or a letter to each value.

Numbers are usually a better choice than letters, because they can be increased without limit as more values are added. Enumeration schemes might be a good choice for a short list of values, but they are a bad choice for a long list. It is too hard to remember a long list of codes, and very soon any natural ordering principle is violated as new values are tacked on the end.

A good heuristic is to order the values in some natural manner, if one exists in the data, so that table look-up will be easier. Chronological order (event 1 occurs before event 2) or procedural order (1 must be done before 2) is often a good choice. Another good heuristic is to order the values from most common to least common. That way you will have shorter codes for the most common cases. Other orderings could be based on physical characteristics such as largest to smallest, rainbow-color order, and so on.

After arguing for a natural order in the list, I must admit that the most common scheme is alphabetical order, because it is simple to implement on a computer and makes it easy for a person to look up values in a table. ANSI standard X3.31, "Structure for the Identification of Counties of the United States for Information Interchange," encodes county names within a state by first alphabetizing the names, then numbering them from 1 to whatever is needed.

Another trick is to use leading zeros in such schemes. It has nothing to do with the meaning of the encoding, but people seeing a leading zero will know that this is NOT a numeric value to be used for computation. This also tells the application developer the size of the display field needed.

3.2.2. Measurement Encoding

A measurement encoding is a number given in some unit of measure, such as pounds, meters, volts, or liters.

This can be done in one of two ways. The column contains an implied unit of measure and the numbers represent the quantity in that unit. But sometimes the column explicitly contains the unit. The most common example of the second case would be money fields, where a dollar sign is used in the column; you know that the unit is dollars, not pounds or yen, by the sign.

Ideally, you want to avoid storing mixed units in a column. That makes computations much more complex than uniformly reported data.

3.2.3. Abbreviation Encoding

Abbreviation codes shorten the attribute values to fit into less storage space, but the reader easily understands them. The codes can be either of fixed length or of variable length, but computer people tend to prefer fixed length. The most common example is the two-letter postal state abbreviations ("CA" for California, "AL" for Alabama), which replaced the old variable-length abbreviations ("Calif." for California, "Ala." for Alabama).

A good abbreviation scheme is very handy, but as the set of values becomes larger, the possibility for misunderstanding increases. The three-letter codes for airport baggage are pretty obvious for major cities: "LAX" for Los Angeles, "SFO" for San Francisco, "BOS" for Boston, "ATL" for Atlanta. But nobody can figure out the abbreviations for the really small airports. Would you guess that "LHV" stands for the W. T. Piper Memorial Airport in Clinton County, Pennsylvania? But then O'Hare Airport in Chicago is ORD; you would have to know that this is from the original name, Orchard Field.

As another example, consider the ISO 3166 country codes, which come in two-letter, three-letter, and nonabbreviation numeric forms. The RIPE Network Coordination Centre maintains these codes.

3.2.4. Algorithmic Encoding

Algorithmic encoding takes the value to be encoded and puts it through an algorithm to obtain the encodings. The algorithm should be reversible, so that the original value can be recovered. Though it is not required, the encoding is usually shorter (or at least of known maximum size) and more uniform in some useful way compared to the original value.

Technically, compression is algorithmic encoding, but data is not displayed in a compressed format. The system will pack and unpack it without any special actions from the user.

Encryption is the most common example of an algorithmic encoding scheme. But it is so important it needs to be considered as a topic in itself. The explicit goal of encryption is to be unreadable by humans and to be difficult to read even with computer help.

Computer people are used to using Julianized dates, which convert a date into an integer. As an aside, please note that astronomers use the "Julian date," which is a large number that represents the number of days since a particular heavenly event. The Julianized date is a number between 1 and 365 or 366, which represents the ordinal position of the day within the year.

Algorithms take up computer time in both data input and output, but the encoding is useful in itself because it allows searching or calculations to be done that would be hard using the original data. Julianized dates can be used for computations.

Soundex, Metaphone, and other algorithms take names or other text and give a result that attempts to do phonetic matching from the original text. For example, "Celko," "Selco," and "Selko" are pronounced the same way but are not spelled the same way.

Another example is hashing functions, which convert values into numeric values. They are used for retrieving the location of the data in physical storage. Rounding numeric values before they go into the database is also a case of algorithmic encoding.

To reiterate, the differences between an abbreviation and an algorithm are not that clear. An abbreviation can be considered a special case of an algorithm, which tells you how to remove or replace letters. The tests to tell them apart are:

1. When a human can read it without effort, it is an abbreviation.

2. An algorithmic encoding is not easily human-readable.

3. An algorithmic encoding might return the same code for more than one value, but an abbreviation is always one-to-one because a human will correct it.

3.2.5. Hierarchical Encoding Schemes

A hierarchy partitions the set of values into disjoint categories, and then partitions those categories into subcategories, and so forth until some final level is reached. Such schemes are shown either as nested sets or as tree charts. Each category has some meaning in itself and the subcategories refine meaning further.

The most common example is the ZIP code, which partitions the United States geographically. Each digit, as you read from left to right, further isolates the location of the address, first by postal region, then by state, then by city, and finally by the post office that has to make the delivery. For example, in the ZIP code 30310, we know that the 30000 to 39999 range means the southeastern United States. Within in the southeastern codes, we know that the 30000 to 30399 range is Georgia and that 30300 to 30399 is metropolitan Atlanta. Finally, the whole code, 30310, identifies substation A in the West End section of the city. The ZIP code can be parsed by reading it from left to right, reading first one digit, then two, and then the last two digits.

Another example is the Dewey Decimal Classification (DDC) system, used in public libraries. The 500 number series covers "Natural Sciences"; within that, the 510s cover "Mathematics"; finally, 512 deals with "Algebra" in particular. The scheme can be carried further, with decimal fractions for kinds of algebra.

Hierarchical encoding schemes are great for large data domains that have a natural hierarchy. They organize the data to make searching and reporting along that natural hierarchy very easy. But there can be problems in designing these schemes. First of all, the tree structure does not have to be neatly balanced, so some categories may need more codes than others and hence may have more break-downs. Eastern and ancient religions are shortchanged in the DCC system, reflecting a prejudice toward Christian and Jewish writing. Asian religions were pushed into a small set of codes. Today, the Library of Congress has more books on Buddhist thought than on any other religion on Earth.

Second, you might not have made the right choices as to where to place certain values in the tree. For example, in the DDC system, books on logic are encoded as 164, in the philosophy section, and not under the 510s, mathematics. In the 19th century, there was no mathematical logic. Today, nobody would think of looking for logic under philosophy. Dewey was simply following the conventions of his day. And like today's programmers, he found that the system specifications changed while he was working.

3.2.6. Vector Encoding

A vector is made up of a fixed number of components. These components can be ordered or unordered, but they are always present. They can be of fixed or variable length. The components can be dependent on or independent of each other, but the code applies to a single entity and makes sense only as a whole unit or vector. Punctuation, symbol-set changes, or position within the code can determine the components of the vector.

The most common example is a date, whose components are year, month, and day. The parts have some meaning by themselves, but the real meaning is in the vector—the ordered date components—as a whole because it is a complete entity. The different date formats used in computer systems give examples of all the options. The three components can be written in year-month-day order, month-day-year order, or just about any other way you wish.

The limits on the values for the day are dependent on the year (is it a leap year or not?) and the month (28, 29, 30, or 31 days?). The components can be separated by punctuation (12/1/2005, using slashes and American date format), symbol-set changes (2005-DEC-01, using digits-letters-digits) or position (20051201, using positions 1 to 4, 5 to 6, and 7 to 8 for year, month, and day, respectively).

Another example is the ISO code for tire sizes, which is made up of a wheel diameter (scaled in inches), a tire type (abbreviation code), and a width (scaled in centimeters).

Thus, 15R155 means a 15-inch radial tire that is 155 millimeters wide, whereas 15SR155 is a steel-belted radial tire with the same dimensions. In spite of the mixed American and ISO units, this is a general physical description of a tire in a single code.

Vector schemes are very informative and allow you to pick the best scheme for each component. But they have to be disassembled to get to the components (many database products provide special functions to do this for dates, street addresses, and people's names). Sorting by components is hard unless you want them in the order given in the encoding; try to sort the tire sizes by construction, width, and diameter instead of by diameter, construction, and width.

Another disadvantage is that a bad choice in one component can destroy the usefulness of the whole scheme. Another problem is extending the code. For example, if the standard tire number had to be expanded to include tread thickness in millimeters, where would that measurement go? Another number would have to be separated by a punctuation mark. It could not be inserted into a position inside the code without giving ambiguous codes. The code cannot be easily converted to a fixed-position vector encoding without changing many of the database routines.

3.2.7. Concatenation Encoding

A concatenation code is made up of a variable number of components that are concatenated together. As in a vector encoding, the components can be ordered or unordered, dependent on or independent of each other, and determined by punctuation, symbol-set changes, or position.

A concatenation code is often a hierarchy that is refined by additions to the right. These are also known as facet codes in Europe. Or the code can be a list of features, any of which can be present or missing. The order of the components may or may not be important.

Concatenation codes were popular in machine shops at the turn of the century: A paper tag was attached to a piece of work, and workers at different stations would sign off on their parts of the manufacturing process. Concatenation codes are still used in parts of the airplane industry, where longer codes represent subassemblies of the assembly in the head (also called the root or parent) of the code.

Another type of concatenation code is a quorum code, which is not ordered. These codes say that (n) out of (k) marks must be present for the code to have meaning, as when three out of five inspectors must approve a part before it passes.

The most common use of concatenation codes is in key-word lists in the header records of documents. The author or librarian assigns a list of keywords that describe the material covered by each article in the system. The keywords are picked from a limited, specialized vocabulary that belongs to a particular discipline.

Concatenation codes fell out of general use because their variable length made them harder to store in early computer systems, which used fixed-length records (think of a punch card). The codes had to be ordered and stored as left-justified strings to sort correctly.

These codes could also be ambiguous if they were poorly designed. For example, is the head of 1234 the 1 or the 12 substring? When concatenation codes are used in databases, they usually become a set of "yes/no" check boxes, represented as adjacent columns in the file. This makes them Boolean vector codes, instead of true concatenation codes.

3.3. ATOMIC VERSUS SCALAR

Depending on which book you read to learn relational database management systems (RDBMS), the definition of first normal form (1NF) is that all columns contain only scalar values or atomic values. There is a difference between atomic and scalar. The word "atomic" comes from the Greek, meaning "without parts" or "indivisible"; the idea was that if you split a piece of matter any further than its atoms, it ceased to exist. Scalar values are units on a scale and have to be atomic by their nature. Now consider (longitude, latitude) pairs. Each member of the pair is a scalar (planar degrees), but if the pair is broken up, meaning is lost.

Database designers will often find it is better to model an atomic data element in separate columns rather than making it a single column. This can make data integrity easier to enforce. It can also make computations much easier—would you really like to compute distances on the globe without separate longitude and latitude columns?

The most common example in databases is splitting the names of people into (last_name, middle_name, first_name) to make sorting and editing easier.

3.4. TRANSITION STATES

Another aspect of encoding data is temporal changes. The status of an entity varies over time in a particular pattern of state transitions. Before you die, you must be born. An account moves from various states ("late," "overdue," "collections," "lawsuit," "write-off," etc.) based on the time between payments to the account. While it is not required, it is a good idea to have an encoding that has a semiordering to it. That means that early states are a lower number or alphabetic string, so there is a natural order to the transitions.

3.4.1. State Transitions

Constraints are often modeled as a state transition diagram. There is an initial state, flow lines that show what are the next legal states, and one or more termination states. As a very simple example, consider the usual person's marital life. Notice that we have to start with birth and you are single. It is important to have one initial state, but you can have many termination states. The reason for an initial state is that it can be set as a default in the DDL of a schema. It is also conceptually easier to have a single starting point.

Following up on my example, after you are born, you can die or get married, but you have to be married to get a divorce. The state diagram is shown in Figure 3-2.

In this example, we have only one (very) termination state, death. But this is not always the case. For example, possible jury verdicts in the Scottish system are ("guilty," "not guilty," "not proven"). The first two, ("guilty," "not guilty") are final states, but ("not proven") leaves the case open to a new trial with new evidence, until a statue of limitations is reached. We will get back to the temporal aspects later.

3.4.2. State Transition DDL

Let's start with a table skeleton and try to be careful about the possible states of our life:

```
CREATE TABLE MyLife
( ..
marital_status VARCHAR(15)
   DEFAULT'Birth'
   NOT NULL
CHECK (marital_status IN ('Birth', 'Married',
   'Divorced', 'Death')),
..);
```

We are being good programmers, using a `DEFAULT` and a `CHECK()` constraint. But this does not prevent us from turning birth directly to death, converting `Divorced` to `Married`,

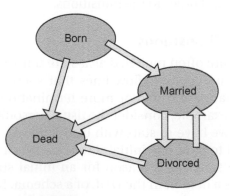

■ **FIGURE 3-2:** State transition diagram.

and so on. You can actually use CHECK() constraints, but you have to store the current and previous states.

```
CREATE TABLE MyLife
(..
previous_state VARCHAR(10) NOT NULL,
current_state VARCHAR(10) DEFAULT 'Birth' NOT NULL,
CHECK (CASE WHEN (previous_state = 'Birth'
            AND current_state IN ('Married',
              'Birth', 'Divorced'))
          THEN 'T'
          WHEN (previous_state = 'Married'
              AND current_state IN ('Divorced',
              'Death')
          THEN 'T'
          WHEN (previous_state = 'Divorced'
              AND current_state IN ('Married',
                'Death')
          THEN 'T' ELSE 'F'  = 'T')
..);
```

In effect, the transition diagram is converted into a search condition. This procedure has advantages; it will pass information to the optimizer, is portable to another SQL product, and will usually run faster than procedural code.

3.4.3. State Transition Tables

Another declarative way to enforce transition constraints is put the state transitions into a table and then reference the legal transitions. This requires that the target table have both the previous and the current state in two columns. Using this example, we would have something like this skeleton table:

```
CREATE TABLE StateChanges
(previous_state VARCHAR(15) NOT NULL,
 current_state VARCHAR(15) NOT NULL,
PRIMARY KEY (previous_state, current_state));

INSERT INTO StateChanges
VALUES ('Birth', 'Birth'), -- initial state
       ('Birth', 'Married'),
       ('Birth', 'Death'),
```

```
                    ('Married', 'Divorced'),
                    ('Married', 'Death'),
                    ('Divorced', 'Married'),
                    ('Divorced', 'Death'),
                    ('Death', 'Death'); -- terminal state
```

The number of rows should be (n + k), where (n) is the number of arrows in the transition diagram and (k) is the number of initial and terminal states. The (k) count is based on requiring (<terminal state>, <terminal state>) and (<initial state>, <initial state>) rows in the table to assure that a row cannot leave a terminal state.

The target table skeleton looks like this:

```
CREATE TABLE SomeStatusAttribute
(..
 previous_<something>_state VARCHAR(15)
   DEFAULT 'Birth' NOT NULL,
 current_<something>_state VARCHAR(15)
   DEFAULT 'Birth' NOT NULL,
 FOREIGN KEY (previous_<something>_state,
   current_<something>_state)
   REFERENCES StateChanges (previous_<something>
     _state, current_<something>_state)
   ON UPDATE CASCADE,
..);
```

If you want to hide this from the users, then you can use an updatable view:

```
CREATE VIEW CurrentSomethingStatus (..,
  marital_status, ..)
AS
SELECT .., current_state, ..
  FROM ..
 ;
```

The immediate advantages to doing so is to pass information to the optimizer, port, as with the CHECK() constraint version. Since the rules are separated from the table declaration, you can maintain them easily. Remember the first rule of professional programming: Write code that is easy to maintain. The few seconds of "hardware time" that you will save with clever code will not make up for "human time" in the long run. Over 80% of the total cost of a system is in maintaining it, not in the design and creation of the code.

3.4.4. Automatic State Transition Tables

One not-so-obvious advantage is that the StateChanges table can contain other data and conditions, such as temporal change data. Your "Birth" cannot change to "Married" until you are of legal age. You cannot go from "Married" to "Divorced" for (n) days and so forth. Likewise, the duration is often between automatic changes is a constant. A very common rule is that your account status is "overdue" when the last payment was over 30 days ago and you do not have a credit balance.

This can be done with some extra columns:

```
CREATE TABLE StateChanges
(previous_<something>_state VARCHAR(15) NOT NULL,
 current_<something>_state VARCHAR(15) NOT NULL,
 <something>_state_duration CHAR(2) DEFAULT '30'
NOT NULL, - number of days for this state
 PRIMARY KEY (previous_state, current_state));
```

If you wish to actually make a change to the base tables (which you should—truth is important!), you will probably have to use a TRIGGER rather than CASCADE declarative referential integrity (DRI) actions. Otherwise, use a VIEW with a CURRENT_DATE to display the actual current status of your base data until you can update it properly.

3.5. GENERAL GUIDELINES FOR DESIGNING ENCODING SCHEMES

These are general guidelines for designing encoding schemes in a database, not firm, hard rules. You will find exceptions to all of them.

3.5.1. Use Existing Encoding Standards

Maybe this rule is hard-coded. The use of existing standard encoding schemes is always recommended. If everyone uses the same codes, data will be easy to transfer and collect in a uniform manner. Also, someone who sat down and did nothing else but work on this scheme probably did a better job than you could while trying to get a database up and running.

As a rule of thumb, if you do not know the industry in which you are working, ask a subject area expert. While that sounds obvious, I have worked on a media library database project where the programmers actively avoided talking to the professional librarians who were on the other side of the project. As a result, recordings were keyed on GUIDs (globally unique identifiers—a Microsoft tool that creates a 16-byte number which is most probably unique because of its wide range) and there were no Schwann or RIAA catalog numbers in the system.

If you cannot find an expert, then go to the Internet and Google for standards. First, check to see if ISO, ANSI, or another national organization has a standard; second, check the U.S. government; third, check industry groups and organizations.

3.5.2. Allow for Expansion

Allow for expansion of the codes. The ALTER statement can create more storage when a single-character code becomes a two-character code, but it will not change the spacing on the printed reports and screens. Start with at least one more decimal place or character position than you think you will need. Visual psychology makes "01" look like an encoding, whereas "1" looks like a quantity.

3.5.3. Use Explicit Missing Values to Avoid NULLs

Rationale: Avoid using NULLs as much as possible by putting special values in the encoding scheme instead. SQL handles NULLs differently from values and NULLs do not tell you what kind of missing value you are dealing with. Most encoding schemes have missing values and miscellaneous value codes.

All zeros are often used for missing values; all nines are often used for miscellaneous values. For example, the ISO gender codes are 0 = Unknown, 1 = Male, 2 = Female, and 9 = Not

Applicable. "Not applicable" means a lawful person, such as a corporation, that has no gender.

Versions of FORTRAN before the 1977 standard read blank (unpunched) columns in punch cards as zeros, so if you did not know a value, you skipped those columns and punched them later, when you did know. Likewise, using encoding schemes with leading zeros was a security trick to prevent blanks in a punch card from being altered.

The FORTRAN 77 standard fixed the "blank versus zero" problem, but it lives on in SQL in badly designed systems that cannot tell a NULL from a blank string, an empty string, or a zero.

The use of all nines or all Zs for miscellaneous values will make those values sort to the end of the screen or report. NULLs sort either always to the front or always to the rear, but which way they sort is implementation-defined.

Exceptions: NULLs cannot be avoided as a missing value token all the time. They are too much a part of SQL. For example, consider the column "termination_date" in the case of a newly hired employee. The use of a NULL makes computations easier and correct. The code simply leaves the NULL date or uses COALESCE() as is appropriate. For example, if you want to know the length of employment in a personnel table, then COALESCE (termination_date, CURRENT_TIMESTAMP) will give the right data for all current and past employees.

3.5.4. Translate Codes for the End User

As much as possible, avoid displaying pure codes to the user, but try to provide a translation. Translation is not required for codes if they are common and well known to the users. For example, most people do not need to see the two-letter state abbreviation written out in full. At the other extreme, however, nobody could read the billing codes used by several long distance telephone companies.

A part of translation is formatting the display so that it can be read by a human being. Punctuation marks, such as dashes, commas, currency signs, and so forth, are important.

However, in a tiered architecture, display is done in the front end, not the database. Trying to put leading zeroes or adding commas to numeric values is a common newbie error. Suddenly, everything is a string and you lose all temporal and numeric computation ability.

These translation tables are one kind of auxiliary table; we will discuss other types later. They do not model an entity or relationship in the schema but are used like a function call in a procedural language. The general skeleton for these tables is:

```
CREATE TABLE SomeCodes
(encode <data type> NOT NULL PRIMARY KEY,
  definition <data type> NOT NULL);
```

Sometimes you might see the definition as part of the primary key or a CHECK() constraint on the "encode" column. But since these are read-only tables, which are maintained outside the application, we generally do not worry about having to check their data integrity in the application itself.

3.5.5. One True Look-up Table

Sometimes a practice is both so common and so stupid that it gets a name. And much like a disease, if it is really bad, it gets an abbreviation. I first ran into the "one true lookup table" (OTLT) design flaw in a thread on a CompuServe forum in 1998, but I have seen it rediscovered in newsgroups every year since.

In the OTLT design, instead of keeping each encoding and its definition in its own table, we put all the encodings in one huge table. The schema for this table looks like this:

```
CREATE TABLE OneTrueLookupTable
(code_type INTEGER NOT NULL,
encoding VARCHAR(n) NOT NULL,
definition VARCHAR(m) NOT NULL,
PRIMARY KEY (code_type, encoding));
```

In practice, m and n are usually something like 255 or 50—default values particular to their SQL product.

The rationale for having all encodings in one table is that it would let you write a single front-end program to maintain all of the encodings. This method really stinks and I want to spend some time discouraging it. Without looking at the following paragraphs, sit down and make a list of all the disadvantages and see if you found anything that I missed.

1. Normalization: The real reason that this approach does not work is that it is an attempt to violate 1NF. Yes, I can see that these tables have a primary key and that all the columns in an SQL database have to be scalar and of one data type. But I would argue that it is not a 1NF table. The fact that two domains use the same data type does not make them the same attribute. The extra "code_type" column changes the domain of the other columns and thus violates 1NF because the column is not atomic. A table should model one set of entities or one relationship, not hundreds of them. The Law of Identity says, "To be is to be something in particular; to be nothing in particular is to be nothing."

2. Total storage size: The total storage required for the OTLT is greater than the storage required for the "one encoding, one table" approach because of the redundant encoding type column. Imagine having the entire ICD and the DDC system in one table. Only the needed small single encoding tables have to be put into main storage with single auxiliary tables, while the entire OTLT has to be pulled in and paged in and out to of main storage if you want to jump from one encoding to another.

3. Data types: All encodings are forced into one data type, which has to be a string of the largest length that any encoding—present and future—uses in the system. But VARCHAR(n) is not always the best way to represent data. The first thing that happens is that someone inserts a huge string that looks right on the screen but has trailing blanks or an odd character to the far right side of the column. The table quickly collects garbage.

CHAR(n) data often has advantages for access and storage in many SQL products. Numeric encodings can take advantage of arithmetic operators for ranges, check digits, and so forth with CHECK() clauses. Dates can be used as codes that are translated into holidays and other events. Data types are not a "one size fits all" affair.

If one encoding allows NULLs, then all of them must in the OTLT.

4. Validation: The only way to write a CHECK() clause on the OTLT is with a huge CASE expression of the form:

```
CREATE TABLE OneTrueLookupTable
(code_type CHAR(n) NOT NULL
            CHECK (code_type IN (<type 1>, ...,
                <type n>)),
encoding VARCHAR(n) NOT NULL
        CHECK (CASE WHEN code_type = <type 1>
                        AND <validation 1>
                    THEN 1
                ...
```

—Assume that your SQL product can support a huge CASE expression:

```
                    WHEN code_type = <type n>
                        AND <validation n>
                    THEN 1
                    ELSE 0 END = 1),
definition VARCHAR(m) NOT NULL,
PRIMARY KEY (code_type, encoding));
```

This means that validation is going to take a long time, because every change will have to be considered by all the WHEN clauses in this oversized CASE expression until the SQL engine finds one that tests TRUE. You also need to add an CHECK() clause to the "code_type" column to be sure that the user does not create an invalid encoding name.

5. Flexibility: The OTLT is created with one column for the encoding, so it cannot be used for (n) valued encodings where (n > 1). For example, if I want to translate (longitude, latitude) pairs into a location name, I would have to carry an extra column.

6. Maintenance: Different encodings can use the same value, so you constantly have to watch which encoding

you are working with. For example, both the ICD and DDC system have three digits, a decimal point, and three digits.

7. Security: To avoid exposing rows in one encoding scheme to unauthorized users, the OTLT has to have VIEWS defined on it which restrict a user to the "code_ type"s that he is allowed to update. At this point, some of the rationale for the single table is gone because the front end must now handle VIEWs in almost the same way that it would handle multiple tables. These VIEWs also have to have the WITH CHECK OPTION clause so that the user does not make a valid change that is outside the scope of his permissions.

8. Display: You have to CAST() every encoding for the front end. This can be a lot of overhead and a source of errors when the same monster string is CAST() to different data types in different programs.

3.6. KEEP THE CODES IN THE DATABASE

There should be a part of the database that contains all of the codes stored in tables. These tables can be used to validate input, to translate codes in displays, and as part of the system documentation.

I was amazed to go to a major hospital in Los Angeles in mid 1993 and see the clerk still looking up codes in a dog-eared loose-leaf notebook instead of bringing them up on her terminal screen. The hospital was still using a very old IBM mainframe system, which had "dumb" 3270 terminals, rather than a client/server system with workstations. There was not even a help screen available to the clerk.

The translation tables can be downloaded to the workstations in a client/server system to reduce network traffic. They can also be used to build pick lists on interactive screens and thereby reduce typographical errors. Changes to the codes are then propagated in the system without anyone having to rewrite application code. If the codes change over time, the table for a code should have to include a pair of "date effective" fields. This will allow a data warehouse to correctly read and translate old data.

3.7. MULTIPLE CHARACTER SETS

Some DBMS products can support ASCII, EBCDIC, and Unicode. You need to be aware of this, so that you can set proper collations and normalize your text.

The predicate " <string> IS [NOT] NORMALIZED" in SQL-99 determines if a Unicode string in one of four normal forms (D, C, KD, and KC). The use of the words "normal form" here are not the same as in a relational context. In the Unicode model, a single character can be built from several other characters. Accent marks can be put on basic Latin letters. Certain combinations of letters can be displayed as ligatures ("ae" becomes "æ"). Some languages, such as Hangul (Korean) and Vietnamese, build glyphs from concatenating symbols in two dimensions. Some languages have special forms of one letter that are determined by context, such as the terminal sigma in Greek or the accented "ú" in Czech. In short, writing is more complex than putting one letter after another.

The Unicode standard defines the order of such constructions in their normal forms. You can produce the same results with different orderings and sometimes with different combinations of symbols. But it is very handy when you are searching such text to know that it is normalized rather than trying to parse each glyph on the fly. You can find details about normalization and links to free software at http://www.unicode.org.

4

Scales

"Where is the wisdom? Lost in the knowledge.
Where is the knowledge? Lost in the information."

—T. S. Eliot

"Where is the information? Lost in the data.
Where is the data? Lost in the #@$%?!& database."

—Joe Celko

There are different types of scales. And not all data can be measured with a scale. We like to think in terms of "something physical" that can be detected with a device, like mass, length, or electrical current, so that we can look for a known scale. But life is not that easy.

In the commercial world, some of the most important data is stored as text. Contracts, laws, regulations, manuals, and so forth are vital for any enterprise. There are some de jure and de facto search standards for text, but we are dealing with semantics and not syntax with text. Computers are good with formal syntax, but still cannot handle semantics, interpretation, and certainly not inspiration. No computer is going to "read" an article on underwater basket-weaving and figure out the techniques given in it will be useful for liver repair surgery. That example is not as absurd as it sounds. A modern technique for skin grafting was invented by a doctor who was looking at the expanded metal grid on his barbeque grill (Meek technique of skin expansion).

Today, we also store other media in databases even though we have limited direct searching techniques. Pictures can be matched, but accurate facial recognition is still slow and costly. Music and sound is easier because it can be made linear.

4.1. BIT FLAGS ARE NOT SCALES

Let me do a flashback to the early days of EDP (Electronic Data Processing) when we had punch cards and magnetic tape files. Primary storage was *very* limited—many mainframe machines had less storage than a modern home computer or even a wristwatch. There was no random access secondary storage. You cannot do random access on a tape or a deck of punch cards by its physical nature. Only sequential access is possible and this shaped the mind-set of the programmers.

The speed of the media was limited by physical movement of punch cards, tape, and time to physically read and write a byte. That meant the time that it took to magnetize the tape or to punch a hole in a card. The concept of the nanosecond did not exist in EDP; neither did the word nanosecond.

This is a model in which physical and logical data are intertwined. Tapes have to be sorted to be useful because display and merging depend on that sequence. A tape or card deck can obviously be sorted in only one order at a time; another ordering requires another sort operation.

This tape sorting key concept is where SQL got the rule of having a PRIMARY KEY for every properly defined table. Later, Dr. Codd would realize that all relational keys have the same power as any other relational key and changed this part of his relational model. But it was too late for SQL to change its syntax. Many early SQL products were built on older file systems that had sequentially ordered indexes and other legacy access methods.

We did our work in sequential process steps, passing tapes from one step to another until we have an output. But how do I tell process step (n + 1) what process step (n) had done? We set a flag in each record to mark completion of a step, usually bit flags.

In particular, each record on a tape file would have a bit flag at the front to show if it was active or inactive. It was not reasonable to physically delete the record, so we flagged it. Later, a garbage collection routine or a procedure that merged another file would delete them from output of that process step. The old tape was retired or archived and the new tape became the file to use.

It did not matter what data was in the record. The flag is at the metadata level and had nothing to do with a data model. The modern concept of a data model did not really exist; this was file design instead.

4.1.1. BITs

Let's define BIT as an abstract data type that always has one of two states, usually shown by {0, 1} in classic switching theory. In hardware, we think of it as a circuit being on or off, a hole in a paper tape, a magnetic spot on a tape or disk. For now, ignore questions about high versus low end architecture and the use of ones complement or twos complement math. Just realize how low-level and physical this is and that it has no place in a high-level abstract data model.

In RDBMS, all data types have to be NULL-able. Exactly what would a NULL mean in a classic physical bit? Does it make it into a "trit" (three-state data type) or something else? How would you handle classic bit-wise operations on such a data type?

Microsoft SQL Server actually has a proprietary BIT data type. In one release of their product, it was implicitly declared NOT NULL, violating the rules for data types in SQL. Then it was "fixed" in the next release by making BIT a NULL-able numeric data type. Unfortunately, if it is numeric, then you can do math with it and that it not how a bit is supposed to work.

This also messed up DDL that was ported from one release to another. Dialect programmers (i.e., someone who writes SQL in a dialect and not standard—"Caesar: Pardon him, Theodotus. He is a barbarian and thinks the customs of his tribe and island are the laws of nature."—*Caesar and Cleopatra*, George Bernard Shaw, 1898) suddenly ran into NULLs where they had expected a default one or zero to be generated by SQL Server.

4.1.2. BITs and Booleans

SQL is a predicate language and uses scalar data. That means that we write a predicate to test for a "state of being" based on the values in attributes. For example, (sex_code = 2 AND (CURRENT_DATE - birth_date >= INTERVAL '18' YEAR)) gives us the characteristic function for females of legal age. This predicate will be true each time you invoke it.

On the other hand, a "legal_age_flg" in each row would have to be recomputed each time we access the table. One of the basic software engineering concepts is cohesion. A module of code with strong functional cohesion can be invoked in any environment and produce the same results. With flags, we have horrible cohesion; the validity of the data depends on executing an UPDATE before the table with flags can be used, so the flags are known to be correct. Even more than that, you cannot allow the table to be accessed by another process that might change it.

Cohesion:

This is how well a module does one and only one thing; that it is logically coherent. The modules should have strong cohesion. You ought to name the module in the format "<verb><object>", where the "<object>" is a specific logical unit in the data model. There are several types of cohesion. We rank them going from the worst form of cohesion to the best

1. Coincidental
2. Logical
3. Temporal
4. Procedural
5. Communicational
6. Informational
7. Functional

Coupling:

If modules have to be executed in a certain order, then they are strongly coupled. If they can be executed independently of each other and put together like Lego blocks, then they are loosely or weakly coupled. There are several kinds of coupling, which are ranked from worse to best:

1. Content
2. Common

3. Control
4. Stamp
5. Data

This is covered briefly in a chapter on writing stored procedures in my book on SQL programming style.

Even worse, an OO (Object Oriented) programmer will write a user defined function in SQL/PSM like "is_legal()" because it looks like the procedural code he knows. The optimizer cannot deal with a procedure or function call because it cannot look inside the body of the procedure. The function is invoked one row at a time, as it computes the legal age status of each row.

BITs are not quite Booleans, but they are used to mimic Booleans by newbies (novice programmers). In the Microsoft world, you have to worry if $+1$ or -1 map to TRUE; their two most popular proprietary languages, Visual Basic (VB) and C# (pronounced "C sharp" and not "C octothorp" as spelled) disagree on the mapping.

Another serious problem with a bit data type is its limited, fixed range. You will often see OO newbies mimic Boolean functions from their OO languages by creating columns with names like "is_male" rather than the "male_flag" that SQL would use under ISO-11179 rules. So they think that setting this bit flag to one means it is a male and setting it to zero means it is a female.

But, the ISO sex-code is (0 = Unknown, 1 = Male, 2 = Female, 9 = Lawful Person, such as a corporation). We cannot use NULL for zero or nine and still have a true bit data type. What happens is that the flag becomes a BIT vector.

4.1.3. BIT Vectors

BIT vectors are not a solution but a bigger problem. Realizing that bit flags have lead to playing "20 Questions" and that the column names are vague, the newbie tries to combine many related bits into one vector, usually modeled with an INTEGER data type.

This requires finding low-level proprietary features and/or complicated integer math to do bit vector operations. For example, consider expressing the ISO sex_code with two bits, you cannot come up with good names for those columns; perhaps "is_male" and "is_human" or worse? In this case, all four of the combinations are legal values, so instead of using an INTEGER, you use two bits and have to convert "11" to 9 when you display a report or join to external data. The saving in physical storage was not worth the extra computations, and the DML code is difficult to maintain.

But imagine a vector with illegal combinations; try to write and maintain a CHECK() constraint to prevent them. The simple math is that (n) bit flags require testing for (2^n) cases. The complexity of working at this low-level of programming increases the real cost of maintaining the DDL code.

Trying modeling a simple five position ranking scale on an air conditioner with radio buttons, labeled ("cold," "cool," "normal," "warm," and "hot"). The nondatabase programmer will mimic the buttons with a flag for each, and then have to make sure that only one of them is "pushed" by constraints. Compare that to a column with the ranking scale in it.

4.1.4. Replacing BITs

The root problem is that the newbie programmer does not know that a bit is not a scalar. When I say "80°C" I know that this value measures temperature and I know the scale is Celsius. The "yes/no" values of a flag can be insanely broad; think about how lawyers ask loaded questions and demand a yes/no answer to trap a witness. They are at a "meta level" and not at a data level. They depend on a context and are often vague even in context.

Is it possible to have a scale with just two values? Yes; consider the Rh, or rhesus, factor in blood typing, which has plus or minus shown by a superscript after the alphabetic blood type code (A, B, AB, and O). This is a particular attribute on a nominal scale with particular validation and verification rules.

You will often see a bit flag used for a status of some kind, say, marking accounts as active or inactive. This mimics the record flag on old magnetic tape records. The flag does not tell us WHY the account is active or inactive and freezes you into two states.

There are two situations:

1. The status of the account is set externally, without any way to verify that decision in the database. I only do database stuff, so I will not deal with business processes. A flag without a constraint can be set to either value, regardless of any business rules. We have lost validation and have to depend on external verification for all data integrity. While this is possible, it means two identical situations can have opposite status and we have no way of knowing why.

2. Usually there are some business rules that determine the account status within the database. These include such things as not paying your bill for a certain length of time, dropping below a certain balance, requesting the account be closed, having an account closed by a legal authority, and so forth. A flag lumps all these business rules (and any future rules) into one bit. As a general statement, it is not good to lose data that might be of use for business decisions and legal requirements.

If I had a well-designed account status, it would tell me which business rule applied. But a status has a temporal component to it; an account is opened, becomes active, and stays that way for some duration. The account can then change status according to certain rules. For example, martial status has a pattern of change: you cannot get married before you are born or after you are dead. You must be married to get a divorce and so forth.

Each of these states has duration, shown as (start_date, end_date) pairs. I can capture the business rules that were in effect then. But if I simply reset the flag according to the new rules, I destroy history.

An actual example of this occurred when the legal age to serve alcohol jumped from 18 to 21 years of age in the United States. A simple personnel system I worked with used flags rather than the birthdates for legal age because it made the staffing schedule staff at a restaurant a little easier in a version of BASIC that had arrays (this is pre-SQL). An illegal staff schedule was in effect the night that the state Alcoholic Beverage Control agency made a visit and shut down the restaurant.

4.2. DIMENSIONLESS MEASUREMENTS

A dimensionless measurement is a measurement without any physical units; it is a pure number. They are usually defined as a product or ratio of quantities which do have units. Percentages need a base measurement from which it is derived. On the other hand, constant pi simply exists as an abstraction which appears from laws of nature and mathematics.

Database people do not like these creatures. They look more like information than data by their nature, so they are out of our expertise. We want to compute them from base data and have control of them. But this is not reasonable and often not even possible.

The Richter number for earthquakes has a complex formula based on many parameters. Only seismologists even knows the names of the three or four measurements that go into it. But people have a rough idea what that dimensionless number means in their world.

Likewise, a percentage with a moving base is hard for people to turn into information. If I tell you that 50% of the steam locomotive engineers in the United States have a PhD, but I do not tell you that the base year for the percentage was 1810 or 2010, the information is useless. Why, half the people in your neighborhood earn below the neighborhood median household income!

4.3. TYPES OF SCALES

The lack or presence of precision and accuracy determines the kind of scale you should choose. Scales are either quantitative or qualitative. The quantitative scales are what most people mean when they think of measurements, because these scales can be manipulated and are usually represented as numbers. Qualitative scales attempt to impose an order or a differentiation on an attribute, but they do not allow for computations—just comparisons.

4.3.1. Nominal Scales

The simplest scales are the nominal scales. They simply assign a unique symbol, usually a number or a name, to each member of the set that they attempt to measure. In illiterate societies, these symbols very often were glyphs of some kind. Rudolf Koch (1876–1934) had a section in his *The Book of Signs* (Dover Publications, ISBN: 0486201627) devoted to the monograms and glyphs used by Renaissance stone cutters for the artist to whom each piece of raw marble was sold. A more modern example would be a list of city names is a nominal scale.

Right away we are into philosophical differences, because many people do not consider listing to be measurement. Since there is no clear property being measured, that school of thought would tell us this cannot be a scale.

There is no natural origin point for a list, and likewise there is no natural ordering. We tend to use alphabetic ordering for names, but it makes just as much sense to use frequency of occurrence or increasing size or almost any other attribute that does have a natural ordering.

The only meaningful operation that can be done with such a list is a test for equality: "Is this city New York or not?" The answer will be TRUE, FALSE, or UNKNOWN.

Nominal scales are very common in databases because they are used for unique identifiers, such as names and descriptions.

4.3.2. Categorical Scales

These ambiguities, redundancies, and deficiencies recall those attributed by Dr. Franz Kuhn to a certain Chinese encyclopedia entitled Celestial Emporium of Benevolent Knowledge. On those remote pages it is written that animals are divided into (a) those that belong to the Emperor, (b) embalmed ones, (c) those that are trained, (d) suckling pigs, (e) mermaids, (f) fabulous ones, (g) stray dogs, (h) those that are included in this classification, (i) those that tremble as if they were mad, (j) innumerable ones, (k) those drawn with a very fine camel's hair brush, (l) others, (m) those that have just broken a flower vase, (n) those that resemble flies from a distance.

—Jorge Luis Borges (from "The Analytical Language of John Wilkins")

The next simplest scales are the categorical scales. They place an entity into a category that is assigned a unique symbol, usually a number or a name. For example, animals might be categorized as reptiles, mammals, and so forth. Finer details would use the binomial nomenclature (http://en.wikipedia.org/wiki/Binomial_nomenclature). The categories have to be within the same class of things to make sense (see the quote from Jorge Luis Borges at the start of this section).

Again, many people do not consider categorizing to be measurement. The categories are probably defined by a large number of properties and there are two potential problems with them.

The first problem is that an entity might fall in one or more categories. For example, a platypus is a furry, warm-blooded egg-laying animal. Mammals are warm-blooded but give live birth and, optionally, have fur. The second problem is that an entity might not fall into any of the categories at all. If we find an animal with chlorophyll and fur on Mars, we do not have an Earthly category of animal in which to place him.

The two common solutions are either to create a new category of animal (monotremes for the platypus and echidna), or to allow an entity to be a member of more than one category. These approaches have problems. The entity without a category gets lost from the data. A "miscellaneous" category that gets too big or too varied does not provide information. An entity is more than one category can be reported more than one time.

The next problem is handling things that do not fit into the categories at all. A Martian animal is discovered that has warm chlorophyll blood, no bones, and reproduces by fusion. Any place you put him is arbitrary.

There is no natural origin point for a collection of subsets, and likewise there is no ordering of the subsets (we will get to nesting subsets with hierarchical encoding). We tend to use alphabetic ordering for names, but it makes just as much sense to use frequency of occurrence or increasing physical size or almost any other attribute that does have a natural ordering.

The only meaningful operation that can be done with such a scale is a test for membership: "Is this animal a mammal or not?" This will test TRUE, FALSE, or UNKNOWN.

4.3.3. Absolute Scales

An absolute scale is a count of the elements in a set. Its natural origin is zero, or the empty set. The count is the ordering (a set of five elements is bigger than a set of three elements, and so on). Addition and subtraction are metric functions. Each element is taken to be identical and interchangeable. For example, when you buy a dozen "Grade A" eggs, you assume that for your purposes any "Grade A" egg will do the same job as any other "Grade A" egg.

Again, absolute scales are very common in databases because they are used for quantities. However, they often have traditional units associated with them. Sheets of paper are sold in reams (500 sheets) or quires (20 sheets). Beverages are sold in a six-pack, which is being replaced with an eight-pack or other multiple packages based on a count of six or eight units. Eggs and other food items are sold in dozens. You can probably add to this list.

People can become strongly attached to a traditional packaging. When decimalization started in the United Kingdom, a dairy offered eggs in 10-packs with a lower cost per egg than the traditional dozen. People would not buy eggs in a nontraditional package because it was too strange. A similar effect occurred in the United States when Coca-Cola first introduced liter-sized bottles. Americans had a vague idea that a liter was a little more than a quart (1 liter = 1.057 quarts) but that a half-gallon was smaller than two liters (2 liters = 0.53 gallons).

I think the liter soft drink bottle won out because it did not look physically different from a quart bottle. Familiarity seems to outweigh savings.

4.3.4. Ordinal Scales

Ordinal scales put things in order but have no origin and no operations. For example, geologists use a scale to measure the hardness of minerals using Moh's Scale for Hardness (MSH, for short). It is based on a set of standard minerals, which are ordered by relative hardness from softest to hardest (talc = 1, gypsum = 2, calcite = 3, fluorite = 4, apatite = 5, feldspar = 6, quartz = 7, topaz = 8, sapphire = 9, diamond = 10).

To measure an unknown mineral, you try to scratch the polished surface of one of the standard minerals with it; if it scratches the surface, the unknown is harder. Notice that I can get two different unknown minerals with the same measurement that are not equal to each other, and that I can get minerals that are softer than my lower bound or harder than my upper bound. There is no origin point and operations on the measurements make no sense (e.g., if I add 10 talc units I do not get a diamond).

A common use we see of ordinal scales today is to measure preferences or opinions. You are given a product or a situation and asked to decide how much you like or dislike it, how much you agree or disagree with a statement, and so forth. The scale is usually given a set of labels such as "strongly agree" through "strongly disagree," or the labels are ordered from 1 to 5.

Consider pairwise choices between ice cream flavors. Saying that "Vanilla" is preferred over "Rotting Leather" in our taste test might well be expressing a universal truth, but there is no objective unit of "likeability" to apply. The lack of a unit means that such things as opinion polls that try to average such scales are meaningless; the best you can do is a histogram of respondents in each category.

Many times an ordinal scale can be made more precise. Dr. Wilbur Scofield developed the Scofield scale in 1912 to measure the strength of peppers. Before the Scofield scale, peppers were informally rated by the personal preferences of cook book authors. There is a long joke (http://www. dabearz.com/forums/f56/yankee-chili-cookoff-33291/) about a New Yorker volunteering to be a judge at a Texas chili competition. While the two native judges can report on the ingredients, the New Yorker is dying from chemical burns.

Likewise, temperature scales on an air conditioner are shown as cool to warm instead of a degree on a Celsius temperature scale.

Another problem is that an ordinal scale may not be transitive. Transitivity is the property of a relationship in which if R(a, b) and R(b, c) then R(a, c). We like this property, and expect it in the real world where we have relationships like "heavier than," "older than," and so forth. This is the result of a strong metric property.

The most common example is the finger game "scissors, paper, stone" in which two players make their moves simultaneously (see *The Official Rock Paper Scissors Strategy Guide* by Douglas and Graham Walker). There are also Efron dice and other recreational mathematic puzzles that are nontransitive.

This problem tends to show up with human preferences in the real world. Imagine an ice cream taster who has just found out that the shop is out of vanilla and he is left with squid, wet leather, and wood as flavor options. He might prefer squid over wet leather, prefer wet leather over wood, and yet prefer wood over squid ice cream, so there is no metric function or linear ordering at all. Again, we are into philosophical differences, since many people do not consider a nontransitive relationship to be a scale.

4.3.5. Rank Scales

Rank scales are like an ordinal scale; they have an origin and an ordering but no natural operations. The most common example of this would be military ranks. Nobody is lower than a private and that rank is a starting point in your military career, but it makes no sense to somehow combine three privates to get a sergeant.

Rank scales have to be transitive: a sergeant gives orders to a private, and since a major gives orders to a sergeant, he can also give orders to a private. You will see ordinal and rank scales grouped together in some of the literature if the author does not allow nontransitive ordinal scales. You will also see the same fallacies committed when people try to do statistical summaries of such scales.

4.3.6. Interval Scales

Interval scales have a metric function, ordering, and meaningful operations among the units, but no natural origin. Calendars are the best example; some arbitrary historical event is the starting point for the scale and all measurements are related to it using identical units or intervals. Time, then, extends from a past eternity to a future eternity.

The metric function is the number of days between two dates. Looking at the three properties: (1) $M(a, a) = 0$: there are zero days between any day and that same day. (2) $M(a, b) = M(b, a)$: there are just as many days from today to next Monday as there are from next Monday to today. (3) $M(a, b) + M(b, c) >= M(a, c)$: the number of days from today to next Monday plus the number of days from next Monday to Christmas is the same as the number of days from today until Christmas, perhaps with a plus or minus sign involved. Ordering is very natural and strong: 1900-07-01 occurs before 1993-07-01. Aggregations of the basic unit (days) into other units (weeks, months, and years) are also arbitrary. Romans and much of Africa used a 10-day week before the Common Era calendar.

Please do not think that the only metric function is simple math; there are log-interval scales, too. The measurements are assigned numbers such that ratios between the numbers reflect ratios of the attribute. You then use formulas of the form $(c * m^d)$, where c and d are constants, to do transforms and operations. For example, density = (mass/volume), fuel efficiency is expressed in Miles per Gallon (mpg) or Kilometers per Liter (kpl), decibel scale is used for sound and the Richter scale for earthquakes are exponential, so their functions involve logarithms and exponents.

Historically, interval scales can evolve into ratio scales. Temperature scales were once considered to have no upper or lower bounds. But that changed with the discovery of Absolute Zero (0°K or −273.15°C) and the invention of the Kelvin temperature scale.

4.3.7. Ratio Scales

Ratio scales are what people think of when they think about a measurement. Ratio scales have an origin (usually zero units), an ordering, and a set of operations that can be expressed in arithmetic. They are called ratio scales because all measurements are expressed as multiples or fractions (ratios) of a certain unit.

Length, mass, and volume are examples of this type of scale. The unit is what is arbitrary; the weight of a bag of sand is still weight whether it is measured in kilograms or in pounds. Another nice property is that the units are identical; a kilogram is still a kilogram whether it is measuring feathers or bricks.

Finally, ratio and interval scales can be used to build compound units, such as square meters and kilometers-per-hour.

4.4. USING SCALES

Absolute and ratio scales are also called extensive scales because they deal with quantities, as opposed to the remaining scales, which are intensive because they measure qualities.

Quantities can be added and manipulated together; qualities cannot.

Type of Scale	Natural Ordering	Natural Origin	Meaningful Functions	Example
Nominal	No	No	No	City names (Atlanta)
Category	No	No	No	Species (dog, cat)
Absolute	Yes	Yes	Yes	Eggs (dozen)
Ordinal	Yes	No	No	Preferences (1 to 5 stars)
Rank	Yes	Yes	No	Races (win, place, show)
Interval	Yes	No	Yes	Calendar
Ratio	Yes	Yes	Yes	Length, Mass

The origin for the absolute scale is numeric zero and the natural functions are simple arithmetic. However, things are not always this simple. Temperature has an origin point at absolute zero and its natural functions average heat over mass. This why you cannot defrost a refrigerator, which is at 0 degrees Celsius, by putting a chicken whose body temperature is 35 degrees Celsius inside of it. The chicken does not have enough mass relative to its body heat. However, a bar of white-hot steel will do a nice job.

4.5. SCALE CONVERSION

Scales can be put in a partial order based on the permissible transformations:

Strength	Scale Type
weakest	Nominal
..	Ordinal
..	Rank
..	Interval & Log-interval
..	Ratio
strongest	Absolute

An attribute might not fit exactly into any these scales. For example, you mix nominal and ordinal information in a single scale, such as in questionnaires that have several non-response categories. It is common to have scales that mix ordinal and an interval scale by assuming the attribute is really a smooth monotone function. Subjective rating scales ("strongly agree," "agree," . . . "strongly disagree") have no "equally spaced intervals" between the ratings, but there are statistical techniques to assure that the difference between two intervals is within certain limits. A binary variable is at least an interval scale and it might a ratio or absolute scale, if it means that the attribute exists or does not exist.

The important principle of measurement theory is that you can convert from one scale to another only if they are of the same type and measure the same attribute.

Absolute scales do not convert, which is why they are called absolute scales. Five apples are five apples, no matter how many times you count them or how you arrange them on the table. The most you can do with them is add similar things together and perhaps convert the results to a traditional unit.

Nominal scales are converted to other nominal scales by a mapping between the scales.

That means you look things up in a table. For example, I can convert my English city names to Chinese names with a dictionary. The problem comes when there is not a one-to-one mapping between the two nominal scales. For example, English vocabulary uses the word "cousin" to identify the offspring of your parents' siblings, and Western tradition treats them all pretty much alike.

Chinese language and culture have separate words for the same relations based on the genders of your parents' siblings and the age relationships among them (e.g., the oldest son of your father's oldest brother is a particular type of cousin and you have different social obligations to him). Something is lost in translation.

Ordinal scales are converted to ordinal scales by a monotone function. That means you preserve the ordering when you convert. Looking at the MSH scale for geologists, I can pick another set of minerals, plastics, or metals to scratch, but rock samples that were definitely softer than others are still softer.

Again, there are problems when there is not a one-to-one mapping between the two scales. My new scale may be able to tell the difference between rocks where the MSH scale could not. But what I want for precise work is the Rockwell scale (abbreviated RHx, where x is a letter in {A, B, C, D, E, F, G} for different forms of the scale). The Rockwell test determines the hardness by measuring the depth of penetration of an indenter (shown by the letter) under a large load compared to the penetration made by a preload.

Rank scales are converted to rank scales by a monotone function that preserves the ordering, like ordinal scales. Again, there are problems when there is not a one-to-one mapping between the two scales. For example, different military branches have slightly different ranks that don't quite correspond to each other. Warrant officers in the U.S. Army have officer privileges, but warrant officers in the British Army do not.

In both the nominal and the ordinal scales, the problem was that things that looked equal on one scale were different on another. This has to do with range and granularity, which was discuss in section 1 of this book.

Interval scales are converted to interval scales by a linear function; that is, a function of the form $y = a*x + b$. This preserves the ordering, but shifts the origin point when you convert. For example, I can convert temperature from degrees Celsius to degrees Fahrenheit using the formula $F = (9.0/5.0 * C) + 32$.

Ratio scales are converted to ratio scales by a constant multiplier, since both scales have the same ordering and origin point. For example, I can convert from pounds to kilograms using the formula $p = 0.4536 * k$. This is why people like to use ratio scales.

4.6. DERIVED UNITS

Many of the scales that we use are not primary units but derived units. These are measures that are constructed from primary units, such as miles per hour (time and distance), or square miles (distance and distance). You can use only ratio and interval scales to construct derived units.

If you use an absolute scale with a ratio or interval scale, you are dealing with statistics, not measurements. For example, using weight (ratio scale) and the number of people in New York (absolute scale), we can compute the average weight of a New Yorker, which is a statistic, not a unit of measurement.

The SI measurements use a basic set of seven units (meter for length, kilogram for mass, second for time, ampere for electrical current, degree Kelvin for temperature, mole for molecules, and candela for light) and construct derived units. ISO standard 2955 ("Information Processing—Representation of SI and other units for use in systems with limited character sets") has a notation for expressing SI units in ASCII character strings. The notation uses parentheses, spaces, multiplication (shown by a period), division (shown by a solidus, or slash) and exponents (shown by numerals immediately after the unit abbreviation). There are also names for most of the standard derived units. For example, "100 kg.m/s2" converts to 10 Newtons (the unit of force), written as "10 N" instead.

Base Quantity	Name	Symbol
length	meter	m
mass	kilogram	kg
time	second	s
electric current	ampere	A
thermodynamic temperature	kelvin	K
amount of substance	mole	mol
luminous intensity	candela	cd

For ease of understanding and convenience, 22 SI derived units have been given special names and symbols.

Derived Quantity	SI Derived Unit			
	Name	Symbol	Expression in SI Units	Expression in SI Base Units
plane angle	radian [a]	rad	-	$m·m^{-1} = 1$ [b]
solid angle	steradian [a]	sr [c]	-	$m^2·m^{-2} = 1$ [b]
frequency	hertz	Hz	-	s^{-1}
force	newton	N	-	$m·kg·s^{-2}$
pressure, stress	pascal	Pa	N/m^2	$m^{-1}·kg·s^{-2}$
energy, work, quantity of heat	joule	J	$N·m$	$m^2·kg·s^{-2}$
power, radiant flux	watt	W	J/s	$m^2·kg·s^{-3}$
electric charge, quantity of electricity	coulomb	C	-	$s·A$
electric potential difference, electromotive force	volt	V	W/A	$m^2·kg·s^{-3}·A^{-1}$

(Continued)

	SI Derived Unit			
Derived Quantity	**Name**	**Symbol**	**Expression in SI Units**	**Expression in SI Base Units**
capacitance	farad	F	C/V	$m^{-2} \cdot kg^{-1} \cdot s^4 \cdot A^2$
electric resistance	ohm	Ω	V/A	$m^2 \cdot kg \cdot s^{-3} \cdot A^{-2}$
electric conductance	siemens	S	A/V	$m^{-2} \cdot kg^{-1} \cdot s^3 \cdot A^2$
magnetic flux	weber	Wb	V·s	$m^2 \cdot kg \cdot s^{-2} \cdot A^{-1}$
magnetic flux density	tesla	T	Wb/m^2	$kg \cdot s^{-2} \cdot A^{-1}$
inductance	henry	H	Wb/A	$m^2 \cdot kg \cdot s^{-2} \cdot A^{-2}$
Celsius temperature	degree Celsius	°C	-	K
luminous flux	lumen	lm	cd·sr [c]	$m^2 \cdot m^{-2} \cdot cd = cd$
illuminance	lux	lx	lm/m^2	$m^2 \cdot m^{-4} \cdot cd = m^{-2} \cdot cd$
activity (of a radionuclide)	becquerel	Bq	-	s^{-1}
absorbed dose, specific energy (imparted), kerma	gray	Gy	J/kg	$m^2 \cdot s^{-2}$
dose equivalent [d]	sievert	Sv	J/kg	$m^2 \cdot s^{-2}$
catalytic activity	katal	kat		$s^{-1} \cdot mol$

4.7. PUNCTUATION AND STANDARD UNITS

Database stores measurements as numeric data represented in a binary format, but when the data is input or output, a human being wants readable characters and punctuation.

Punctuation serves to identify the units being used, and can be used for prefix, postfix, or infix symbols. It can also be implicit or explicit.

If I write "$25.15," you know that the unit of measure is the dollar because of the explicit prefix dollar sign. If I write "160 lbs.," you know that the unit of measure is pounds because of the explicit postfix abbreviation for the unit. If I write "1989MAR12," you know that this is a date because of the implicit infix separation among month, day, and year, achieved by changing from numerals to letters. The ISO and SQL defaults represent the same date, using explicit infix punctuation, with "1989-03-12" instead. Likewise, a column header on a report that gives the units used is explicit punctuation.

Databases do not generally store punctuation. There was a proprietary MONEY or CURRENCY data type found in a few old SQL implementations. But they are considered bad programming practices. As of this writing, there are only two nondecimal currencies left on Earth (Mauritania and Madagascar), and they are so worthless that nobody uses them. Instead, DECIMAL(s,p) is preferred since the precision can be adjusted to follow rules and regulations about computations. Punctuation wastes storage space and the units can be represented in some internal format that can be used in calculations. Punctuation is only for display, which is supposed to be done outside of the database.

It is possible to put the units in a column next to a numeric column that holds their quantities. This is awkward and wastes storage space. If everything is expressed in the same unit, the unit's column is redundant. If things are expressed in different units, you have to convert them to a common unit to do any calculations. Why not store them in a common unit in the first place? The database administrator (DBA) has to be sure that all data in a column of a table is expressed in the same units before it is stored. There are horror stories about multinational companies sending the same input programs used in the United States to their European offices, where SI and Imperial measurements were mixed into the same database without conversion.

Ideally, the DBA should be sure that data is kept in the same units in all the tables in the database. If different units are needed, they can be provided in a VIEW that hides the conversions (thus the office in the United States sees Imperial measurements and the European offices see SI units and date formats; neither is aware of the conversions being done for it).

4.8. GENERAL GUIDELINES FOR USING SCALES IN A DATABASE

The following are general guidelines for using measurements and scales in a database and not firm hard rules. You will find exceptions to all of them.

1. The more unrestricted the permissible transformations on a scale are, the more restricted the statistics in general. Almost all statistics are applicable to measurements made on ratio scales, but only a very limited group of statistics may be applied to measurements made on nominal, ordinal and ranking scales.

2. Use `CHECK()` clauses on table declarations to make sure that only the allowed values appear in the database. If you have the `CREATE DOMAIN` feature of SQL-92, use it to build your scale types. Nominal scales would have a list of possible values; other scales would have range checking.

   Likewise, use the `DEFAULT` clauses to be sure that each scale starts with its origin value, a `NULL`, or a default value that makes sense.

3. Declare at least one more decimal place than you think that you will need for your smallest units. In most SQL implementations, rounding and truncation will improve with more decimal places.

4. Declare at least one order of magnitude more than you think that you will need. This gives you a safety margin and room for expansion for a relatively small cost.

   The downside of SQL is that the rules for precision, truncation, and rounding are implementation-dependent, so a query with calculations might not give the same results on another SQL product. However, SQL is more merciful than older file systems, since the DBA can ALTER a numeric column so it will have more precision and a greater range without destroying existing data or queries. Host programs may have to be changed to display the extra characters in the results.

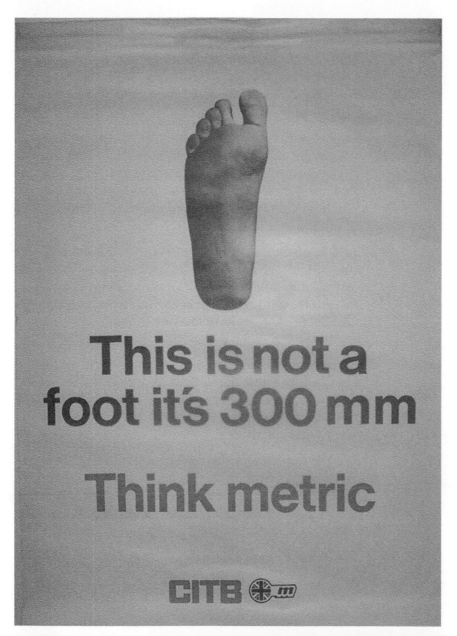

■ FIGURE 4-1: When the United Kingdom converted from Imperial to SI units of measurement, the various trade organizations ran advertising campaigns. This one is from Construction Industry Training Board (CITB). The three nonmetric countries on Earth are Liberia, Myanmar, and the United States.

However, you also need to consider laws and accounting rules that deal with currencies. The European Union has rules for computing with euros and the United States has similar rules for dollars in the GAAP (Generally Accepted Accounting Practices).

5. Try to store primary units rather than derived units. This is not always reasonable or even possible, since you might not be able to measure anything but the derived unit. Look at your new tire gauge; it is set for Pascals (Newtons per square meter) and will not tell you how many square meters you have on the surface of the tire or the force exerted by the air.

And you simply cannot figure these things out from the Pascals given. A set of primary units can be arranged in many different ways to construct any possible derived unit desired. Never store both the derived and the primary units in the same table.

Not only is this redundant, but it opens the door to possible errors when a primary-unit column is changed and the derived units based on it are not updated. Also, most computers can recalculate the derived units much faster than they can read a value from a disk drive.

6. Use the same punctuation whenever a unit is displayed. For example, do not mix ISO and ANSI date formats, or express weight in pounds and kilograms on the same report. Ideally, everything should be displayed the same way in the entire system and use industry standard terms.

Data with Ignorance

The great truth is that we don't know everything. I have already discussed the need for special values in encoding schemes to allow for missing data, miscellaneous categories, and so forth. But what do you do when the data value is either absurd or missing completely? What if the "exception codes" built into the encoding scheme cannot be used for computations?

Statistics has techniques for replacing bad data with approximations that let us continue on at the aggregate level, even though the individual data might be wrong or at least not verified. The purpose of this chapter is not to be a class in statistics but only to make you aware of their existence. If you don't understand some of the terms, you can either skip this chapter or look up the definitions in any elementary textbook.

5.1. GET IT RIGHT

Consider loading a data warehouse with a row that says the customer is a 1000-year-old man. One choice is to drop the entire row at the expense of missing a lot of correct data in that row. This is not always a bad thing from a business viewpoint. If enough of the columns for this customer are also absurd, then it might well be garbage data that needs to be rejected.

Or the cost of correcting the error might be more than the value realized. Anyone who has run a small retail store knows that the cash register seldom balances to the penny at the end of the day. You simply live with the till being over or under

Doi: 10.1016/B978-0-12-374722-8.00005-0

and show it as an expected error in your bookkeeping. When the amount of error is consistently out of balance by significant amounts, then you worry and take corrective actions.

Ideally, we want to go back and recreate the data from the source. In this case, we would ask the customer what his birthdate is and change the data. But you cannot ask all of yesterday's customers at a small retail store to count the change that you gave them.

Graeme Simsion (http://www.simsion.com.au/) has a wonderful quote about data quality; first you mop the floor, then you fix the leak. Craig Mullens also reminded me that sometimes you need to shut off the water supply before you can even start to mop the floor! Once you find a systematic source of errors, you must first correct the bad data and then prevent it from happening again. This is a whole topic in itself, so let me get back on topic.

5.2. REPLACE BAD VALUES WITH A GENERAL DUMMY VALUE

It is usual to replace an obviously bad value with a dummy value, especially when the encoding scheme has a code for "unknown," "missing," and so forth that can be put into place during data scrubbing. It is easy to set the age of all customers who have some absurd birthdate to a dummy date that makes them all 1000+ years old.

For such dummy dates, programmers seem to like to use the earliest date that their favorite SQL product can store. Since products do not agree on this "Beginning of the Universe" date, porting code is difficult. It also has the problem of being a real date, and computations done with it will return valid, even if absurd, answers.

5.3. REPLACE BAD VALUES WITH A STATISTICAL DUMMY VALUE

We usually know something about the statistical distribution of an attribute. Let's say that we know that our customers are between 18 and 95 years of age based on sampling the existing data. We can reject the 0-year-old man and the

1000-year-old man as being out of range. But what do we substitute for their ages?

One of the most common solutions is to use the average of the incoming data, not the average of the whole database. The rationale is that the new data items are probably drawn from the same population and will be similar. For example, if my incoming data is from a retirement community in Florida, then the average sample age will be over 55 years. If my incoming data is from a college spring break in the same town in Florida, then the average sample age will be closer to 21 years.

If the population is skewed (the spring break data included a lot of senior citizens who were at the beach for a real estate marketing show), then the median might be a better replacement value. The median is a better measure of central tendency, but it is harder to compute. Random sampling can often come up with a good quick estimate of the median, but you have to know what you are doing.

5.4. REPLACE BAD VALUES TO COMPLETE A STATISTICAL DISTRIBUTION

Our knowledge of the statistical distribution of an attribute goes beyond the minimum, maximum, and average value. There is a very good chance that the values fall into a normal distribution (aka "bell curve"), so we can compute the standard deviation (shown with the Greek letter sigma). We know that the ages of ~99.7% of our customers fall inside plus or minus three standard deviations of the mean (average), but we can be happy with two sigma (95.4%) coverage.

Instead of looking at the replacement value one row at a time, we can look at the data as a whole. The goal of the replacement values is to fill in "holes" in the normal distribution. In effect, we are saying that we know we should have (n) customers of age (x), so I will assign age (x) to missing data until I get (n) customers of that age.

This is better than just grabbing the average or a dummy value, but we are still inventing values under assumptions about the data as a whole.

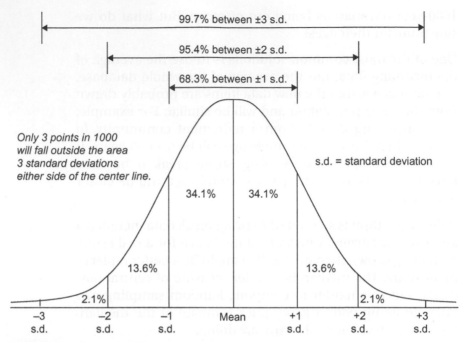

99.7% between ±3 s.d.

95.4% between ±2 s.d.

68.3% between ±1 s.d.

Only 3 points in 1000 will fall outside the area 3 standard deviations either side of the center line.

s.d. = standard deviation

34.1%　34.1%

13.6%　13.6%

2.1%　2.1%

| −3 s.d. | −2 s.d. | −1 s.d. | Mean | +1 s.d. | +2 s.d. | +3 s.d. |

■ **FIGURE 5-1:** Statistical distribution with values that fall into a normal distribution.

5.5. REPLACE BAD VALUES WITH STATISTICAL PROFILING

You can pick values that match a profile using correlation methods. Look at what you know about your customer and use a Bonferroni tree or other method to generate rules. Without going into the math, these techniques give you if-then rules to predict a value. You get things like "if he buys denture cream, then his age is between 60 and 90 years" or "if he buys energy drinks and condoms, then his age is between 18 and 25 years" and you can refine them further. Given that the denture cream buyer is also buying adult diapers then we can narrow his age to the 75-to-90 year age range. Then you can use the average within these subpopulations as the replacement value.

This is the most expensive method and it is probably the best. The replacement values in other methods can be as absurd as the rejected value, and we have created a 21-year-old man who uses denture cream and adult diapers to fill out a curve.

Keys

Keys are fundamentally different from other attributes. They have to be "stronger" than nonkey attributes because relationships in an RDBMS depend on the keys. That strength comes from properties that we want in a key.

6.1. UNIQUENESS

A key by definition is unique. This is why you cannot use a person's name for a key in any system larger than a PDA contact list. It is up to me to find some way to tell one "John Smith" from another. In the case of a PDA or cell phone, I change the name of one of them to "John Smith Jr." or something else. In a larger database, I will need a different key.

In the old days, other data values were hashed with the name to get a unique identifier. In the case of the Internet, many Web sites use the e-mail address of their customers.

6.2. A KEY CANNOT BE NULL

A key cannot be NULL by definition. But people often forget that a key can be multipart and that none of the parts can be NULL-able. This is a special case of uniqueness in disguise. If we allowed a NULL, then we would never be sure that it does not resolve to an existing value and give us a duplicate.

This bothers SQL newbies. You often have part of a multipart key or an entity that needs to go into the schema. If this was a manufacturing situation and a vehicle was missing the engine, nobody would call this an automobile. The same reasoning applies to a row in a table—if it has no key, then it is not finished.

But you can borrow some tricks from manufacturing. Hold the data aside until you have a key and can release a "finished product" into the schema. This is this is the classic "work in progress" items of a manufacturing inventory. Another trick is to create temporary identifiers that have to be replaced with real ones. I will discuss open codes later in this book.

6.3. INVARIANT OR UNIVERSALLY CONTROLLED VALUES

Ideally, we would love to have a key that is invariant for all eternity. The (longitude, latitude) of a location is such an example—assuming that you planed to stay in business until the Earth blows up. However, things are not always that easy. In 2006, the retail industry in the United States switched from the 10-digit UPC barcode on products to the 13-digit EAN system, and the ISBN (International Standard Book Number) is falling under the same scheme.

But the retail industry is still alive and well. Why? The most important property of a key is that it must ensure uniqueness. But that uniqueness does not have to be eternal. Nor does the format have to be fixed for all time. They simply have to be universally verifiable at the time I ask my question.

The retail industry assured that the old and the new barcodes would identify the same products by a carefully planned migration path. This is what allowed us to change the values and the formats of one of the most common identifiers on earth. The migration path started with changing the length of the old UPC code columns from 10 to 13 and padding them with leftmost zeros.

The migration added leading digits for the country of origin of the product and changed the check digit computation (it actually made it weaker!). If you look at the back cover of a book for the next few years, you will see both an ISBN and the new ISBN-13 codes.

On January 1, 2010, the GTIN (Global Trade Item Number) standards to go into effect for the retail industry. You can get details and tools at http://www.GS1.org.

The hard work in this massive conversion was not so much on the database side of the industry as it was in applications. Printouts, display screens, reports, and so on needed extra space to handle the longer codes.

6.4. SURROGATE AND PHYSICAL LOCATORS KEYS

This is one of the most misunderstood concepts in RDBMS. Newbies fake surrogate keys with various proprietary autonumbering features in their database product. For example, the `IDENTITY` property of a table in the Sybase/SQL Server family is a count of attempted physical insertions; it has nothing to do with the logical data model and exists only in one schema on one machine. ROWID in Oracle is the track and sector on the physical disk. Imagine that you are identifying an automobile by the current parking space number at one store instead of the VIN.

Dr. Codd gave a definition of Surrogate Keys, to quote:

Database users may cause the system to generate or delete a surrogate, but they have no control over its value, nor is its value ever displayed to them . . . (Dr. Codd in ACM TODS, pp. 409–410) and Codd, E. (1979), Extending the Database Relational Model to Capture More Meaning. ACM Transactions on Database Systems, 4(4). pp. 397–434.

This means that a surrogate ought to act like an index: created by the user, managed by the system, and never seen by a user. That means never used in queries, DRI, or anything else that a user does. Autonumbering is an exposed physical locator and not a surrogate.

Dr. Codd also wrote the following: "There are three difficulties in employing user-controlled keys as permanent surrogates for entities:

1. The actual values of user-controlled keys are determined by users and must therefore be subject

to change by them (e.g. if two companies merge, the two employee databases might be combined with the result that some or all of the serial numbers might be changed).

2. Two relations may have user-controlled keys defined on distinct domains (e.g. one uses social security, while the other uses employee serial numbers) and yet the entities denoted are the same.

3. It may be necessary to carry information about an entity either before it has been assigned a user-controlled key value or after it has ceased to have one (e.g. and applicant for a job and a retiree).

6.4.1. Physical Locators for Performance

The two arguments usually made for machine generated physical locators ("fake pointers") are weak. The first is that a multicolumn key is so lengthy that performance is adversely affected.

In practice, I have not found a multicolumn key that runs past five columns. Such keys are usually two or three columns with an obvious relationship among them, such as coordinate systems. I have seen five columns in a data warehouse that used organizational and temporal data as part of the key. The estimate, as of 2006, was that a human being has between 20,000 and 25,000 genes, so if you wanted to use a full human genome as a key, then you would be in trouble.

If the multicolumn key is an actual constraint, you still have to assure its uniqueness with a constraint. Creating a redundant one-column pseudo-key is not an option. This only means more overhead for inserts, deletes, and updates. Perhaps the funniest example of this mindset was the use of a GUID/UUID (16 bytes) for an IP address that had been modeled as four TINYINTs (a TINYINT or nybble is a 4-bit aggregation or half an 8-bit byte for a total of 16 bytes). The GUID/UUID was supposed to save space. All it did was double it and give a value that cannot be used in partial address searches.

The performance argument only applies to certain implementations. In the SQL Server family, the FOREIGN KEY column(s) repeat the referenced PRIMARY KEY value and use B-tree indexes on each table. This is a legacy problem in which each table is treated as if it were a stand-alone file.

Sybase SQL Anywhere uses pointers from the FOREIGN KEY to the single appearance of the PRIMARY KEY value in the schema. This was from network database architectures.

Teradata and SQLs that use hashing will work better with longer keys because they hash with fewer collisions. There are other architectures that do not depend on the length of the keys for access speed.

6.4.2. Physical Locators for Lack of a Proper Key

The second argument is that no suitable natural key exists and we have to do something locally. A natural key has to exist by the Law of Identity (all things in the universe are unique). But it might not be a suitable key. More times than not, this is a result of a bad design—or the designer is too lazy to look for industry standards.

Today, you can Google ANSI, ISO, DIN, and industry standards. These standards are available online or in machine-readable formats. If you bother to look for these standards, the problem is the opposite! There are too many of them! Do you want to organize your library with Dewey Decimal Classification or Library of Congress? Or, if you deal with Asian languages, you might want to use the Nippon Decimal Classification (NDC), Chinese Library Classification (CLC), or Korean Decimal Classification (KDC).

Do I market my wine in the European or the U.S. system of bottle sizes? Does your music collection use the ISRC (International Standard Recording Code) code (http://www.ifpi.org/content/section_resources/isrc.html) or the Schwann catalog number?

I suggest that you look at http://www.nationmaster.com, which is a Web site devoted to national information for anyone who has to do international business.

If you honestly cannot find industry standards and have to create an identifier, then you need to take the time to design one, with validation and verification rules, instead of returning to 1950s-style magnetic tape files.

6.4.3. Trusted Sources

We have already talked about validation (done internally in the database) and verification (done externally). But then this leads to the concept of a "trusted source" that can give us verification. And then that leads to the concept of "How trusted?" is my source.

My ATM believes the four-digit PIN when it gives me money. My local grocery store believes that the check I cash is good and that the address on the check and Texas driver's license number are correct. If I produced a license with the picture that did not match my face or the name on the check, the store would question or refuse my check.

When I go to travel to certain countries, I need a birth certificate and a passport. This is a higher degree of trust. For some security clearances, I need to provide fingerprints. For some medical tests, I need to provide DNA—that is probably the highest degree of trust, since even identical twins have different DNA (http://www.nytimes.com/2008/03/11/health/11real.html).

An industry standard has an external trusted source—the governing organization that controls the standard. Locally created identifiers also need a single internal trusted source. This internal trusted source ought to be accessible by both database and application programmers.

One of the most common mistakes is the failure of IT to talk to internal departments so that everyone uses the same codes. The accounting department is probably the least used source. Accounting defines the fiscal calendar, identifiers for commercial documents, and so forth.

Do not be afraid of the accounting department; they can be our friends.

Part 7

A Sampling of Standards

These ambiguities, redundancies, and deficiencies recall those attributed by Dr. Franz Kuhn to a certain Chinese encyclopedia entitled Celestial Emporium of Benevolent Knowledge. On those remote pages it is written that animals are divided into (a) those that belong to the Emperor, (b) embalmed ones, (c) those that are trained, (d) suckling pigs, (e) mermaids, (f) fabulous ones, (g) stray dogs, (h) those that are included in this classification, (i) those that tremble as if they were mad, (j) innumerable ones, (k) those drawn with a very fine camel's hair brush, (l) others, (m) those that have just broken a flower vase, (n) those that resemble flies from a distance.

The Analytical Language of John Wilkins,
by Jorge Luis Borges

The first part of this book discussed the principles of designing data encoding schemes and some of the history of standardization. This second part will give examples of actual standards used in a variety of industries. Although my choices are not quite as weird as the "Celestial Emporium of Benevolent Knowledge" quoted at the beginning of this part, I tried to give standards for common things and for specialized things.

The common things are more complex than people think that they are. Because they are common, there are often several ways to measure and encode them.

The specialized things are unknown to people outside a particular trade. When a database has to interface with that trade or industry, the DB designer will invent his own encodings and create huge problems. If you want an example of what can happen, read "The Data Model That Nearly Killed Me" by Joe Bugajski, March 17, 2009 (http://www.syleum .com/2009/03/17/healthcare-data-model/). It is the story of a medical emergency that was almost fatal to the author because of poor data modeling and the inability to exchange data within the hospital system.

In the pre-Internet days, when systems were isolated and documentation was only on paper, it was hard to find standards to use. This is assuming that such standards even existed. Things such as standardized screws, bolts, nuts, and springs did not show up until the 1900s. A Sunday newspaper feature article in the *New York Times* for April 18, 1915, had the verbose title: "AUTOMOBILE STANDARDS TOPIC OF DETROIT MEET; S.A.E. to Discuss Many Points of Importance to Consumers at Gathering This Week—What Standards Have Meant." Leaf springs were a very complicated automobile part in 1915.

Today, you should do "Google diligence" and "Wikipedia diligence" at the start of a project when you are not a subject matter expert. Most of the second part of this book is taken from Google, Wikipedia, newsgroups, company Web sites, and contributions from friends.

My choices might be grouped as standards that have to do with people, with locations in time and space, and commercial things. There are thousands more that I might have covered, but I hope that I picked interesting ones.

Chapter

7

Dates

Until fairly recently, nobody agreed on the proper display format for dates. Every nation seems to have its own commercial conventions. Most of us know that Americans put the month before the day and the British do the reverse, but do you know any other national conventions? National date formats may be confusing when used in an international environment. Slashes, dashes, dots, or spaces can separate the three fields. The order of the fields varies and sometimes the year is two digits or four digits.

Of course, the names of the months and time zones disagree across language, so we prefer numbers and not full words or abbreviations. At one time, NATO tried to use Roman numerals for the month to avoid language problems among treaty members; this was because of the French membership at the time.

7.1. ISO-8601 STANDARD

The ISO-8601 standard consolidated older ISO standards for dates and times. We can do Common Era (CE) dates, time of day, combined date and time of day, and time intervals. The Common Era was formerly known as the Georgian calendar and dates in it were expressed with AD ("Anno Domini" or "In the year of (the/Our) Lord" in English) and BC ("Before Christ"), depending if they were after or before an estimated date for the birth of Jesus Christ. There is no "Year Zero," so 1 BC is before 1 AD. This is obviously biased toward the Christian religion, but the world agreed on its usage with the rise of Western civilization and globalization.

The display formats are a mix of digits for the temporal units of time, zone displacements, and other common temporal representations. These fixed-length fields are separated by punctuation marks or uppercase letters. The standard does not deal with temporal data shown in a particular language and it should not.

The date information is ordered from left to right, the most significant to the least significant unit: year, month (or week), day, hour, minute, second, and fractional second. This gives you a natural sort order, but you have to remember that current version of the standard allows negative dates for historical usage before the Common Era (BCE).

Each date and time value has a fixed number of digits that must be padded with leading zeros.

7.1.1. Year Field

The year has to be at least four digits; this is a result of the "Y2K Crisis" in the year 2000. If you want to represent years before 0000 or after 9999, you can expand the year field to extra digits and prefix it with a + for years CE or − sign for years BCE with the convention that year 0 is positive.

MySQL has an extension to this that uses "YYYY-00-00," where the zeros are a placeholder for a unspecified month within the year or the whole year. It is not part of the ISO standards, but you should be aware of it.

ISO 8601 fixes a reference calendar date to the Common Era calendar of 1875-05-20, which is the date the "Convention du Mètre" (Meter Convention) was signed in Paris and the SI system started. However, ISO calendar dates before the Convention are still compatible with the Common Era calendar all the way back to the official introduction of the Gregorian calendar on 1582-10-15. Earlier dates, in the proleptic Common Era calendar, are used by mutual agreements.

You probably have never of a proleptic calendar. It is a calendar that is extended backward in time from the official starting date by following the rules of that calendar.

The Julian calendar was introduced in 45 BCE, but when historians date events before that year, they normally extend the Julian calendar backward in time. This is the "Julian Proleptic Calendar." Similarly, it is possible to extend the Gregorian calendar backward in time before 1582.

Since the ISO scheme has a year 0000, the year 3 BC in the Gregorian calendar scheme is represented by –0002. This all means that you have to be careful when looking at historical data.

7.1.2. Month Field

The month values are shown as two digits in the range of 01–12. The month cannot be used by itself but has to have a year attached to it. The format is "YYYY-MM" but not "YYYYMM" to avoid confusion.

MySQL has an extension to this that uses "YYYY-MM-00," where the zeros are a placeholder for an unspecified day within the month or the whole month.

7.1.3. Week Field

```
Week dates
Main article: ISO week date
YYYY-Www  or  YYYYWww
YYYY-Www-D  or  YYYYWwwD
```

Week date representations are in the format as shown in the box to the right. YYYY indicates the ISO week-numbering year, which is slightly different to the calendar year (see below). Www is the week number prefixed by the letter "W," from W01 through W53. D is the weekday number, from 1 (Monday) through 7 (Sunday). Since weeks do not align to year boundaries, we need to have a rule for which week is week 01. The ISO definition is that it has the Thursday of its year in it (the formal ISO definition). But there are equivalent rules:

- the week with 4 January in it
- the first week with four or more of its days in the year

■ the week starting with the Monday in the period December 29 thru January 04

7.1.4. Day Field

The day is the one unit of time on which calendars agree. After that, cultures aggregate days in "weeks" of 5, 7, 14, or 15 days. Likewise, the "month" varies in size and there are days outside of months and weeks altogether.

7.1.4.1. Day within Month

The standard allows both the "YYYY-MM-DD" and "YYYYMMDD" formats for complete calendar date representations. The SQL standards use only the first format, but vendors may allow others, usually national variants.

The months in the Common Era calendar vary from 28 to 31 days in each month, so certain "MM-DD" combinations are not allowed. Years are actually 365.2422 days. The fractional day accumulates leads to leap years to correct the error. Every four years the 0.24 days give us a February 29; every 400 years the 0.0022 days give us another day to correct. A year is a leap year if it is divisible by 4 but not by 100. If a year is divisible by 4 *and* by 100, it is *not* a leap year *unless* it is also divisible by 400. This was one of the problems with the year 2000—it was a leap year, but nobody alive had seen a 400-year cycle. Some spreadsheets had the computation wrong!

7.1.4.2. Day within Year

This is called the ordinal date. Their format is "YYYY-DDD" or "YYYYDDD," where DDD maps from 001 to 365 or 366 in leap years. This is the ordinal position of a day within its year. This is *not* a Julian date; that is a count of the days from January 1, 4713 BCE, at Greenwich noon on the Julian proleptic calendar; only astronomers use it. This is a *Julianized* date within a year. You can Julianize longer periods in your own look-up tables for calculations across years.

This format is usually embedded in encoding schemes that depend on a timestamp of some kind. The best example was an old IBM magnetic tape label format that used "YYDDD," which fell out of favor in the "Y2K crisis" years. The advantage of the format before 2000 was that the labels were in temporal order and the math was easy; tapes had to be archived in a certain number of days.

7.1.5. Time Field

ISO 8601 uses the 24-hour clock system. A day starts at "00:00:00" (zero hour) and ends just before the start of the following day. The model is a half-open interval in mathematical terms.

The basic format uses an optional colon separator, an American convention that is not followed in other countries.

7.1.5.1. Hour Field

Hours are two digits between 00 and 23, but you will see "24" used as the "00" of the following day. The easiest way to think of it is that is like converting 12 inches into 1 foot. DB2 will accept 24 as input and do the conversion to the proper format when the time is displayed.

7.1.5.2. Minute Field

Minute are shown as two digits between "00" and "59," but you will see "60" used as the "00" of the following hour.

7.1.5.3. Second Field

Second are shown as two digits between "00" and "59," mostly. To keep the official atomic clock for the world and the astronomical clock aligned, we created a "leap second" to adjust them. This means that you might have a minute with 59, 60, or 61 seconds in duration.

The world runs on two clocks, UTC (Coordinated Universal Time) and UT1 (mean solar time—observed Earth rotation). The UTC is based on an atomic clock, which is very stable and consistent. UT1 is based on the Earth's rotation. But the Earth wobbles and gives small random fluctuations in its rotation. UT1 was known as GMT (Greenwich Mean Time) before the ISO standards, but that term is obsolete.

Starting the 1972, the International Earth Rotation and Reference System Service (IERS) has added a second on the UTC during some years to keep the difference between UTC and UT1 less than 0.9 seconds. You can get more details at Timeanddate.com.

At the time of this writing, there are proposals to do away with the leap second altogether—2008 may be the last year that they are used. It is unpredictable and most of the world's time is kept by machines and not by sundials.

It is also acceptable to omit lower order time elements for reduced accuracy: hh:mm, hhmm, and hh are all used.

7.1.6. Time Zones and Daylight Saving Time

The letter "Z" separates the time fields from the Zone codes:

<time> = The time is assumed to be local time when no Zone is given.

<time>Z = The time is UTC. This is also known as "Zulu" time in the Military because "Zulu" is the NATO phonetic alphabet word for "Z".

<time>±hh = the time is displaced from UTC by plus or minus hh hours.

<time>±hh:mm or <time>±hhmm == the time is displaced from UTC by plus or minus hh hours and mm minutes. Yes, there are still local times that are fractional hours off of the standard time zones.

On December 07, 2007, Venezuela created own time zone. President Hugo Chavez wanted to be in a different time zone from the United States. Of course, Venezuela was put out of step with all of its neighboring nations and trade was messed up.

Canada's Newfoundland province is half an hour out of step with other Atlantic provinces.

Pakistan is 30 minutes behind India, while Nepal is 15 minutes ahead of India.

Western Australia and South Australia observe a 90-minute time difference across the state boundary. It gets even worse in the Australian town of Eucla, which has about 200 people and its own time zone, 45 minutes ahead of Western Australia and 45 minutes behind South Australia.

7.2. PUTTING IT ALL TOGETHER

The syntax for a complete date and time is " <date> T <time> ," where the letter "T" shows the start of the time component. Notice that there are no spaces in the string. The SQL standard was based on an older version of ISO-8601 and a space was used instead of the "T" to separate them. As of this writing, I am not sure if the SQL standards will change.

7.3. DURATIONS AND INTERVALS

Durations of time are a bit trickier. The first letter is always a "P," then each component is a number (no leading zeros) followed by a one-letter code for the temporal unit used. The syntax is:

```
PnYnMnDTnHnMnS
PnW
P<date>T<time>

* P = required letter which originally stood for
"period".
* Y = Year(s)
* M = Months(s)
* W = Week(s)
* D = Day(s) designator that follows the value for
the number of days.
* T = Time separator. This has to be used if there
are parts less than one day.
* H = Hour(s)
* M = Minute(s)
* S = Second(s) with possible decimal places.
```

Any number-letter combination can be dropped if its value is zero. You have to watch for the letter "M" so that you know "P1M" is a one-month duration and "PT1M" is a one-minute duration (note the time designator, T, that precedes the time value). The smallest value used may also have a decimal fraction, as in "P0.5Y" to indicate half a year. You do not have to reduce a temporal expression to its lowest terms; that is, you can use 36 hours instead of one day and 12 hours.

7.3.1. Time Intervals

An interval has a start and end time. You can express it as a pair of points in time, a starting time and duration, or duration and an ending time. The two parts are separated by a solidus (slash), thus:

```
<start>/<end>
<start>/<duration>
<duration>/<end>
```

A time interval is the intervening time between two time points. The amount of intervening time is expressed by a duration (as described in the previous section). The two time points (start and end) are expressed by either a combined date and time representation or just a date representation.

Repeating intervals prefixed with the letter "R," an optional number, and a solidus. Here is the syntax:

```
Rnn/<interval>
R/<interval>
```

The number is the number of repetitions and if it is not given then there is no upper limit.

Chapter 8

Sex Codes

ISO 5218 sets up a simple list of single-digit numeric codes for human sexes. The four codes are:

```
* 0 = not known
* 1 = male
* 2 = female
* 9 = not applicable. This means a "lawful person"
such as a corporation, organization, government
and so forth.
```

It is referenced by the term "sex" and not "gender" in data processing. This standard is embedded in several national identification numbers.

8.1. SEX CODES

Notice that the ISO system is a legal encoding and not a medical or biological one. There are other standards for this, which are "more medical" than the ISO model.

- CDC = Center for Disease Control
- NETSS & NCHS & ECML & NCVHS & JC3IEDM & ICAO
- NAACCR = North American Association of Central Cancer Registries

Doi: 10.1016/B978-0-12-374722-8.00008-6

Code	Definition
1	Male
2	Female
3	Other (hermaphrodite)
4	Transsexual
9	Not stated

■ ANSI ASC X12 = American National Standards Institute

Code	Definition
F	Female
M	Male
N	Nonsexed gender is not known because observation or examination for such was not recorded or requested by the protocol
U	Gender could not be determined because of ambiguity in external or internal genitalia

■ ASTM E1633 = Standard Specification for Coded Values Used in the Electronic Health Record

Code	Definition
M	Male
F	Female
U	Unknown sex
MP	Male Pseudo-hermaphrodite
FP	Female Pseudo-hermaphrodite
H	Hermaphrodite
MC	Male changed to Female
FC	Female changed to Male
A	Ambiguous sex

With the United States and other countries moving to electronic health records and companies having to pay for sex changes, these codes might become more important.

8.2. OTHER SOURCES

- DICOM = Digital Imaging and Communications in Medicine. This code deals with humans but in a medical context.

These three have to do with biology and you will not see them:

- ZIMS = Zoological Information Management System uses a International Species Information System sex code with a lot of combinations that do not appear in humans

- OBIS = The Ocean Biogeographic Information System has a Census of Marine Life, which includes transitional and indeterminate sex statuses

- UBIF = Unified Biosciences Information Framework has another sex code system that covers all the transitions and combinations that occur in nature

9

Ethnicity and Race Codes

In the United States, the Constitution requires that citizens be enumerated every 10 years for the purpose of assigning congressional representation. This also affects the number of votes that states receive in the Electoral College for the presidential election.

The Bureau of the Census will also collect other information that can be used for court challenges, planning, and other purposes. It is the only federal level guide we have to use. The data is available in electronic format on "TIGER Tapes."

Race and ethnicity are self-reported in the U.S. Census. Race has no real basis in biology, science, genealogy, or anthropology. There is more genetic variation within a racial group than between them. Most Americans have mixed ancestry. Ethnicity is a political concept.

9.1. RACE VERSUS ETHNICITY

The U.S. population is shifting, thanks to legal and illegal immigration from South America, aging factors, and fertility rates. African, Americans are much more assimilated into "the mainstream" today. This is why Barack Obama could be elected president in the 21st century but not before.

The seventh Census (1850) categorized people by "color" and gave the choices "white," "black," or "mulatto" without a reference to the Amerindian population in the Americas. By 1880, "Chinese" and "Indian" had been added to the categories. Categories tend to increase, not decrease.

Doi: 10.1016/B978-0-12-374722-8.00009-8

For the 2010 Census, race and ethnicity are separate attributes. So in addition to your race (or races), you can be in "Hispanic or Latino" and "Not Hispanic or Latino" categories. The Census is also considering removing the "other races" category. Interracial and multiracial categories will be used for the first time in 2010. Illegal immigrants also will be counted.

Can you see some problems already? Then add the way that the categories have been changed over the lifetime of the Census. And, finally, add social changes. I saw the end of racial segregation in my youth—I remember "Colors Seat From The Rear; Whites Seat From The Front" signs on Atlanta Transit System buses. An African, American (or black? or colored? or Negro? and so on?) friend of 30+ years complaining about the changing names in the 1960–1970 time period in the United States. She told me that I was lucky to always be a "Wonder Bread and Clorox White honky" all my life.

9.2. U.K. ETHNIC GROUPS

U.K. ethnic group coding from their ONS U.K. Census for 2001 was more detailed. It is more political than the U.S. systems; it reflects the racial model in Anglo-Saxon culture as well as political voter blocks within the United Kingdom and places where the British empire held sway.

White

- 01 British
- 02 Irish
- 03 English
- 04 Scottish
- 05 Welsh
- 06 Cornish
- 07 Cypriot (part not stated)
- 08 Greek (including Greek Cypriot)
- 09 Turkish (including Turkish Cypriot)
- 10 Mediterranean (including Italian, Portuguese, and Spanish)
- 11 All republics that made up the former Yugoslavia
- 12 All republics that made up the former USSR (including Russian, Kazakh, Ukrainian, Armenian, and Uzbek, to name a few)
- 13 Other White European

- 14 Irish Traveler
- 15 Jewish
- 19 Other White, Mixed White, White Unspecified

Mixed
- 21 White and Black Caribbean
- 22 White and Black African
- 23 White and Asian
- 24 Black and Asian
- 25 Black and Chinese
- 26 Black and White
- 27 Chinese and White
- 28 Asian and Chinese
- 29 Other Mixed, Mixed Unspecified

Asian or asian british
- 41 Indian or British Indian
- 42 Pakistani or British Pakistani
- 43 Bangladeshi or British Bangladeshi
- 44 Mixed Asian
- 45 Hindu
- 46 Moslem
- 47 Sikh
- 48 Punjabi
- 49 Kashmiri
- 50 East African Asian
- 51 Other Asian, British Asian, Asian Unspecified

Black or black british
- 61 Caribbean
- 62 African
- 63 Mixed Black
- 64 Somali
- 65 Other Black, Black British, Black Unspecified

Chinese or other
- 81 Chinese
- 82 Africa—color not defined
- 83 Middle East
- 84 Arab
- 85 Vietnamese
- 86 Any Other Groups

- 14 Irish Traveler
- 15 Jewish
- 16 Other White, Mixed White, White Unspecified

Mixed
- 21 White and Black Caribbean
- 22 White and Black African
- 23 White and Asian
- 24 Black and Asian
- 25 Black and Chinese
- 26 Black and White
- 27 Chinese and White
- 28 Asian and Chinese
- 29 Other Mixed, Mixed Unspecified

Asian or asian british
- 41 Indian or British Indian
- 42 Pakistani or British Pakistani
- 43 Bangladeshi or British Bangladeshi
- 44 Mixed Asian
- 45 Hindu
- 46 Moslem
- 47 Sikh
- 48 Punjabi
- 49 Kashmiri
- 50 East African Asian
- 51 Other Asian, British Asian, Asian Unspecified

Black or black british
- 61 Caribbean
- 62 African
- 63 Mixed Black
- 64 Somali
- 65 Other Black, Black British, Black Unspecified

Chinese or other
- 71 Chinese
- 72 Africa - color not defined
- 73 Middle East
- 74 Arab
- 75 Vietnamese
- 76 Any Other Groups

ISO-3166 and Other Country Codes

ISO 3166 is a three-part standard for encoding the names of countries, dependent territories, and special areas of geographical interest and their principal subdivisions (e.g., provinces or states). It began in 1974 and has been updated on a regular basis as countries change names, disappear, or are reabsorbed into other nations.

10.1. ISO 3166-1

Part one of the standard is a set of codes: a two-letter alpha code, a three-letter alpha code, and a three digit code. The two-letter alpha code is the most important. It is embedded in lots of other standards and we computer geeks know it has the Internet's country code for top-level domains.

Except for the numeric codes, ISO 3166 codes have been adopted in the United States as FIPS 104-1. But there is also an old Federal Information Processing Standard, FIPS 10. It is also a two-letter code, but it does not match the ISO 3166 in many places. It has either a different abbreviation code or a different political division. Beware of it for historical reasons.

10.2. ISO 3166-2

ISO 3166-2 goes down to the principal subdivisions (e.g., provinces or states) within a country as encoded by the two-letter ISO 3166-1 with a separator followed by up to three more characters. It was first published in 1998.

Doi: 10.1016/B978-0-12-374722-8.00010-4

The problem is that multinational statistical agencies like to divide the world up differently. There is the "Nomenclature of Territorial Units for Statistics" (NUTS) standard developed by the European Union (http://ec.europa.eu/eurostat/ramon/nuts/codelist_en.cfm?list=efta).

The United Nations also a hierarchical three-digit numeric scheme that starts at the continental level, then goes to regions within continents, and finally resolves to countries (http://unstats.un.org/unsd/methods/m49/m49regin.htm).

STANAG 1059 is the version of ISO 3166 used by the North Atlantic Treaty Organization (NATO).

10.3. ISO 3166-3

These are the codes for formerly used names of countries. Each former country name in has a four-letter alphabetic code. The first two letters are the ISO 3166-1 two-letter code of the former country, while the last two letters tell us why the name disappeared or changed.

If the country changed its name, the new ISO 3166-1 two-letter code is used (e.g., Burma changed its name to Myanmar, whose new two-letter code is MM), or the special code AA is used if its two-letter code is not changed (e.g., Byelorussian SSR changed its name to Belarus, which has kept the same two-letter code).

If the country merged into an existing country, the ISO 3166-1 two-letter code of this country is used (e.g., the German Democratic Republic merged into Germany, whose two-letter code is DE).

If the country split into several parts, the special code HH is used to indicate that there is no single successor country (e.g., Czechoslovakia split into the Czech Republic and Slovakia), with the exception of Serbia and Montenegro, for which XX is used to avoid confusion.

The old name also carries the time period when it was valid as part of the standard, so you can use historical data.

Language Codes

The ISO-639 has a two-letter (639-1) and a three-letter (639-2) code for languages. The two-letter codes are favored by computer people because they encode current languages and are embedded in other standards. The three-letter codes are favored by librarians because they cover a wide range of existing, dead, and ancient languages.

The three-letter codes include "mis" for uncoded languages and "zbl" for Blissymbolics. The later is a pictographic system used mostly for the handicapped. The Library of Congress registers the three-letter codes and Infoterm is the agency for the two-letter codes. You can find a current list on the Library of Congress Web site.

However, there are more parts to the standard for linguists.

Part 3: Alpha-3 code for comprehensive coverage of languages. The goal was to cover all known natural languages. The standard was published by ISO on 2007-02-05.

Part 4: Implementation guidelines and general principles for language coding. It is not an encoding scheme, so don't care about it.

Part 5: Alpha-3 code for language families and groups. This is more for linguists than database users.

Part 6: Alpha-4 representation for comprehensive coverage of language variation (i.e., British versus American English). Considering the differences in spelling, grammar choices, and so forth, this could be useful in a database. Many years ago I wrote a column on computing in an IT trade paper in the United Kingdom. I had a good editor who changed my spelling from American to British (of course), but he also changed my sentence structures. It was a subtle but importance difference in the final product.

You can download a list of current codes at http://www. loc.gov/standards/iso639-2/php/code_list.php

Currency Codes

ISO 4217 is the three-letter international standard currency code. You will see it used in newspapers for the current exchange rates, in banking, and on airline and international train tickets.

The first two letters of the code are the two letters of ISO 3166-1 country and the third is usually the initial of the currency itself.

Lots of countries use the same name for their currency, but they have no relationship to each other, as with the U.S. dollar and the Canadian dollar. Sometimes the same currency symbol is used; some currencies have no special symbol as do the U.S. dollar ($), yen (¥), euro (€), and British pound (£) signs.

If a currency is revalued, the currency code's last letter is changed to distinguish it from the old currency. For example, the Russian ruble changed from RUR to RUB.

There is also a three-digit code number assigned to each currency based on the three-digit country in the ISO 3166 standard. For example, USD (U.S. dollar) is numeric code 840.

With two exceptions, all currencies are based on the decimal system. The major currency unit and any minor currency unit are expressed with decimals. Often, the minor currency unit has a value that is 1/100 of the major unit (1.00 USD = 100 cents), but 1/1000 is also common.

Before you ask, Mauritania sets 1 ouguiya (UM) = 5 khoums, and in Madagascar 1 ariary = 5 iraimbilanja.

Doi: 10.1016/B978-0-12-374722-8.00012-8

12.1. NONCURRENCY UNITS

Supranational currencies, such as the euro, have codes. This is probably the only one that you will find outside a region.

ISO 4217 also includes codes for precious metals (gold, silver, palladium, and platinum) weighed in troy ounces. They begin with the letter "X" and end with their chemical symbol (i.e., "XAG" for silver).

Currencies that no longer exist or are printed for commemorative purposes might also have codes.

Finally, there are codes for "no currency" that begin with the letter "X," allocated for testing purposes (XTS) and to indicate no currency transactions (XXX). Since ISO 3166 does not allow a country code to start with "X," this is safe.

National Identification Numbers

Many countries have a National Identification Number assigned to their citizens and other residents. These various national systems usually grew out of taxation systems that needed to assess individual persons and then mutated into general person identification tools within the country.

Finland and other Nordic countries use a variant of the Swedish design. The Finnish personal identification number (Finnish: henkilötunnus [HETU], Swedish: personbeteckning) uses the format DDMMYYCZZZQ, where DDMMYY is the date of birth, C is the century identification sign (+ for the 19th century, – for the 20th, and A for the 21st), ZZZ is the personal identification number (even for females, odd for males) and Q is a check digit.

The Finnish check digit character is calculated using a stronger algorithm than most. The birth date and person number are taken as a single nine-digit number x, and then you compute $Q = MOD(x, 31)$ and return the $(n + 1)$th character in the string "0123456789ABCDEFHJKLMNPRSTUVWXY"; notice that the letters "O" and "I" are left out to avoid confusion with the digits 1 and 0.

In Hungary, there is no national identification number and it was ruled to be unconstitutional to establish one in 1991. In India, there is no national identification number. The closest thing in India is the Permanent Account Number (PAN), issued by the Income Tax Office.

In Italy, the Fiscal Code (Codice Fiscale) issued by the Ministry of Treasure has an elaborate scheme based on a three-letter abbreviation code for the family name, followed by the same three-letter abbreviation code for the family name, followed by a birthdate in a "YYMDD," with an alpha code for the birth month, and the birth day encodes the gender by adding 40. This is then followed by a four-character area code and a check digit letter based on a MOD 26 algorithm. There an exception algorithm for handling duplicate fiscal codes. It is easy to create a fictional fiscal code or to steal a real one based on simple personal data.

I cannot cover every nation on Earth in this book, so let me pick the United States and Canada (most of my readers are there) and Sweden. The Swedish system is fairly typical of many other nations. In many countries, the number is created from the person's birthdate, sex, a geographic location (political or administrative unit within the country), and a sequence (or, better, "unique-ifier") of some kind. The sequence possibly encodes other information such as legal status. Most of the systems have a check digit and it is usually a Luhn algorithm.

13.1. SOCIAL SECURITY NUMBERS

The closest thing the United States has to a universal identification number is the Social Security Number (SSN). You are supposed to validate the SSN when you hire a new employee, but a lot of programmers have no idea how to do that validation. I am not going to go into the privacy issues, recent laws, or anything to do with legal aspects.

The SSN is composed of three parts, all digits and separated by dashes in the format "XXX-XX-XXXX" when displayed. These parts are called the Area, Group, and Serial.

13.1.1. SSN Area Numbers

For the most part (there are a few exceptions), the Area is determined by where the individual applied for the Social Security Number (before 1972) or resided at time of application (after 1972). The chart below shows the Area numbers used in the United States and its possessions.

Area Range	Residence or application location
000–000	Invalid code
001–003	New Hampshire
004–007	Maine
008–009	Vermont
010–034	Massachusetts
035–039	Rhode Island
040–049	Connecticut
050–134	New York
135–158	New Jersey
159–211	Pennsylvania
212–220	Maryland
221–222	Delaware
223–231	Virginia
691–699	
232–236	West Virginia
232	North Carolina
237–246	
681–690	
247–251	South Carolina
654–658	
252–260	Georgia
667–675	
261–267	Florida
589–595	
766–772	
268–302	Ohio
303–317	Indiana
318–361	Illinois

(Continued)

Area Range	Residence or application location
362–386	Michigan
387–399	Wisconsin
400–407	Kentucky
408–415	Tennessee
756–763	
416–424	Alabama
425–428	Mississippi
587–588	
752–755	allocated, but not issued yet
429–432	Arkansas
676–679	
433–439	Louisiana
659–665	
440–448	Oklahoma
449–467	Texas
627–645	
468–477	Minnesota
478–485	Iowa
486–500	Missouri
501–502	North Dakota
503–504	South Dakota
505–508	Nebraska
509–515	Kansas
516–517	Montana
518–519	Idaho
520	Wyoming
521–524	Colorado
650–653	

(Continued)

Area Range	Residence or application location
525,585	New Mexico
648–649	
526–527	Arizona
600–601	
764–765	
528–529	Utah
646–647	
530	Nevada
680	
531–539	Washington
540–544	Oregon
545–573	California
602–626	
574	Alaska
575–576	Hawaii
750–751	
577–579	District of Columbia
580	Virgin Islands
580–584	Puerto Rico
596–599	
586	Guam
586	American Samoa
586	Philippine Islands
666	permanently unassigned
700–728	Railroad Board – discontinued in 1963
729–733	Enumeration at Entry, see note below
734–899	unassigned, for future use
900–999	Invalid code, see the note below

No SSNs with an Area number above 728 have been assigned in the 700 series, except for 729 through 733 and 764 through 772.

If an Area number is shown more than once, it means that certain numbers have been transferred from one state to another, or that an Area has been divided for use among certain geographic locations. The actual assignment is done based on the ZIP code given on the application. You can blame population shifts for this. You do not have to have an SSN to work in the United States. Since 1996, the IRS issued over 8 million tax-payer identification numbers to foreign workers without an SSN. In 2004 alone there were 900,000 such numbers issued.

While 900–999 are not valid Area numbers, they were used for program purposes when state aid to the aged, blind, and disabled was converted to a federal program administered by the Social Security Administration. You might also see this range of Area numbers used to construct student id numbers for foreign students in the days when schools used the SSN as the student identification number.

13.1.2. SSN Group Numbers

The Group portion of the SSN has no meaning other than to determine whether or not a number has been assigned. There was an urban myth that the ethnicity of the card holder was coded in the Group number; I have no idea how that one got started. The Social Security Administration publishes a list of the highest group assigned for each Area once a month. You can download this data at: http://www.ssa.gov/employer/highgroup.txt. They also provide some free software for employers at http://www.socialsecurity.gov/employer/software.htm.

The only validation check on the SSN is the way that the Group numbers are issued. which is in the following order:

    Odd numbers from 01 to 09
    Even numbers from 10 to 98
    Even numbers from 02 to 08
    Odd numbers from 11 to 99

For example, if the highest group assigned for area XXX is 72, then we know that the number XXX-04-XXXX is an invalid Group number because Even Groups under 9 have not yet been assigned.

In 1938, wallets by the E. H. Ferree Company came with fake SSN cards already in them to make them look good when they were on display—much like the photos of a family in a dime store picture frame that looks better than your real family. Many people simply used these fake cards. The numbers look valid, but the IRS and other government agencies have a list of them.

A list of bad SSNs has expanded over the years for various reasons, some similar to this story and some involving identity theft and fraud. You need to consider it when doing validation. You can find it online at http://www.socialsecurity.gov/history/ssn/misused.html.

13.1.3. SSN Serial Numbers

The Serial portion of the Social Security Number has no meaning. The Serial number ranges from 0001 to 9999, but it is not assigned in strictly numerical order. The Serial number 0000 is never assigned, so the "dummy SSN" is "000–00–0000" for display purposes, much like dummy telephone numbers that have "555" as their exchange code.

13.1.4. SSN Validation

The SSN has no check digits, making it one of the worst systems in the world. Other than knowing the "700 + rule," there is no obvious way to look at the person and his SSN and see if they are grossly misaligned.

There are commercial firms and nonprofit Web sites that will verify SSNs for living and deceased persons. They usually tell you if the person holding that number is alive or dead, along with the year and place of issue. Some of these sites are set up by government agencies or universities to help employers, hospitals, or other concerned parties validate SSNs. The commercial sites can do bulk validations from files that you submit to them, at a cost of about one cent per SSN.

Here is a small sample to get you started. I am not recommending one source over another in this listing:

http://www.veris-ssn.com

http://www.searchbug.com/peoplefinder/ss.aspx

http://privacy.cs.cmu.edu/dataprivacy/projects/ssn watch/

http://info.dhhs.state.nc.us/olm/manuals/dma/eis/ man/Eis1103.htm

http://www.comserv-inc.com/products/ssndtect.htm

You can also find which SSNs belong to dead people at:

http://ssdi.rootsweb.ancestry.com/cgi-bin/ssdi.cgi.

13.2. SOCIAL INSURANCE NUMBER

A Social Insurance Number (SIN) is the Canadian version of the U.S. SSN. It was not meant to be a national identification number, but it has worked out that way. The SIN was created in 1964 for the Canada Pension Plan and Canada's varied employment insurance programs. In 1967, Revenue Canada (now the Canada Revenue Agency) started using the SIN for tax reporting purposes. SINs are issued by Human Resources and Social Development Canada (previously Human Resources Development Canada).

The SIN is formatted as three groups of three digits (e.g., 123–456–789).

13.2.1. SIN First digit

The first digit of a SIN indicates the province in which it was registered:

1. Nova Scotia, New Brunswick, Prince Edward Island, Newfoundland, and Labrador
2. Quebec
3. Quebec
4. Ontario (including overseas forces)
5. Ontario

6. Manitoba, Saskatchewan, and Alberta), Northwest Territories, and Nunavut
7. British Columbia and Yukon
8. Not used
9. Temporary resident: foreign students, individuals on work visas, etc., which have an expiry date.
10. used for fictitious SIN numbers

Note: While the first digit usually identifies the location of registration, the government has found it necessary in the past to supply certain regions with SIN numbers assigned to other regions.

13.2.2. SIN Validation

The SIN has a simple Luhn check digit, as it was created after the advent of computers. The weights are applied left to right:

```
0 * 1 = 0
4 * 2 = 8
6 * 1 = 6
4 * 2 = 8
5 * 1 = 5
4 * 2 = 8
2 * 1 = 2
8 * 2 = 16 = 7
6 * 1 = 6
================
Total = 50 MOD (50, 10) = 0
```

13.3. SWEDISH PERSONAL IDENTITY NUMBER

The Swedish personnummer was introduced in 1947 and started as an identifier for all public agencies, from health care to the tax authorities. Today, it is used for commercial purposes such as bank accounts, insurance, automobile rentals, and so forth.

13.3.1. Personnummer Format

The original personnummer is 10 digits and a hyphen. The first six digits are the person's birthday, in YYMMDD form, followed by a hyphen. Positions seven, eight, and nine are a serial number; if the ninth digit is odd, the person is a male; if even, then female. Originally, the seventh and eighth digits were the codes for the county of issue, with foreign-born citizens having a 9 in the seventh digit.

In some counties, such as Stockholm, the official Swedish ID cards, and some banks, have started using 12-digit numbers to allow the use of the YYYYMMDD ISO-8601 date format.

The 10th digit is a check digit, which was introduced in 1967 when the system was computerized. At that time, IBM dominated the computer market and they had the Luhn algorithm. It follows the usual pattern by starting with 2 as the weight for the first (leftmost) digits and alternating between 1 and 2. Obviously, given the birthdate, county of birth, sex, and check digit algorithm, you can build a personnummer for someone.

Originally, when the personal identity number was introduced, it had nine digits and the seventh and eighth denoted the county (Swedish: län) in which the person was born. The seventh digit was 9 for foreign-born, who did not have a county. This led to charges of discrimination and was changed in 1990.

This system was replaced with the current system in 1990. People who have no Swedish personal identity number can receive a coordination number (Swedish: samordningsnummer) for people staying less than a year in the country. It is structured along the same lines, but with the day in the date of birth advanced by 60 (giving a number between 61 and 91).

13.4. EU BIOMETRIC PASSPORTS

The European Parliament voted to implement biometric passports starting June 29, 2009. The passports have fingerprints as well as the usual photograph.

Children will carry their own passports but without fingerprints because young children's fingerprints change as they get older. People with no hands would obviously be exempt from the new fingerprint-based biometric passport system.

Instead, they would have to apply for temporary, 12-month passports in order to travel. There are some people, such as bricklayers, who erase their fingerprints in the course of their occupation. I cannot believe that either situation is common.

Both Norway and Sweden store digital facial images on smart cards embedded into the passports. The problem is that passport control centers in the world will have to the readers to read the chips.

A European Parliament decision in December 2004 prohibited the creation of a central database of biometric information collected from EU passports and travel documents. In Sweden, the digital image on the chips will not be stored in any database nor stored in the readers. While this gives more privacy, it also means that law enforcement agencies will not be able to track known criminals.

The chips being used in Norway and Sweden employ a security feature recommended by the International Civil Aviation Organization (ICAO), but the method isn't entirely secure. Passport control officials must first scan the machine-readable portion of the passport to obtain a key that is made up of the passport number, date of birth of the passport holder, and the expiration date of the passport. Once that key is created, the information stored on the chip can be unlocked and accessed. If that information is available and you have the algorithm for the key, you have access.

13.4.1. Fingerprint Classification Systems

There are two major fingerprint classifications used in the world, the Vucetich system and the Henry system.

The Vucetich system was developed in Argentina by Juan Vucetich, a statistician who was in charge of immigration in the 1800s when more than half of the population was immigrants. Vucetich's method is still taught at an institute bearing his name in Mendoza, Argentina.

About 10 years after the Vucetich system was set up in Argentina, Sir Edward Richard Henry devised a similar system in India for the British government. When he transferred to London, he took his classification system to Scotland Yard and it spread to the rest of the English speaking world. In the United States, there were variants of the Henry system in use by various police agenciesm which was not straightened out until the 1940s when the federal government had a centralized physical card file system in Washington.

When it came time to computerize this database, the options investigated were: (1) write software for the Henry system. (2) write software for the Vucetich system. or (3) write software for a Henry-Vucetich hybrid system.

All three options lost because both systems just don't work very well with computerized pattern recognition. This is when the Federal Bureau of Investigation (FBI) came up with the International Automated Fingerprint Identification System (IAFIS).

The IAFIS database includes almost all convicted criminals, federal civil servants, and military personnel. This makes sense because the FBI is a police organization. Both a Henry and Vucetich want to have a full "ten card"—a collection of all 10 fingerprints to assign a category number for *identification* and not *forensics*. For example, the Henry system has a version of a weights check digit in which each finger is assigned a number to identify it and a weight. If the fingerprint pattern is a whorl (the three major types of prints are arches, loops and whorls), then that weight is summed and run through a formula. If you have only one fingerprint at the crime scene, it is hard to get the right category code, much less search millions of records.

The classic textbook for fingerprint technology is:

Maltoni D., D. Maio, A.K. Jain, and S. Prabhakar, "Handbook of Fingerprint Recognition"; DVD included, ISBN-13: 978–0387954318

Chapter

14

Occupations

The Dictionary of Occupational Titles (DOT) began in 1939 and was used by the U.S. Employment Service to match jobs and job seekers. It has a strong basis toward the textile industry at first but grew more general over the years. Unfortunately, it did not keep up with the changing labor market, and the fourth and last edition was published in 1991.

The Web site http://www.occupationalinfo.org/ has an online look-up of the Dictionary of Occupational Titles (DOT) revised fourth edition, as supplied electronically by the U.S. Department of Labor.

The DOT was replaced by O*NET (http://online.onetcenter .org/), which has a more modern taxonomy of jobs. But DOT lives on because the Social Security Administration kept using it for disability claims and it was used by immigration. O*Net classifies jobs in job families, so it is less useful for determining disability eligibility or job-specific benefits analysis. It is tied to the Standard Occupational Classification (SOC) codes used by the U.S. Department of Labor. This scheme has 23 major groups encoded by the leading two digits and refined by four more digits after a dash. Decimal places can also be added for the finest resolution.

Within these major groups are 96 minor groups, 449 broad occupations, and 821 detailed occupations. Occupations with similar skills or work activities are grouped at each of the four levels of hierarchy to facilitate comparisons.

Doi: 10.1016/B978-0-12-374722-8.00014-1

SOC Major Groups

- 11-0000 Management Occupations
- 13-0000 Business and Financial Operations Occupations
- 15-0000 Computer and Mathematical Occupations
- 17-0000 Architecture and Engineering Occupations
- 19-0000 Life, Physical, and Social Science Occupations
- 21-0000 Community and Social Services Occupations
- 23-0000 Legal Occupations
- 25-0000 Education, Training, and Library Occupations
- 27-0000 Arts, Design, Entertainment, Sports, and Media Occupations
- 29-0000 Healthcare Practitioners and Technical Occupations
- 31-0000 Healthcare Support Occupations
- 33-0000 Protective Service Occupations
- 35-0000 Food Preparation and Serving Related Occupations
- 37-0000 Building and Grounds Cleaning and Maintenance Occupations
- 39-0000 Personal Care and Service Occupations
- 41-0000 Sales and Related Occupations
- 43-0000 Office and Administrative Support Occupations
- 45-0000 Farming, Fishing, and Forestry Occupations
- 47-0000 Construction and Extraction Occupations
- 49-0000 Installation, Maintenance, and Repair Occupations
- 51-0000 Production Occupations
- 53-0000 Transportation and Material Moving Occupations
- 55-0000 Military Specific Occupations

For example, a DBA would be classified with this hierarchy.

- 15-0000 Computer and Mathematical Occupations
- 15-1000 Computer Specialists
- 15-1060 Database Administrators
- 15-1061 Database Administrators

14.1. NATIONAL OCCUPATIONAL CLASSIFICATION (NOC)

In Canada, the National Occupational Classification (NOC) serves the same purpose for their labor market. The NOC is developed in collaboration with Statistics Canada, as are many other standard encodings.

The NOC is a four-digit code based on skill type in the left-most digits and skill level on the right side of the code (e.g., 3113 Dentists—"31" indicates that this is a health occupation and it requires university-level education). The system is used by Job Futures, the widely used source of information about occupational outlooks, and the national JobBank®, an electronic listing of jobs, work, or business opportunities provided by Canadian. There are more details at (http://www5 .hrsdc.gc.ca/NOC/English/NOC/2006/Welcome.aspx).

Occupational Structure by Skill Type
- 0 Management Occupations
- 1 Business, Finance and Administration Occupations
- 2 Natural and Applied Sciences and Related Occupations
- 3 Health Occupations
- 4 Occupations in Social Science, Education, Government Service and Religion
- 5 Occupations in Art, Culture, Recreation and Sport
- 6 Sales and Service Occupations
- 7 Trades, Transport and Equipment Operators and Related Occupations
- 8 Occupations Unique to Primary Industry
- 9 Occupations Unique to Processing, Manufacturing and Utilities

Following this hierarchy, a DBA would be:

- 2 Professional Occupations in Natural and Applied Sciences
- 21 Major Group
- 217 Computer and Information Systems Professionals
- 2172 Database Analysts and Data Administrators

Color is something that people understand as a sensory primary. At one extreme, we have color blindness (total, red-green, and blue-yellow color blindness) and at the other extreme there are people with hyper–color vision who can see millions more colors than a normal person.

Most color codes are formulas for mixing new colors from a set of base colors. Some systems are additive and some are subtractive. This makes the encoding really useful.

The RGB color model is a common additive system that uses red, green, and blue light to create new colors. Because phosphorus for cathode ray tube displays comes in those colors, the system is popular with older electronic devices.

The CMYK is used with inks and is called the "four-color process" printing. The letters stand for cyan, magenta, yellow, and key (black). New colors are formed by a subtractive process. The inks are put on white paper and mask out colors from that background. Black could be created with the other three colors, but it is cheaper and easier to use black to darker tones.

In the printing trades, proprietary Pantone colors have been an industry standard for mixing inks. In addition to the usual CMYK color model, Pantone has Hexachrome (also known as CMYKOG), a six-color printing process that adds orange and green inks.

HTML colors are an RGB system that uses three numbers between 0 and 255 for each color. Thus (255, 255, 255) is white and (0, 0, 0) is black. The triplets can be expressed as hexadecimal numbers, too.

15.1. INTERNATIONAL COLOR CONSORTIUM

Managing color across systems with different color models and hardware is difficult, so we have color management systems that try to guarantee that the colors you see on one display screen are identical or very close to the colors on another screen.

The International Color Consortium (ICC) sets open standards for cross-platform color management systems via ISO 15076-1. The current version is Version 4 and it is nearly universal.

16

Telephone Numbers

The Telecommunication Standardization Sector (ITU-T, formerly known as the International Telegraph and Telephone Consultative Committee or CCITT from the French), of the International Telecommunication Union (ITU) standardizes the international telephone number formats.

The defining standard is E.164 and its subdocuments. The numbers are up to 15 digits (excluding prefixes) and could be modeled with a regular expression that looks for a single string of digits.

The single string is not a good idea because the format is a vector encoding (see Section 03.02.06. Vector Encoding) and the components of the telephone number have meaning that can be useful. The display convention for putting punctuation separating the vector components of the numbers vary from country to country. Validation with punctuation is hard work. It is much easier to validate a telephone number if you have separate vector components and can avoid writing a parser.

16.1. THE INTERNATIONAL TELEPHONE NUMBER COMPONENTS

The International Telephone Number Components are:

- Country Code: The number begins with an international access code (00 or 011) followed by a country code. The country is one to three digits based on a hierarchical

Doi: 10.1016/B978-0-12-374722-8.00016-5

(see Section 03.02.05. Hierarchical Encoding Schemes) encoding of geographic zones:

- Zone 1—North American Numbering Plan Area (NANPA) controls this zone
- Zone 2—Mostly Africa, some Atlantic and Indian Ocean islands
- Zone 3—Europe
- Zone 4—Europe
- Zone 5—Mexico, Central America, South America, and French dependencies
- Zone 6—Southeast Asia and Oceania
- Zone 7—Russia and Kazakhstan
- Zone 8—East Asia and Special Services
- Zone 9—West, South and Central Asia
- Zone 0—unassigned
- Zone 10 Locations with no country code
- City Code or Area Code

This code is under local national control. In North America, we use a three-digit area code that is approximately geographic; before cell phones freed the device from a physical wire, this was more so. Area codes start at "201" to avoid conflicts with the country code part of the number. Most, but not all, of the three-digit combinations are in use, so you are better off with a shortlist of unassigned area codes to exclude certain codes when you validate a North American telephone number. Here is a skeleton DDL:

```
CREATE TABLE North_American_Phonebook
( ...
   area_code CHAR(3) NOT NULL
       CHECK (area_code NOT IN (<list of missing
         area codes>)
               AND area_code BETWEEN '201' AND '989'
               AND area code SIMILAR TO
                 '[0-9][0-9][0-9]'),
   phone_exchange CHAR(3) NOT NULL
       CHECK (phone_exchange SIMILAR TO
         '[0-9][0-9][0-9]')
```

```
phone_nbr CHAR(4) NOT NULL
    CHECK (phone_nbr SIMILAR TO
       '[0-9][0-9][0-9][0-9]'),
 ..);
```

Do not think this is universal! For example, in Brazil (country code: 55), the local telephone numbers are eight digits, broken into two groups of four digits, plus a two-digit area code. If the first digit of the local telephone number is 2 to 5, it is a land line; if it is 6 to 9 it is a mobile telephone.

This is why international telephone numbers are hard to validate. The components have to be VARCHAR(n) and have look-up tables or ugly CASE expressions.

16.2. SUBSCRIBER LOCAL EXCHANGE OR PREFIX

Certain exchanges are reserved for special purposes in NANPA and form a complete phone number in themselves. The strangest one is the "555" exchange; it is fictional and never used for a real telephone number. Its purpose is to allow movies, television shows, and so on that need a fictional number to be used, so that a real person is not bothered by crank calls. Originally, telephone exchanges had names and you dialed the first two letters of that name and digit (Klondike-5 was the favorite in old American movies). However, if you dial "<area code>-555-1212," you get the information operator for that area code.

There is also a series of "x11" numbers to access special services in the United States and Canada:

- 211—Community information or social services
- 311—City government or nonemergency police matters
- 411—Local telephone directory
- 511—Traffic, road, and tourist information
- 611—Telephone line repair service
- 711—Hearing or speech disabilities relay service
- 811—Telephone company buried line information
- 911—Emergency services: fire, ambulance, police, etc.

Please note that this scheme is not universal. For example, the United Kingdom uses "999" for emergencies and other countries have separate codes for particular emergency services. However, the use of "800" for toll-free dialing is worldwide now.

Technically, there ought to be a look-up table for (area_code, phone_exchange) in NANPA since not all combinations are valid. Frankly, it is a lot of work to validate because so many telephone numbers are issued and reissued constantly. Only telephone companies need to be that current.

- Subscriber Local Number

In NANPA, this is the four digits that get to the individual subscriber telephone within the exchange. There are not really any restrictions on these digits.

- Internal Extension

If the subscriber has a local switchboard on his line, then these digits go to device on that switchboard.

International telephone number validation is a complex operation; I would recommend that you consider doing it in an external routine written in a language more suited for string handling than SQL. One source is:

http://www.quentinsagerconsulting.com/documents/10025.htm

E-Mail Addresses

The use of e-mail addressees as identifiers is now the dominate method used in e-commerce to identify the customers. The simply fact that someone is ordering from an e-commerce Web site implies that they have computer access. That implies that they probably have an e-mail account. If they don't have an e-mail account, they can apply for a free account at Google, Yahoo, or other Web sites.

The advantages of it as a personal identifier are:

1. The user creates it himself, so he is more likely to remember it easily. Compare this to learning all of your credit card numbers.

2. The string can be quite long and complex for security.

3. An e-mail address can be validated with a regular expression in the application programs as well as the database. Here is a regular expression from David Huyck that includes some of the newer top-level-domain extensions, such as info, museum, name, and so forth. It also allows for e-mails tied directly to IP addresses.

```
^[_a-zA-Z0-9-]+(\.[_a-zA-Z0-9-]+)*@[a-zA-Z0-9-]
+(\.[a-zA-Z0-9-]+)*\.(([0-9]{1,3})|([a-zA-Z]{2,3})|
(aero|coop|info|museum|name))$
```

What it does not do is handle invalid two-letter country codes and other things that have a valid format but are not actually used. Compare this to five-digit strings that are not used as ZIP codes.

©2010, Elsevier Inc. All rights reserved.
Doi: 10.1016/B978-0-12-374722-8.00017-7

There are other versions of such regular expressions for e-mails, and you can find some of them at http://regexlib .com. As the name implies, this is a library of contributed regular expressions in many different programming languages. It is usually not too hard to translate one dialect to another mechanically. This is one of the most useful Web sites that a database designer can know about.

4. An e-mail address is easy to verify. You send an e-mail to that address and ask if they really meant to place an order with your company. You can also give them a temporary password or set up challenge questions.

If you don't want to actually contact the email address, you can "ping" it. Ping is a network tool that tests whether a particular host is reachable across an Internet Protocol network and gives some statistics about the packet traffic that was used to make a round-trip time.

18

Universal Postal Union

The Universal Postal Union in Berne, Switzerland, is an international organization that coordinates the worldwide postal system as an agency of the United Nations. It actually goes back to an international postal congress in 1863.

The UPU has a standards board to develop and maintain international standards for postal-related information exchange in such areas as Electronic Data Interchange (EDI), mail encoding, postal forms, and meters.

Having said all that, we do not have a universal street address scheme. There is no universal postal code system.

Even in the same national postal system, you can find differences. In the U.S. Postal Service, for example, rural delivery is only now getting conventional street addresses because of E9-1-1 Emergency Services requirements for emergency services. The Puerto Rico addresses have an extra "urbanization" field in them.

Japan uses an addressing system established after World War II, but it is an update of the addressing system used since the Meiji era (1868–1889). It starts with the Prefecture (roughly a state or county), followed by the municipality within the Prefecture—but not quite; if the municipality is large, we have wards. The next address line is the location within the municipality. That could be wards or other smaller units with special names. The final part is the city district, the block, and finally the house number with an apartment number. Street names are seldom used in postal addresses. The houses within a block are numbered by age, not by physical sequence on the street.

Doi: 10.1016/B978-0-12-374722-8.00018-9

I cannot review all of the postal addresses on Earth. Showing a cultural basis, I will look at the United States, Canada, and the United Kingdom. They are all English-speaking nations with a common heritage, so you might expect some commonality. Wrong again.

18.1. ZIP CODE

The Zone Improvement Plan (ZIP) code is a postal code system used by the U.S. Postal Service (USPS). The term "ZIP code" was a registered servicemark (a type of trademark) held by the USPS, but the registration expired. Today the term has become almost a generic name for any postal code, and almost nobody remembers what it originally meant. The basic format is a string of five digits that appear after the state abbreviation code in a U.S. address. An extended "ZIP + 4" code was introduced in 1983, which includes the five digits of the ZIP code, a hyphen, and four more digits that determine a more precise location than the ZIP code alone.

18.1.1. Basic ZIP Code

The code is based on geography, which means that locations with the same ZIP code are physically contiguous. The first digit is a contiguous group of states.

The first three digits identify the Sectional Center Facility (SCF). An SCF sorts and dispatches mail to all post offices with those first three digits in their ZIP codes. Most of the time, this aligns with state borders, but there are some exceptions for military bases and other locations that cross political units or that can be best served by a closer SCF.

The last two digits are an area within the SCF. But this does not have to match to a political boundary. They tend to identify a local post office or station that serves a given area.

18.1.2. ZIP + 4

In 1983, the USPS began using an expanded ZIP code system called "ZIP + 4," often called "plus-four codes," "add-on codes," or "add ons." This code uses the basic five-digit code plus four additional digits to identify a geographic segment

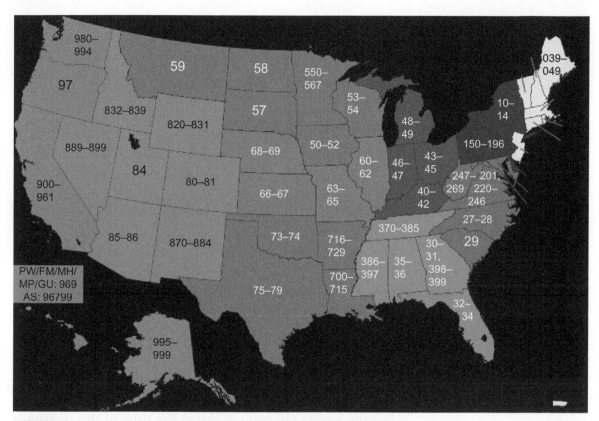

■ **FIGURE 18-1:**   Map showing how zip codes are geographically identified.

within the five-digit delivery area, such as a city block, post office boxes, apartment complexes, an individual high-volume receiver of mail, or any other unit that could use an extra identifier to aid in efficient mail sorting and delivery. The ZIP + 4 is not required for private mail but is used mostly on bulk mailings to speed up delivery and sorting. If the address is in the approved format, multiline optical character readers (MLOCR) can add the correct ZIP + 4 code and put it in a barcode on the piece of mail.

ZIP codes are only loosely tied to cities.

18.1.3. Postal Zone Charts

Shipments of parcel post packages made by the USPS are priced based on Zone tables. This is a list of ZIP codes by linear distance from a given ZIP code. There are eight possible zones, with Zone one or "Local Delivery" being in the same ZIP code; eight is the furthest away.

This is another advantage of geographical postal code system. They give you a simple table look-up distance estimation.

18.1.4. ZIP Code Validation

The first temptation is to write a simple CHECK() constraint such as:

```
zip_code SIMILAR TO '[:DIGIT:][:DIGIT:][:DIGIT:]
[:DIGIT:][:DIGIT:]'
```

This does not quite work. Not all five digit strings are actually used as ZIP codes. There is an Urban Myth among old programmers that 99999 used to be an Eskimo village in Alaska when the system was first implemented. COBOL programmers traditionally use all 9s in a field to signify a missing value (you will see that convention in many standard encoding schemes today). The result was that the village was swamped with bags of improperly encoded bulk mail because nobody had validation routines for the new system.

You might want to use 00000 and 99999 for special purposes, but the lowest ZIP code in use at the time of this writing is 00601 for Adjuntas, PR (Puerto Rico is a U.S. territory). The highest ZIP code in use is 99950 for Edna Bay, Kassa, and Ketchikan, AK.

While several towns might be put under one official name (in the last paragraph, Edna Bay and Kassa are considered part of Ketchikan), a ZIP code will belong to only one state, territory, or military postal unit.

The USPS also publishes a list of preferred abbreviations for states, street suffixes, and other parts of an address (http://www.usps.com/ncsc/lookups/usps_abbreviations.html). You can find commercial software to edit your addresses to USPS standards.

18.2. CANADIAN POSTAL CODES

Canada (http://www.canadapost.ca) was one of the last Western countries to get a nationwide postal code system

(1971). A Canadian postal code is a string of six characters that forms part of a postal address in Canada. This is an example of an alphanumeric system that has less of a geographical basis than the ZIP codes used in the United States. The format is:

```
postal_code SIMILAR TO '[:UPPER:][:DIGIT:]
[:UPPER:] [:DIGIT:] [:UPPER:][:DIGIT:]'
```

Notice the space separating the third and fourth characters. The first three characters are a Forward Sortation Area (FSA), which is geographical; A0A is in Newfoundland and Y1A in the Yukon.

But this is not a good validation. The letters "D," "F," "I," "O," "Q," and "U" are not allowed because handwritten addresses might make them look like digits or other letters when they are scanned. The letters "W" and "Z" are not used as the first letter.

```
'[ABCEGHJKLMNPRSTVXY][:DIGIT:][ABCEGHJKLMNPRSTVW
XYZ][:SPACE:][:DIGIT:] [ABCEGHJKLMNPRSTVWXYZ]
[:DIGIT:]'
```

The first letter of an FSA code denotes a particular "postal district," which, outside of Quebec and Ontario, corresponds to an entire province or territory. Because of Quebec's and Ontario's large populations, those two provinces have three and five postal districts, respectively, and each has at least one urban area so populous that it has a dedicated postal district ("H" for Laval and Montréal and "M" for Toronto).

At the other extreme, Nunavut and the Northwest Territories (NWT) are so small that they share a single postal district. The digit specifies if the FSA is rural (zero) or urban (nonzero). The second letter represents a specific rural region, entire medium-sized city, or section of a major metropolitan area.

The last three characters denote a local delivery unit (LDU). An LDU denotes a specific single address or range of addresses, which can correspond to an entire small town, a significant part of a medium-sized town, a single side of a city block in larger cities, a single large building or a portion of a very large one, a single (large) institution such as a university or a hospital, or a business that receives large volumes of mail on a regular basis. LDUs ending in zero are postal facilities, from post offices and small retail postal outlets all the way up to sorting centers.

In urban areas, LDUs may be specific postal carriers' routes. In rural areas where direct door-to-door delivery is not available, an LDU can describe a set of post office boxes or a rural route. LDU 9Z9 is used exclusively for Business Reply Mail. In rural FSAs, the first two characters are usually assigned in alphanumerical order by the name of each community.

LDU 9Z0 refers to large regional distribution center facilities, and is also used as a placeholder, appearing in some regional postmarks such as the "K0H 9Z0" on purely local mail within the Kingston, Ontario, area.

18.3. POSTCODES IN THE UNITED KINGDOM

These codes were introduced by the Royal Mail over a 15-year period from 1959 to 1974 and are defined in part by British Standard BS-7666 rules. Strangely enough, they are also the lowest level of aggregation in census enumeration. U.K. postcodes are variable-length alphanumeric, making them hard to computerize. The format does not work well for identifying the main sorting office and suboffice. They seem to have been based on what the Royal Post looked like several decades or centuries ago by abbreviating local names at various times in the 15-year period when they began.

Postcodes have been supplemented by a newer system of five-digit codes called Mailsort, but only for bulk mailings of 4,000 or more letter-sized items. Bulk mailers who use the Mailsort system get a discount, but bulk delivery by postcode is not discounted.

18.3.1. Postcode Formats

The format of U.K. postcode is generally given by the regular expression:

```
(GIR 0AA|[A-PR-UWYZ]([0-9]{1,2}|([A-HK-Y][0-9]|
[A-HK-Y][0-9]([0-9]|[ABEHMNPRV-Y]))|[0-9]
[A-HJKS-UW]) [0-9][ABD-HJLNP-UW-Z]{2})
```

It is broken into two parts with a space between them. It is a hierarchical system, working from left to right—the first letter or pair of letters represents the area, the following digit or digits represent the district within that area, and so on. Each postcode generally represents a street, part of a street, or a single address. This feature makes the postcode useful to route-planning software.

The part before the space is the "outward code" and identifies the destination sorting office. The outward code can be split further into the area part (letters identifying 1 of 124 postal areas) and the district part (usually numbers); the letters in the inward code exclude "C", "I", "K", "M", "O", and "V" to avoid confusing scanners. The letters of the outward code approximate an abbreviation of the location (London breaks this pattern). For example, L is Liverpool, EH is Edinburgh, AB is Aberdeen, and BT is Belfast and all of Northern Ireland.

The remaining part is the "inward code" and it is used to sort the mail into local delivery routes. The inward code is split into the sector part (one digit) and the unit part (two letters). Each postcode identifies the address to within 100 properties (with an average of 15 properties per postcode), although a large business may have a single code.

18.3.2. Greater London Postcodes

In the London Postal Area, postcodes are based on the 1856 system of Postal Districts as refined in 1918. They do not match the current boundaries of the London boroughs and can overlap into counties in the Greater London area. The numbering system appears arbitrary on the map because it is historical rather than geographical.

Most central London areas needed more postcodes than were possible in an orderly pattern, so codes like "EC1A 1AA" were devised to make up the shortage. Then some codes are constructed by the government for their use, without regard to keeping a pattern. For example, in Westminster:

- SW1A 0AA - House of Commons
- SW1A 0PW - House of Lords, Palace of Westminster
- SW1A 1AA - Buckingham Palace

- SW1A 2AA - 10 Downing Street, Prime Minister and First Lord of the Treasury
- SW1A 2AB - 11 Downing Street, Chancellor of the Exchequer
- SW1A 2HQ - HM Treasury headquarters
- W1A 1AA - Broadcasting House
- W1A 1AB - Selfridges
- N81 1ER - Electoral Reform Society has all of N81

There are also nongeographic postcodes, such as outward code BX, so that they can be retained if the recipient changes physical locations. Outward codes beginning XY are used internally for misaddressed mail and international outbound mail. This does not cover special postcode for the old Girobank, Northern Ireland, Crown dependencies, British Forces Post Office (BFPO), and overseas territories.

In short, the system is so complex that you require software and data files from the Royal Post ("Postcode Address File" or PAF, which has about 27 million U.K. commercial and residential addresses) and specialized software. The PAF is not given out free by the Royal Mail but is licensed for commercial use by software vendors and updated monthly. In the United Kingdom, most addresses can be constructed from just the postcode and a house number, but not in an obvious way, so GIS systems have to depend on look-up files to translate the address into geographical locations.

18.4. CASE EXPRESSION FOR MANY INTERNATIONAL POSTAL CODES

Philipp Post wrote this CHECK() constraint, which does a *quick* validation on the postal codes for 58 countries. It is *not* a complete validation; some codes that pass this pattern matching are not actually valid. You might want to check to be sure that each pattern is current.

```
CREATE TABLE International_Addresses
(address_id INT NOT NULL PRIMARY KEY,
 --other columns
 country_code CHAR(2) NOT NULL, -- ISO 3166
 postal_code VARCHAR(10) NOT NULL,
```

```
CONSTRAINT validate_postal_code
CHECK(postal_code SIMILAR TO
CASE country_code
WHEN 'AR' THEN '[0-9][0-9][0-9][0-9]'
WHEN 'AT' THEN '[0-9][0-9][0-9][0-9]'
WHEN 'BE' THEN '[0-9][0-9][0-9][0-9]'
WHEN 'BR' THEN '_____'
WHEN 'CA' THEN '[A-Z][0-9][A-Z] [0-9][A-Z][0-9]'
WHEN 'CH' THEN '[0-9][0-9][0-9][0-9]'
WHEN 'CN' THEN '[0-9][0-9][0-9][0-9][0-9][0-9]'
WHEN 'CR' THEN '[0-9][0-9][0-9][0-9]'
WHEN 'CY' THEN '[0-9][0-9][0-9][0-9]'
WHEN 'CZ' THEN '[0-9][0-9][0-9] [0-9][0-9]'
WHEN 'DE' THEN '[0-9][0-9][0-9][0-9][0-9]'
WHEN 'DK' THEN '[0-9][0-9][0-9][0-9]'
WHEN 'DZ' THEN '[0-9][0-9][0-9][0-9][0-9]'
WHEN 'ES' THEN '[0-9][0-9][0-9][0-9][0-9]'
WHEN 'FI' THEN '[0-9][0-9][0-9][0-9][0-9]'
WHEN 'FO' THEN '[0-9][0-9][0-9]'
WHEN 'FR' THEN '[0-9][0-9][0-9][0-9][0-9]'
WHEN 'GR' THEN '[0-9][0-9][0-9][0-9][0-9]'
WHEN 'HR' THEN '[0-9][0-9][0-9][0-9][0-9]'
WHEN 'HU' THEN '[0-9][0-9][0-9][0-9]'
WHEN 'ID' THEN '[0-9][0-9][0-9][0-9][0-9]'
WHEN 'IL' THEN '[0-9][0-9][0-9][0-9][0-9]'
WHEN 'IN' THEN '[0-9][0-9][0-9][0-9][0-9][0-9]'
WHEN 'IR' THEN '[0-9][0-9][0-9][0-9][0-9]'
WHEN 'IS' THEN '[0-9][0-9][0-9]'
WHEN 'IT' THEN '[0-9][0-9][0-9][0-9][0-9]'
WHEN 'JP' THEN '[0-9][0-9][0-9][0-9][0-9][0-9][0-9]'
WHEN 'KR' THEN '[0-9][0-9][0-9]-[0-9][0-9][0-9]'
WHEN 'KW' THEN '[0-9][0-9][0-9][0-9][0-9]'
WHEN 'KZ' THEN '[0-9][0-9][0-9][0-9][0-9][0-9]'
WHEN 'LI' THEN '[0-9][0-9][0-9][0-9]'
WHEN 'LS' THEN '[0-9][0-9][0-9]'
WHEN 'LU' THEN '[0-9][0-9][0-9][0-9]'
WHEN 'MX' THEN '[0-9][0-9][0-9][0-9][0-9]'
WHEN 'MY' THEN '[0-9][0-9][0-9][0-9][0-9]'
WHEN 'NO' THEN '[0-9][0-9][0-9][0-9]'
WHEN 'NP' THEN '[0-9][0-9][0-9][0-9][0-9][0-9]'
WHEN 'NZ' THEN '[0-9][0-9][0-9][0-9]'
WHEN 'PH' THEN '[0-9][0-9][0-9][0-9]'
```

```
WHEN 'PL' THEN '[0-9][0-9]-[0-9][0-9][0-9]'
WHEN 'PT' THEN '[0-9][0-9][0-9][0-9]'
WHEN 'RO' THEN '[0-9][0-9][0-9][0-9][0-9][0-9]'
WHEN 'RU' THEN '[0-9][0-9][0-9][0-9][0-9][0-9]'
WHEN 'SA' THEN '[0-9][0-9][0-9][0-9][0-9]'
WHEN 'SE' THEN '[0-9][0-9][0-9] [0-9][0-9]'
WHEN 'SG' THEN '[0-9][0-9][0-9][0-9][0-9][0-9]'
WHEN 'SI' THEN '[0-9][0-9][0-9][0-9]'
WHEN 'SK' THEN '[0-9][0-9][0-9] [0-9][0-9]'
WHEN 'TH' THEN '[0-9][0-9][0-9][0-9][0-9]'
WHEN 'TN' THEN '[0-9][0-9][0-9][0-9]'
WHEN 'TR' THEN '[0-9][0-9][0-9][0-9][0-9]'
WHEN 'TW' THEN '[0-9][0-9][0-9]'
WHEN 'UA' THEN '[0-9][0-9][0-9][0-9][0-9]'
WHEN 'US' THEN '[0-9][0-9][0-9][0-9][0-9]-[0-9]
[0-9][0-9][0-9]'
WHEN 'VE' THEN '[0-9][0-9][0-9][0-9]'
WHEN 'VN' THEN '[0-9][0-9][0-9][0-9][0-9]'
WHEN 'YU' THEN '[0-9][0-9][0-9][0-9][0-9]'
WHEN 'ZA' THEN '[0-9][0-9][0-9][0-9]'
ELSE postal_code END));
```

Hierarchical Triangular Mesh

Most of us are used to locating positions on earth with (longitude, latitude) pairs. But this traditional system has problems as you get closer to either the North or South Pole and the math involved uses spherical trigonometry.

An alternative system is the Hierarchical Triangular Mesh, or HTM for short. While (longitude, latitude) pairs are based on establishing a point in a two-dimensional coordinate system on the surface of the earth, HTM is based on dividing the surface into almost-equal sized triangles with a unique identifier to locate something by a containing polygon.

If you have seen a geodesic dome or Buckminster Fuller's maps, you have some feeling for this approach. HTM start with an octahedron at level zero. To map the globe into eight triangles, align it so that the world is first cut into a Northern and Southern hemisphere. Now slice it along the Prime Meridian, and then at right angles to both those cuts. In each hemisphere, number the spherical triangles from 0 to 3, prefixing them with either N or S.

A triangle on a plane always has exactly 180°, but on the surface of a sphere and other positively curved surfaces it is always greater than 180° and on negatively curved surfaces it is less than 180°. If you want a quick mind tool, think that a positively curved surface has too much in the middle. A negatively curved surface is like a horse saddle or the bell of a trumpet; the middle of the surface is "too small" and curves the shape.

■ **FIGURE 19-1:** The Hierarchical Triangular Mesh (HTM).

The eight spherical triangles are labeled N0 to N3 and S0 to S3 and are called "level 0 trixels" in the system. Each trixel can be split into four smaller trixels recursively. Put a point at the middle of each edge of the triangle. Use those three points to make an embedded triangle with great circle arc segments. This will divide the original triangle into four more spherical triangles at the next level down. Trixel division is recursive and smaller and smaller trixels to any level you desire.

To name the new trixels, take the name of the patent trixel and append a digit from 0 to 3 to it, using a counterclockwise pattern. The (n = {0, 1, 2}) point on the corner of the next level is opposite the same number on the corner of the previous level. The center triangle always gets a 3.

The triangles are close to the same size at each level. As they get smaller, the difference also decreases. At level seven, approximately three-quarters of the trixels are slightly smaller than the average size, and a quarter are larger. The difference is because the three corner trixels (0, 1, 2) are

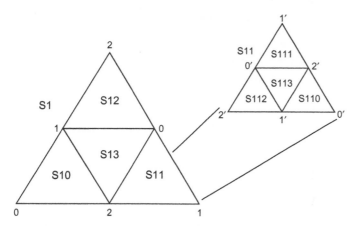

■ **FIGURE 19-2:** Trixels.

smaller than trixel 3 in the center one. The ratio of the maximum over the minimum areas at higher depths is about two.

Smaller trixels have longer names and the length of the name gives its level.

The name can be used to compute the exact location of the three vertex vectors of the given trixel. They can be easily encoded into an integer identifier by assigning two bits to each level and encoding "N" as 11 and "S" as 10. For example, "N01" encodes as binary 110001 or hexadecimal 0x31. The HTM ID (HtmID) is the number of a trixel (and its center point) as a unique 64-bit string (not all strings are valid trixels).

While the recursion can go to infinite, the smallest valid HtmID is eight levels, but it is easy to go to 31 levels in represent in 64 bits. Level 25 is good enough for most applications, since it is about 0.6 meters on the surface of the Earth or 0.02 arc-seconds. Level 26 is about 30 centimeters (one foot) on the Earth's surface. If you want to get any closer than that to an object, you are probably trying to put a bullet in it.

20

Shoe Sizes

National shoe sizes are very different from each other. In the United States, the Branach system was developed in World War II by a private company. The U.S. Army hired the Branach Company to ensure that boots and shoes fit enlisted men. The Branach system was expanded to allow for the width of the foot with alphabetic codes after the size that start at (narrowest) AAA and continue through AA, A, B, C, D, E, EE, and EEE. The widths are 3/16" apart and differ by shoe length.

The Continental European system used in France, Germany, Italy, Spain, and in most other continental European countries is based on the French system. The unit of measure is called a "Paris point" and it is given by the formula:

shoe size = (1.5 * (foot_length + 2))

Foot length is the length of the foot in centimeters. There are also national shoe size systems and you will often see a shoe box label that gives several of them. These national systems did not include width as part of the size. It was simply assumed that the feet in a national population would have the same general foot shape—Germans have square feet, Spaniards have narrow heels, and so on.

Unfortunately, this is not true. If you are right-handed, then your left foot is probably larger than your right foot. Likewise, if you are left-handed, then your right foot is probably larger than your left foot. The population in industrial nationals is taller and fatter than it was in the past.

Doi: 10.1016/B978-0-12-374722-8.00020-7

As an example, a friend is currently wearing a pair of shoes with the label:

```
US UK FR JP
13 12½ 48 310
```

20.1. MONDOPOINT SYSTEM

The Mondopoint system is defined by ISO 9407; it is becoming more popular because it is both metric and more universal across populations. The name (mondo = "world" in Latin) tells you the intent—a worldwide measurement system. The idea is that an idealized model foot can be constructed from the length and width. The standard leaves open the question of how to make the model foot.

Length in millimeters is the first number. Width is the second number and is defined as the distance in millimeters from the first to fifth metatarsophalangeal toe joints. This is the widest part of a normal foot. These measurements are made on a statistically constructed human foot.

Chapter 21

International Clothing Sizes

There have been national systems for clothing sizes for some time. This was fine when the garment industry was local to a given country and foreign-made goods were expensive luxuries (Italian shoes, French dresses, and so forth). Here is an example from http://www.asknumbers.com/ SizeConversion.aspx of one woman's dress size in five different national systems.

Women's dress sizes

US/ Canada	Europe	UK	Australia	Japan
8	38	10	12	11

Almost nothing in the modern world is local, and the garment industry is one of the most globalized. Just look at the labels on virtually any basic clothing item you buy today, especially in the United States where we have almost no native textile or garment industry left after decades of unionization.

U.S. standard clothing sizes were developed from statistical data in the 1940s and 1950s, using physical measurements gathered during and after World War II. But over time, the original system drifted toward larger, fatter people; on average, the current numbers are six sizes smaller than the original standard, which led to the original size 6 becoming size 0 today.

To make things even worse, companies created special categories such as "petite," "juniors," and "women" for women's clothing and "short portly" for men's suits, which have the same numbers with different underlying anatomy models. This is part of the reason why a size from one manufacturer will not match the same size from a second manufacturer.

The European Committee for Standardization or Comité Européen de Normalisation (CEN), is a private nonprofit organization that provides the European economy with an efficient infrastructure of coherent standards and specifications for European trade.

CEN was founded in 1961 to develop European Standards (ENs) in various sectors to build a European internal market for goods and services and to position Europe in the global economy. Some of these standards are voluntary, whereas other standards such as harmonized standards have been made effectively mandatory under EU law. CEN is the officially recognized standardization representative for sectors other than electrotechnical (CENELEC) and telecommunications (ETSI).

CEN (together with CENELEC) owns the Keymark, a voluntary quality mark for products and services that shows that the product conforms to European Standards. You can look for the stylized "CE" on labels.

Many standards are for building materials and other things which will not leave Europe once they are in use. However, the EN 13402 is a European standard for labeling the sizes of clothes which are exported. It is based on body dimensions, measured in centimeters. It aims to replace many older national dress-size systems, most likely before the year 2010.

■ **FIGURE 21-1:** The Keymark shows a product conforms to European Standards.

Acceptance of this form of standardization is likely to vary from country to country.

The system has four parts:

1. **EN 13402-1**: Terms, definitions, and body measurement procedure. This is descriptive and talks about what is being measured in terms of the shape of a male and female body (i.e., men do not have a bust girth).

2. **EN 13402-2**: Primary and secondary dimensions. Using the terms from section 1, this describes which of the measurements are used for what kind of garment. For example, trousers and shorts must use waist girth, but can optionally have (height, inside leg length).

3. **EN 13402-3**: Measurements and intervals. Here we find that the unit of measure is the centimeter, and depending on what is being measured, steps of 2, 4, or 8 centimeters are used. The product should not be labeled with the average body dimension for which the garment was designed (i.e., not "height: 176 cm."). Instead, the label should show the range of body dimensions from half the step size below to half the step size above the design size (e.g., "height: 172-180 cm"). For trousers, the recommended step size for height is 4 cm and the standard defines similar tables for other dimensions and garments. There is also a series of letter codes for "extra extra small" (XXS) to "extra extra extra large" (3XL), and letter codes for bra cups from "AA" to "G" based on ranges of (cup size = bust girth – underbust girth) in steps of 2 centimeters.

4. **EN 13402-4**: The fourth part of the standard is still under review. It will define a compact coding system for clothes sizes. This code was originally intended for industry use in databases, stock-keeping identifiers, and customer catalog ordering numbers. Writing out all of the centimeter figures of all the primary and secondary measures from EN 13402-2 can require up to 12 digits. But garments are not made for people who are wider than they are tall; only certain combinations body measurements occur in human beings.

The same information from the combinations that are actually used can be squeezed into a human usable code with look-up tables. EN 13402-4 will define such tables.

One of these, from the European Association of National Organizations of Textile Traders (AEDT), proposes a five-character alphanumeric code, consisting of the three-digit centimeter figure of the primary body dimension, followed by one or two letters that code a secondary dimension, somewhat like the system already defined for bra sizes. For example, an item designed for:

- Bust girth: 100 cm (100)
- Hip girth: 104 cm (B)
- Height: 176 cm (G)

would bear (in addition to the explanatory pictogram) the compact size code "100BG." This proposal was agreed on in a 2006 March meeting in Florence and a final draft was produced by AEDT on June 6, 2006. If you read Italian, there is a PDF file at http://www.uni-tex.it/webapp/upl/rassegna-Stampa/allegati/2007-03%5CFERRETTI-proposta%20di%20codifcazione%20taglie2_39220.pdf

The measurements from EN 13402-3 are put into two- and three-dimensional look-up tables, and then given a number or letter. It is very easy SQL but there is a lot of it so I will not go into details here.

22

ICD Codes

The real title of the "International Classification of Diseases" or "ICD" is the "International Statistical Classification of Diseases and Related Health Problems," although nobody uses the full honorific in the medical trades. This is the "Dewey Decimal for disease," in that it is a hierarchical scheme to encode diseases, symptoms, abnormal findings, complaints, social circumstances, and external causes of injury or disease. Every health condition can be assigned to a unique category and given a code up to six characters long. Such categories usually include a set of similar diseases. The format of the code is '[:alpha:][:digit:][:digit:]-[:alpha:][:digit:][:digit:]' in the ANSI/ISO Standard SIMILAR TO predicate syntax.

The ICD is published by the World Health Organization (WHO) and used for almost any medical system that deals with the diagnosis of disease. The ICD is one of the WHO Family of International Classifications (WHO-FIC).

At the time of this writing, we are still working on a draft document for the ICD-10, which is the 10th edition of the codes (minor updates are made between major releases). The ICD-10 began development in 1992 and will be replaced with ICD-11 in 2015. In 1893 Jacques Bertillon created the "Bertillon Classification of Causes of Death" at the International Statistical Institute in Chicago. It became popular and led to the current ICD system.

22.1. LOCAL VERSIONS

There are some national adaptations and modifications, but the core document is international. If you work in this area, you will need to know the subtle differences. You will see the abbreviation "CM" or "ICDA" for amended or clinical modifications.

The United States required ICD-9-CM codes for Medicare and Medicaid claims from 1988, and most of the rest of the American medical industry followed suit. The proposed codes come in two parts:

- ICD-10-CM, for diagnosis codes (draft completed in 2003)
- ICD-10-PCS, for procedure codes (draft completed in 2000)

As of this writing, there is a huge push by the Obama administration toward computerizing the U.S. medical system, which may speed up things.

The first draft of the ICD-11 system (authored by WHO) is expected in 2010, with publication following by 2014. WHO has announced that it will to let anyone register for an online group, present and back their suggestions with evidence from medical literature, and participate in online debate over proposed changes to the ICD. Not a bad way to develop such standards when you can use the Internet to get to a specialized community online.

22.2. MENTAL AND BEHAVIORAL DISORDERS

It is better to be sick than to be crazy for reporting purposes. The ICD and the *American Psychiatric Association's Diagnostic and Statistical Manual of Mental Disorders* (*DSM*, currently *DSM-IV*) are trying to use the same codes. The *DSM* is the primary diagnostic system for psychiatric and psychological disorders within the United States and some other countries, and is used as an adjunct diagnostic system in other countries. This is not a matter of different codes for the same data element value. The ICD has personality disorders on the same axis as other mental disorders, unlike the *DSM*. This alignment will take some effort.

Vehicle Identification Number (VIN)

A Vehicle Identification Number (VIN) is used to uniquely identify automobiles and other vehicles. The VIN was originally described in ISO-3779 in 1977 and last revised in 1983. The VIN identifies motor vehicles, trailers, motorcycles, and mopeds. In the early 1980s the U.S. National Highway Traffic Safety Administration (USDOT) required that all road vehicles must have a VIN. Manufacturers put the VIN on the chassis, dashboard, and windows of the vehicle at the factory. Custom-built vehicles are assigned a VIN if they are registered for highway use.

There were some worries about running out of VINs—see *USA Today,* posted 2004 July 1, updated 2004 July 2: "U.S. Auto Industry Running out of Vehicle ID Numbers" by Eric Mayne, and *The Detroit News* and *Automotive News* on a second article in 2007 October 15, "VIN's Numbers Tank Is Running On Empty" by Harry Stoffer. The VIN system was designed to last 30 years, but it did not take into account the growth of the automobile industry.

The details of the VIN can be found in SAE (Society of Automotive Engineers; SAE International, 400 Commonwealth Drive, Warrendale, PA 15096-0001, USA) documents and standards. Since it is universally used, you can find lots of Web sites that track the history (http://www.carfax.com), legal status, recall information, and so forth.

23.1. VIN FORMAT

The VIN is a 17-digit alphanumeric character vector code. The characters used do not include the letters I, O, Q, or Z to avoid confusion with digits. The vector components are fixed length and use this format:

Position 1 identifies the country of manufacture.

For example: U.S. (1 or 4), Canada(2), Mexico(3), Japan(J), Korea(K), England(S), Germany(W), Italy(Z)

Position 2 identifies the manufacturer. For example; Audi(A),

BMW(B), Buick(4), Cadillac(6), Chevrolet(1), Chrysler(C), Dodge(B),

Ford(F), GM Canada(7), General Motors(G), Honda(H), Jaguar(A), Lincoln(L), Mercedes Benz(D), Mercury(M), Nissan(N), Oldsmobile(3), Pontiac(2 or 5), Plymouth(P), Saturn(8), Toyota(T), Volvo(V).

Position 3 identifies vehicle type or manufacturing division.

This substring of 3 characters is called the World Manufacturer Identifier or WMI code.

Positions 4 to 8 are used by the manufacturer to identify vehicle features such as body style, engine type, model, series, etc.

Position 9 is the check digit.

A check digit has been part of each VIN since 1981. The VINs of any two vehicles manufactured within a 30-year period cannot be identical. After all other characters in the VIN have been determined by the manufacturer, the check digit is calculated with a `MOD(11)` weighted sum algorithm, so the check digit will be zero through nine (0–9) or the letter "X" if the remainder is 10.

As usual, the letters have to be mapped to numerical value (remember I, O, and Q are not allowed) and digits use their own values:

```
A: 1    G: 7    N: 5    V: 5
B: 2    H: 8    P: 7    W: 6
C: 3    J: 1    R: 9    X: 7
D: 4    K: 2    S: 2    Y: 8
E: 5    L: 3    T: 3    Z: 9
F: 6    M: 4    U: 4
```

The weights for each position in the VIN except the 9th position, which is where the results of this computation will go, are:

```
1st: X8      5th: X4      10th: X9      14th: X5
2nd: X7      6th: X3      11th: X8      15th: X4
3rd: X6      7th: X2      12th: X7      16th: X3
4th: X5      8th: X10     13th: X6      17th: X2
```

Multiply the weights and the numerical values, sum the resulting products, and perform the MOD(11) computation. If the remainder is 10, the check digit is the letter X. Valid check digits also run through the numbers 0 to 9.

Consider the hypothetical VIN "M8GDM9A_KP042788'," where the underscore will be the check digit:

```
VIN: 1 M 8 G D M 9 A _ K P 0 4 2 7 8 8
Value: 1 4 8 7 4 4 9 1 0 2 7 0 4 2 7 8 8
Weight: 8 7 6 5 4 3 2 10 0 9 8 7 6 5 4 3 2
Products: 8 28 48 35 16 12 18 10 0 18 56 0 24 10 28
  24 16
```

You can play with the algorithm online at http://www.brenz.net/vin_checksum.asp

The substring in positions 4 to 9 is called the Vehicle Descriptor Section or VDS.

Position 10 is the model year. In addition to the three letters that are not allowed in the VIN itself (I, O, and Q), the letters U and Z and the digit 0 are not used for the year code. Note that the year code can be the calendar year in which a vehicle is built, or a model or type year allocated by the manufacturer. Notice that there is a 30-year cycle in this component.

Code	Year	Code	Year	Code	Year	Code	Year
A	1980	L	1990	Y	2000	A	2010
B	1981	M	1991	1	2001	B	2011
C	1982	N	1992	2	2002	C	2012
D	1983	P	1993	3	2003	D	2013
E	1984	R	1994	4	2004	E	2014
F	1985	S	1995	5	2005	F	2015
G	1986	T	1996	6	2006	G	2016
H	1987	V	1997	7	2007	H	2017
J	1988	W	1998	8	2008	J	2018
K	1989	X	1999	9	2009	K	2019

Position 11 identifies the assembly plant for the vehicle.

The last eight characters of the VIN are used for the identification of a specific vehicle. The last four characters are numeric and are the sequence of the vehicle as it rolled off the manufacturer's assembly line.

Positions 10 to 17 are the Vehicle Identifier Section or VIS. This may include information on options installed or engine and transmission choices, but often it is a simple sequential number. In fact, in North America, the last five digits must be numeric.

Chapter 24

Freight Containers

In the old days, freight was shipped in whatever packaging the suppliers wished to use. This meant an incredible amount of manual labor was needed to handle cargo. Freight containers reduced the labor required, but without standardization, automating cargo handling was not possible.

There are a lot of ISO codes for freight containers, but the most important one is ISO 6346. This is the international standard for identifying freight containers.

24.1. FREIGHT CONTAINER CODES

The code starts with a three-letter owner code assigned by Bureau International des Containers (BIC). This is a 1,700 member nongovernmental coordinating organization for the containerization and intermodal transport industries.

This is followed by a one-letter equipment category identifier. Only three letters are used:

- U for all freight containers
- J for detachable freight container-related equipment
- Z for trailers and chassis

Next, there is a six-digit serial number assigned by the owner or operator as they wish. The only requirement is that it is unique within that owner or operator's fleet.

The check digit is a more complex scheme than is usually used in commercial systems. You can go online and get calculators for it, since it is a bit hard to do manually.

24.1.1. Map Letters to Numeric Values

Since the entire alphabet is used, the convention of dropping letters like I and O that might be confused with digit 1 and 0 is not followed. But multiples of 11 are dropped (they are 11, 22, and 33). The letter "A" maps to 10, "B" maps to 12, and, finally, "Z" maps to 38.

24.1.2. Assign Weights to Each Position

The weights are assigned from left to right, but they are powers of two. That means the leftmost position is $1 = (2^0)$, then 2 ,4, 8, 16, and so forth until the 10th position, which is $512 = (2^9)$.

Each of the weights is multiplied by its numeric mapping and the results are added, just like any weighted sum check digit.

24.1.3. Compute the Check Digit from the Weighted Sum

The standard describes a MOD 11 procedure, but if the answer was 10, the check digit becomes 0. The standard recommends but does not require that serial numbers should be picked to avoid a final difference of 10. But this is a recommendation and not a requirement.

24.2. SIZE AND TYPE CODES

ISO 6346 also gives size and type codes for containers. The codes are four characters:

- First character is the length
- Second character is the width and height
- Third and fourth characters are the container type

24.3. RELATED ISO STANDARDS

- ISO 668—Freight containers—Classification, dimensions, and ratings
- ISO 830—Freight containers—Terminology
- ISO 1161—Freight containers—Corner fittings—Specification
- ISO 1496—Freight containers—Specification and testing

- ISO 2308—Hooks for lifting freight containers of up to 30 tons capacity—Basic requirements
- ISO 3874—Freight containers—Handling and securing
- ISO 8323—Freight containers—Air/surface (intermodal) general purpose containers—Specification and tests
- ISO 9669—Freight containers—Interface connections for tank containers
- ISO 9711—Freight containers—Information related to containers on board vessels
- ISO 9897—Container equipment data exchange (CEDEX)
- ISO 10368—Freight thermal containers—Remote condition monitoring
- ISO 10374—Freight containers—Automatic identification

- ISO 2308 – Hooks for lifting freight containers of up to 30 tons capacity – Basic requirements
- ISO 3874 – Freight containers – Handling and securing
- ISO 8323 – Freight containers – Air/surface (intermodal) general purpose containers – Specification and tests
- ISO 9669 – Freight containers – Interface connections for tank containers
- ISO 9711 – Freight containers – Information related to containers on board vessels
- ISO 9897 – Container equipment data exchange (CEDEX)
- ISO 10368 – Freight thermal containers – Remote condition monitoring
- ISO 10374 – Freight containers – Automatic identification

25

Credit Card Numbers

Specifications for credit card numbering are in ISO/IEC 7812-1:1993 and the American National Standards Institute ANSI X4.13. Most credit card numbers are now 16 digits, grouped in blocks of four digits; longer or shorter numbers are historical and you are not likely to see them.

25.1. CARD ISSUERS

The first digit is the Major Industry Identifier (MII), which represents the category of the issuer of the card, according to this table:

MII Digit Issuer Category

- **0** ISO/TC 68 and other industry assignments
- **1** Airlines
- **2** Airlines and other industry assignments
- **3** Travel and entertainment
- **4** Banking and financial
- **5** Banking and financial
- **6** Merchandizing and banking
- **7** Petroleum
- **8** Telecommunications and other industry assignments
- **9** National assignments

The first six digits are complete issuer identifier, which limits us to 1 million possible issuers. Currently you will see the first four-digit block embossed and printed on the face

Doi: 10.1016/B978-0-12-374722-8.00025-6

of the card. Here is a sample of the more common issuer identifiers:

```
Issuer
Identifiers

Diner's Club/Carte Blanche = 300xxx-305xxx,
  36xxxx, 38xxxx

American Express = 4xxxxx, 37xxxx

VISA = 4xxxxx

MasterCard = 51xxxx-55xxxx

Discover = 6011xx
```

If the MII digit is nine, then the next three digits of the issuer identifier are the three-digit ISO-3166 country codes, and the next two digits are defined by the national standards body of that country.

25.2. ACCOUNT NUMBER

Digits 7 to (length − 1) are the account number. The maximum length of the account number field is 12 digits, but in practice today, it is usually nine digits. The final digit is a Luhn check digit.

25.3. OTHER NUMBERS

The Card Security Code (CSC), also known as Card Verification Value (CVV or CV2), Card Verification Value Code (CVVC), Card Verification Code (CVC), or Card Code Verification (CCV) is a three-digit number printed—not embossed—on the back of the card. American Express is the odd man out, putting a four-digit code on the front of its cards and calling it the CID or Unique Card Code.

There are several types of security codes:

- The first code, called CVC1 or CVV1, is encoded on the magnetic stripe of the card and is used for transactions in person.

- The second code, and the most cited, is CVV2 or CVC2. This CSC (also known as a CCID or Credit Card ID) is used for transactions occurring over the Internet, by mail, fax, or over the phone where the card is not physically at the point of the transaction. In many countries in Western Europe, it is now mandatory to provide this code when the cardholder is not present in person.

- Contactless Cards and Chip Cards may supply their own codes generated electronically, such as iCVV or Dynamic CVV. The number is generated when the card is issued, by hashing the card number and expiration date by each issuing bank with its own algorithm.

25.4. PERSONAL IDENTIFICATION NUMBERS

The Personal Identification Number (PIN) is created by the card holder and is never stored on the card itself. It is used to verify the user's identity at ATMs and other computer systems that can access the account at the issuer.

There are some legal issues with having the merchant's computer system hold the PINs from transactions, and many states require that only the last four or five digits of the account number and no expiration date can be displayed on receipts and other documents.

For example, in Minnesota, the Plastic Card Security Act or Minnesota Data Retention Act of 2007 requires merchants to flush security codes, PINs, and the contents of any magnetic stripe with 48 hours of the completed transaction authorization.

25.5. PCI DSS AND RELATED STANDARDS

The Payment Card Industry Data Security Standard (PCI DSS) is an international security standard defined by the Payment Card Industry Security Standards Council (PCI SSC). This council is made up of all the major card companies (American Express, Discover Financial Services, JCB International, MasterCard Worldwide, and Visa Inc.) and many others.

Their goal is to prevent credit card fraud, hacking, and other security vulnerabilities and threats. They issue guidelines and certification for software that handles payment card numbers. Compliance is validated annually.

PCI DSS originally began as five different programs: Visa Card Information Security Program, MasterCard Site Data Protection, American Express Data Security Operating Policy, Discover Information and Compliance, and the JCB Data Security Program. Each company's intentions were roughly similar: to create an additional level of protection for customers by ensuring that merchants meet minimum levels of security when they store, process, and transmit cardholder data. The Payment Card Industry Security Standards Council (PCI SSC) was formed, and on December 15, 2004, these companies aligned their individual policies and released the Payment Card Industry Data Security Standard (PCI DSS).

Companies have had security breaches while being registered as PCI DSS compliant. In 2008 one of the largest payment service providers, Heartland Payment Processing Systems, suffered a data compromise that has been estimated by some as exceeding 100 million card numbers.

Other PCI standards include PIN Entry Device (PED) Security Requirements for manufacturers that make personal identification number (PIN) entry terminals used for payment card financial transactions. The authorized devices are listed at the PCI Web site.

The PA-DSS is for software developers and integrators of payment applications that store, process, or transmit cardholder data as part of authorization or settlement when these applications are sold, distributed, or licensed to third parties. Validated applications are listed at the PCI Web site.

25.6. TOOLS AND MORE INFORMATION

For a good introduction to this industry, Google the online article "Everything You Ever Wanted to Know about Credit Cards" by Joe Ziegler (http://www.eastland.com/everythingCC.html). It gives lots of industry information and has Java source code for credit card number validation. There are many other validation routines in other programming languages in open source software.

Chapter 26

SWIFT and Related Banking Standards

The Society for Worldwide Interbank Financial Telecommunication (SWIFT) operates a secured worldwide financial messaging network. Messages are securely and reliably exchanged between banks and other financial institutions. SWIFT also markets software and services to financial institutions, much of it for use on the SWIFTNet Network, and ISO-9362 bank identifier codes (BICs) are popularly known as "SWIFT codes."

The SWIFT network is the largest international banking message service, covering over 200 countries. An average of 2.4 million messages, with aggregate value of $2 trillion, was processed by SWIFT per day in 1995. It is not a clearinghouse, but the BIC numbers are needed for funds transfers.

It is important to note that SWIFT just transports secured financial messages but does not hold accounts for its members and does not perform any form of clearing or settlement. This is the messenger.

SWIFT is also a registration authority (RA) for the following ISO standards. A registration authority is "Standards Speak" for the group in charge of the standards, even though it is not a national agency. Registration authorities are usually trade organizations, nonprofits in the particular area of expertise, and sometimes affiliated with a university.

- ISO 9362:1994 Banking—Banking telecommunication messages—Bank Identifier Codes

Doi: 10.1016/B978-0-12-374722-8.00026-8

- ISO 10383:2003 Securities and related financial instruments—Codes for exchanges and market identification (MIC)

- ISO 13616:2003 IBAN (International Bank Account Number) Registry

- ISO 15022:1999 Securities—Scheme for messages (Data Field Dictionary) (replaces ISO 7775)

- ISO 20022-1:2004 and ISO 20022-2:2007 financial services—Universal Financial Industry message scheme

26.1. BIC CODES

Bank Identifier Codes (BIC) are defined by ISO-9362 and are sometimes called SWIFT-BIC, BIC code, SWIFT ID, or SWIFT code. They provide a unique identification code of a particular bank. These codes are used when transferring money between banks, particularly for international wire transfers, and also for the exchange of other messages between banks. The codes can sometimes be found on account statements.

The SWIFT code is 8 or 11 characters, made up of:

- Four characters—bank code (alpha)

- Two characters—ISO 3166-1 alpha-2 country code

- Two characters—location code (letters and digits) (if the second character is "1," then it denotes a passive participant in the SWIFT network)

- Optional three characters—branch code, optional ('XXX' for primary office, letters, and digits). If the three characters are missing then this is the primary office.

As an example, consider Deutsche Bank, which has its headquarters in Frankfurt, Germany. The SWIFT code for its primary office is DEUTDEFF:

DEUT identifies Deutsche Bank, DE is the country code for Germany, and FF is the code for Frankfurt

Beyond that, DEUTDEFF500 refers to an office of Deutsche Bank in Bad Homburg. If you need to look up a BIC, you can go to one of several sites such as http://www.swift.com/bsl/ freequery.do

26.2. INTERNATIONAL BANK ACCOUNT NUMBER (IBAN)

The International Bank Account Number (IBAN) is an international standard for identifying bank accounts across national borders. It is defined by ISO-13616:2007 and is maintained by SWIFT.

The IBAN consists of an ISO-3166-1 alpha-2 country code, followed by two check digits and up to 30 alphanumeric characters for the domestic bank account number, called the BBAN (Basic Bank Account Number).

This is where things get messy. Every country gets to design its own national bank account encoding system; the only rule that IBAN imposes is that it is a fixed length for any given country.

The IBAN is transmitted as a string without spaces, which would make it a nightmare to read. The display convention is to break it into blocks of four characters separated by a single space; the last block can be shorter.

- Examples of IBANs include:
- Greek IBAN: GR16 0110 1050 0000 1054 7023 795
- British IBAN: GB35 MIDL 4025 3432 1446 70
- Swiss IBAN: CH51 0868 6001 2565 1500 1

If you know the country and the account number, you can create an IBAN with the help of a free Web site: http://www .ibanconverter.eu/

The two-position check digit is worth a separate mention. Digits carry the expected weight, then A = 10, B = 11, and so forth. ISO-7064 (MOD 97, 10) returns two digits instead of the usual one character. This is the best system that we have right now. It catches just about every possible error at the cost of one extra digit. It evens beats the Dihedral Five check digit (see Section 2.2.2.4. Dihedral Five Check Digit).

It is a basic weighted check digit formula. The check digits are given by `MOD(98—MOD(data * 100, 97), 97)` and the verification is just `MOD(check_number, 97) = 1`.

Banks in the British dependencies, U.S. banks, and some banks outside Europe may not recognize IBAN, but it is coming. Perhaps even the United States will participate. If you do not have an IBAN, then you will probably use the current ISO-9362 Bank Identifier Code system with the BBAN.

Banks in the United States do not use IBAN format account numbers. When we switch it would likely be initiated by ANSI ASC X9, the U.S. financial services standards development. This is one reason that foreign payments to U.S. bank accounts are prone to routing errors.

26.2.1. IBAN Check Digits

The checksum is a basic ISO-7064 MOD 97-10 calculation where the remainder must equal 1. To validate the checksum:

1. Check that the total IBAN length is correct as per the country. If not, the IBAN is invalid.

2. Move the four initial characters to the end of the string.

3. Replace the letters in the string with digits, expanding the string as necessary, such that A = 10, B = 11, and Z = 35. This allows for accented characters, but they are not used in ISO-3166 country codes and most other encodings.

4. Convert the string to an integer and MOD-97 the entire number. There are some math tricks to avoid having to work with a huge integer value.

If the remainder is 1, you have a valid IBAN number.

To calculate the checksum:

1. Check that the total IBAN length is correct as per the country. If not, the IBAN is invalid.

2. Make the checksum digits 00 (e.g. GB00 for the United Kingdom).

3. Move the four initial characters to the end of the string.

4. Replace the letters in the string with digits, expanding the string as necessary, such that A = 10, B = 11, and Z = 35. Each alphabetic character is therefore replaced by two digits.

5. Convert the string to an integer (i.e., ignore leading zeroes) and MOD-97 the entire number minus 1, then add 1.

6. Subtract the remainder from 98 and pad with a leading 0, if necessary.

As few computers can handle numbers that long, an iterative modulus calculation is probably needed:

1. Take the first 8 digits.
2. Perform a modulus calculation on those.
3. Append the next six digits to the result on step 2.
4. Repeat steps 2 and 3 until there are no more digits to append.

This works because `MOD(x, 97x10^n)` is an integer product of (97 + MOD (x, 97)).

4. Replace the letters in the string with digits, expanding the string as necessary such that A = 10, B = 11, and Z = 35. Each alphabetic character is the letter replaced by two digits.

5. Convert the string to an integer (i.e., ignore leading zeros) and MOD-97 the entire number minus 1, then add 1.

6. Subtract the remainder from 98 and pad with a leading 0, if necessary.

As few computers can handle numbers that long, an iterative modulus calculation is probably needed.

1. Take the first 9 digits.
2. Perform a modulus calculation on those.
3. Append the next six digits to the result on step 2.
4. Repeat steps 2 and 3 until there are no more digits to append.

This works because $10(x) \cdot 9 \times 10^n$ is an integer product of $(47 = MOD(x, 97))$.

Chapter 27

Data Universal Numbering System

The Data Universal Numbering System (DUNS) is a numeric identifier controlled by Dun & Bradstreet (D&B) for a single business entity. It has been in use since 1965. It started as part of their credit reporting and it is now a common international standard. It is NOT a national tax identifier. For example, Dell Computers requires all of its suppliers, consultants, and so on to bill by using the DUNS. The Office of Management and Budget (OMB) requires a DUNS for all grant applicants for new or renewal. The United Nations also uses it. There are about 100 million numbers in use.

The DUNS number is a nine-digit random number written without punctuation. Until 2006, it had a MOD 10 check digit, but this feature was stopped to increase the range of numbers. There is no charge for a DUNS number and you can apply for it online (http://www.dnb.com/us/duns_update/index.html); but it can take some time. You can also request one and pay an investigation fee to get it is issued immediately.

A DUNS number is sometimes formatted with embedded dashes to promote readability, such as 15-048-3782. Modern usage typically omits dashes, and shows the number in the form 150483782 (this is the actual D&B).

There have been other business identifier systems, but none of them have the volume and acceptance of the DUNS.

28

Global Trade Item Number

The Global Trade Item Number (GTIN) actually refers to a family of barcodes on retail packaging. For North American companies, the UPC is the most common member of the GTIN. Attempts at machine-readable package codes started in the grocery business. This is quite logical; a grocery store has a low profit margin and a fast inventory turnover. Anything that saves manual labor shows up on the bottom line immediately.

Modern barcode technology began with a graduate student research project in 1948 at Drexel Institute of Technology in Philadelphia, Pennsylvania. But it did not catch on for years. The National Association of Food Chains (NAFC) put out a call for technology to speed the checkout process. In 1967 RCA installed one of the first scanning systems at a Kroger store in Cincinnati. But the real problem was that without an open industry standard encoding scheme, each retailer would be stuck with one proprietary system and labels would have to be affixed by hand.

The NAFC issued Parts 1 and 2 of the Universal Grocery Products Identification Code (UGPIC) in 1970. The U.S. Supermarket Ad Hoc Committee on a Uniform Grocery Product Code was formed and in 1973 the committee defined the UPC system. The first scanners were used in Marsh's supermarket in Troy, Ohio. On June 26, 1974, the first product scanned was a 10-pack of Wrigley's Juicy Fruit chewing gum, which is on display at the Smithsonian Institution's National Museum of American History.

The term "symbologies" refers to the physical barcodes versus the data in the barcode. There are parity checks, shape

Doi: 10.1016/B978-0-12-374722-8.00028-1

and size requirements, and so forth. But as database people, we don't have to worry about the hardware.

28.1. GTIN FAMILY

The GTIN family includes:

- GTIN-12: 12-digit number used primarily in North America.

- GTIN-8: 8-digit number used predominately outside of North America.

- GTIN-13: 13-digit number which was used predominately outside of North America, but now is the Standard for North America.

- GTIN-14: 14-digit number used to identify trade items at various packaging levels. This was used more in wholesale rather than retail, but the shorter codes are put into this format by padding the strings with zeros.

GS1 (http://www.gs1.org/) is the organization that administers the GTIN codes for North America. The original UPC codes are running out, so the retail industry is shifting to EAN. The process is fairly straightforward. You apply to GS1 and get a company prefix, which can vary from 6 to 10 digits. The smaller the number of products a manufacturer needs to identify, the longer the prefix. The rest of the digits are for the products and done locally.

28.1.1. Prefixes for UPC

The first digit indicates a general category of business.

- 0, 1, 6, 7, 8, or 9: These are the most common digits.

- 2: This is an "open code" that is used for items that are made locally in the store or which are sold by weight or similar measurement. Think of meat, fruits, and vegetables, or other food items made in the store rather than being packaged by an external manufacturer. If the items are packaged in the store, the leftmost five digits are the item number, and the next five digits are either the weight or the price, with the first digit in the substring determining the meaning.

- 3: Drugs identified by National Drug Code number (NDC). The rest of the UPC is the NDC code used for pharmaceuticals in the United States. This includes both over-the-counter and prescription drug packages. NDC codes are an 11-digit number in three sections. The first section is assigned by the Food and Drug Administration (FDA) to identify the vendor or labeler of the drug. The manufacturer assigns the second and third sections of the code for a given product. The second section is the product code, which has the generic name, strength, and dosage form. The third section is the package size. Medicaid and Medicare display the code in an 11-digit format with leading zeros.

- 4: Reserved for local use like 2, but it is most often used for loyalty cards or store coupons. The 2 is things we sell and 4 is things we pay out.

- 5: Coupons: The manufacturer code is the usual encoding, but the next three digits after that is a family code set by manufacturer. This tells us to what product line(s) the coupon applies. The last two digits determine the amount of the discount. It is worth mentioning that coupon fraud and counterfeiting is a huge problem. If you can read the barcodes, you can determine if a coupon is actually generic for anything in that product family. Sometimes these generic coupons can work for anything in any product family.

By prefixing these codes with a 0, they become EAN-13 rather than UPC-A. This does not change the check digit.

28.2. ISBN

The International Standard Book Numbers (ISBN) has been brought into the GTIN system. The original ISBN used 10 digits with a MOD 10 check digit that is superior to the Luhn check digit in the new ISBN-13 system. The format consists of a "978" prefix and the new check digit with the old ISBN from positions 1 to 9 in positions 4 to 12.

Chapter 29

Digital Object Identifier (DOI)

The Digital Object Identifier is a way to identify content objects on the Internet. DOI codes are assigned to any entity for use on digital networks. They are used to provide current information, including where they (or information about them) can be found on the Internet. Information about a digital object may change over time, including where to find it, but its DOI name will not change.

The International DOI Foundation (http://www.doi.org/), an open membership consortium including both commercial and noncommercial partners, is trying to become an ISO Standard. As of this writing, approximately 40 million DOI names have been assigned by DOI System Registration Agencies in the United States, Australia, and Europe.

The ISO DOI effort is to use existing ISO Standard identifiers by embedding them into the DOI syntax. The ISBN-A is the first example.

29.1. DOI SYNTAX

DOI name syntax is an NISO standard; Z39.84-2005 DOIs are persistent, as defined in IETF RFC 1737. Functional Requirements for Uniform Resource Names (http://www.ietf.org/rfc/rfc1737.txt): "It is intended that the lifetime of a URN be permanent. That is, the URN will be globally unique forever, and may well be used as a reference to a resource well beyond the lifetime of the resource it identifies or of any naming authority involved in the assignment of its name."

Doi: 10.1016/B978-0-12-374722-8.00029-3

The DOI is composed of the prefix and the suffix. Within the prefix are the Directory Code <DIR> and the Registrant Code <REG >. The suffix is made up of the DOI Suffix String <DSS >:

```
<DIR>.<REG>/<DSS>
```

There is no limit on the length of a DOI string. The character set is ASCII alphanumerics and some punctuation marks. The Alphas are case insensitive, but are kept in uppercase for comparisons. The punctuation marks are: %, ', #, <space>, <, >, {, }, ^, [,], | and \.

The Directory Code is required and currently the only valid value is "10," but other values may be added later.

The Registrant's Code is required and is issued by the International DOI Foundation.

The DOI Suffix string is required and issued by the registrant. The only rules are that you are limited to a character set and that the suffix cannot start with "<character>/" since this is reserved for future use. Because there are so many options here, you have to know something about the rules each registrant uses.

The following are examples of Digital Object Identifiers:

- DOI (incorporating a SICI) from an article in the *Journal of the American Society for Information Science,* published by John Wiley & Sons: 10.1002/(SICI)1097-4571(199806)49:8 <693::AID-ASI4> 3.0.CO:2-0

- The SICI (Serial Item and Contribution Identifier) is an existing standard used by academic journals.

- DOI for an article from *JAMA, the Journal of the American Medical Association:* 10.1001/PUBS.JAMA (278)3,JOC7055-ABSY:

- DOI for the article "ABO Blood Group System" from *Encyclopedia of Immunology Online,* 2nd edition, published by Academic Press: 10.1006/rwei.1999.0001

- DOI Handbook: DOI 10.1000/182, http://www.doi.org/hb.html

29.2. ISBN-A

The ISBN (International Standard Book Number) is a 13-digit code for books. ISBNs were originally 10 digits and applied to just physical books. When were expanded to 13 digits they became part of the UPC/EAN barcode system and expanded to eBooks, software, mixed media, or pretty much anything sold in bookstores.

The ISBN-A ("the actionable ISBN") is an ISBN embedded into the DOI system that enables a book to be tracked in digital formats on networks. Publishers' internal systems and bibliographic agency databases still use the ISBN as the key identifier. An ISBN-A is not automatically created for every ISBN; it has to be registered with the appropriate DOI agency.

The ISBN-A begins with the Handle System DOI (http://www.handle.net/), a period, the ISBN "bookland" prefix, which is always "978" or "979," the two to eight digits that identify the publisher, a solidus prefix/suffix divider, and, finally, the digits that identify the book within publisher with the ISBN check digit.

30

Audiovisual Media

The International Standard Audiovisual Number (ISAN) is a standards identifier for audiovisual works, similar to the International Standard Book Number (ISBN) for books or the International Standard Serial Number (ISSN) for periodicals. The ISAN standard is covered by ISO standard 15706:2002 and ISO 15706-2.

I have a personal interest in this standard because I once consulted for the Belgian National Radio and Television Network (BRTN), which is the national broadcasting agency for Flemish speakers in Belgium. There was no standard for identifying a television or radio show. Sometimes the same show would be renamed and remarketed by another company; each distributor had their own encoding scheme. In short, this was much like the book industry before the ISBN.

The ISAN is recommended or required as the audiovisual identifier of choice for producers, studios, broadcasters, Internet media providers, and video games publishers who need to encode, track, and distribute video in a variety of formats. It is unique, international, and permanent for each work (and related versions) registered in the ISAN system.

ISAN covers the entire life cycle from conception, to production, distribution, and consumption.

ISANs can cover theatrical release prints, DVDs, publications, advertising, and marketing materials and packaging, as well as the original works.

Doi: 10.1016/B978-0-12-374722-8.00030-X

The ISAN identifier is now incorporated in many draft and final standards such as AACS (http://www.aacsla.com/home), DCI, MPEG (http://www.mpeg.org/), DVB (http://www.dvb.org/), and ATSC (http://www.atsc.org/), among others.

30.1. FORMAT

The ISAN is a 96-bit number that is represented in 24 hexadecimal digits. This makes it easy to put into barcodes. The code, like Gaul, is divided into three parts; root, episode, and version.

ISAN-IA (ISAN International Agency) is a nonprofit that was founded in 2003 by AGICOA (http://www.agicoa.org), CISAC (http://www.cisac.org), and FIAPF (http://www.fiapf.org) to run the ISAN standard. The headquarters is in Geneva. The central ISAN central repository is there. But they also can accredit national ISAN registration agencies.

A printed ISAN designed for human reading always begins with the ISAN label at the start, followed by hexadecimal digits separated into groups of digits, and ending with two check characters.

30.1.1. Root

The root is the basis work from which other things are derived. Subsequent film parts or television episodes that relate to the root work can have the same root but a different "episode or part" component.

30.1.2. Episode or Part

This identifies an episode or part within the root work. If a core work has no associated parts or episodes, then the episode segment is filled with zeros.

30.1.3. Version

A version is a modification of the episode or part. This can mean the work (root and their episodes or parts) that have been modified in some way. This includes dubbing or subtitling languages or different versions for international or DVD distribution.

30.2. CATALOGING AV MATERIALS

The ISAN has nothing to do with cataloging AV materials. This falls to other groups associated with libraries, just as the ISBN did with books.

The former standard was the Anglo-American Cataloging Rules version 2 (http://www.aacr2.org), but it has now been replaced by the RDA (Resource Description and Access). It is a very elaborate and detailed file format for describing the content of a work rather than just identifying it. RDA is being developed for library use, but other user communities will find it useful.

AACR2 was first published in 1978. It is a bit dated now and needs updating. The Anglo-American Cataloging groups formed the Joint Steering Committee for Development of RDA (JSC) in 2004. This consists of six major Anglo-American cataloguing communities: the American Library Association (ALA), the Australian Committee on Cataloguing (ACOC), the British Library (BL), the Canadian Committee on Cataloguing (CCC), the Chartered Institute of Library and Information Professionals (CILIP), and the Library of Congress (LC). You can get copies in online and offline products from http://www.aacr2.org/index.html.

ISIN and Related Securities Identifiers

An International Securities Identification Number (ISIN) uniquely identifies a security according to ISO 6166. ISINs are issued for bonds, commercial paper, equities, and warrants. The ISIN code is a 12-character alphanumerical string.

The ISIN identifies the security, not the exchange (if any) on which it trades; it is not a ticker symbol. Stock traded on several different stock exchanges worldwide (and therefore priced in different currencies) will have the same ISIN on each, although not the same ticker symbol. Stock markets are identified by another identifier, MIC (ISO 10383, "Codes for Exchanges and Market Identification"), a four-letter code.

An ISIN consists of three parts: generally, a two-letter country code, a nine-character alphanumeric national security identifier, and a single check digit. The country code is the ISO 3166-1 alpha-2 code for the country of issue, which is not necessarily the country in which the issuing company is domiciled. International securities cleared through Clearstream and Euroclear, which are European rather than national, use "XS" as the country code. In some cases, there will be three letters for the country code and the check digit is left off.

The nine-digit security identifier is the National Securities Identifying Number, or NSIN, assigned by governing bodies in each country, known as the National Numbering Agency (NNA).

The procedure for calculating ISIN check digits is a Luhn code. Letters are converted to numbers by their position starting with A = 10. Starting with the rightmost digit, every

Doi: 10.1016/B978-0-12-374722-8.00031-1

other digit is multiplied by two. (For CUSIP check digits, these two steps are reversed.) The resulting string of digits (numbers greater than 9 becoming two separate digits) are added up. Subtract this sum from the smallest number ending with zero that is greater than or equal to it: this gives the check digit, which is also known as the ten's complement of the sum modulo 10.

31.1. CUSIP

In North America the NNA is the CUSIP organization, meaning that CUSIPs can easily be converted into ISINs by adding the US or CA country code to the beginning of the existing CUSIP (Committee on Uniform Security Identification Procedures) code and a check digit at the end. The CUSIP is a nine-character alphanumeric string. It belongs to American Bankers Association and is operated by Standard & Poor's and serves the United States and Canada.

The first six characters are "base" or "CUSIP-6" and identify the issuer. Issuer codes are assigned alphabetically from a series that includes deliberate built-in "gaps" for future expansion. The last three characters of the issuer code can be letters.

Issuer numbers 990 to 999 and 99A to 99Z in each group of 1,000 numbers are reserved for internal use, like the open codes in the UPC system and others. Digits 7 and 8 identify the type of security (ISO 10962, the CFI [Classification of Financial Instruments] code is a more detailed code). In general, numbers are used for equities and letters are used for fixed income. The first security issued by any particular issuer is numbered "10." Newer issues are numbered by adding ten to the last used number up to 80, at which point the next issue is "88" and then goes down by tens. The issue number "01" is used to label all options on equities from that issuer. Fixed income issues are labeled using a similar fashion, but because there are so many of them they use letters instead of digits. The first issue is labeled "AA," the next "A2," then "2A" and onto "A3." The letters I and O are not used. The check is a Mod 10 Luhn code.

31.2. SEDOL AND OTHER COUNTRIES

In the United Kingdom and Ireland, the NNA is the London Stock Exchange and the NSIN is the SEDOL (Stock Exchange Daily Official List), seven characters in length: a six-character alphanumeric code and check digit.

Most other countries use similar conversions, but if no country NNA exists then regional NNAs are used instead. ISINs are slowly being introduced worldwide. At present, many countries have adopted ISINs as a secondary identifier for securities. A few countries are using ISINs as their primary identifier and the trend will continue. This is because historically most trades occur within national borders and are governed by local laws. But with globalization and freer movement of capital, this is not how it will be in the future.

31.3. CLASSIFICATION OF FINANCIAL INSTRUMENTS

ISO 10962 is the CFI (Classification of Financial Instruments) code. It is an alphabetical code consisting of six letters. The first letter is the category, the second is the group, and the remaining letters show special attributes of the group. The letter X always means Not Applicable/Undefined. For example: FFIXXX is Futures/Financial/Index without any other information.

Chapter

32

Temperature Scales

There are actually several different temperature scales that have been developed for specialized uses. The two most common in commercial use are Celsius and Fahrenheit, and Fahrenheit survives only because the United States has not switched over to Celsius. This table gives a comparison among eight of the scales, using the 0 and 100 degree points on the Celsius scale.

	Celsius	Fahrenheit	Kelvin	Rankine	Delisle	Newton	Réaumur	Rømer
Freeze point	0	32	273.15	491.67	150	0.0	0.0	7.50
Boiling point	100	212	373.15	671.67	0	33.0	80	60.00

Most scales increase as the temperature becomes hotter, but this is not always true, as you can see from the table.

Temperature scales do not add or have simple math since they are interval scales (see Chapter 4). You can get absurd results when you try. One of the famous examples was the Google Calculator result of 1 °C + 1 °C = 275.15 °C because it incorrectly converted to Kelvin.

Temperature depends on mass as well as energy. A chicken's body temperature is about 40 °C, so if you put three chickens in a pot of water, the water will not be 120 °C, and boil.

Doi: 10.1016/B978-0-12-374722-8.00032-3

32.1. CELSIUS SCALE

The Celsius scale (formerly known as "centigrade") is named after the Swedish astronomer Anders Celsius (1701–1744), who developed a similar temperature scale two years before his death. From 1744 until 1954, 0 °C was defined as the freezing point of water and 100 °C was defined as the boiling point of water, both at a pressure of one standard atmosphere.

This is still a good mental model for the scale, but technically the Celsius scale is now defined by two different points: absolute zero and the triple point of VSMOW (specially prepared water). The reason for this definition is to relate the Celsius scale to the Kelvin scale, which is the SI base unit of temperature (symbol: K). Absolute zero, the hypothetical but unattainable temperature at which matter exhibits zero entropy, is defined as being precisely 0 K and −273.15 °C. The temperature value of the triple point of water is defined as being precisely 273.16 K and 0.01 °C.

The term "centigrade" was also the Spanish- and French-language name for a unit of angular measurement (1/10000 of a right angle) and had a similar connotation in other languages, in 1948, the term "degree Celsius" (symbol: °C) in 1948. There is a single Unicode character for the degree Celsius at U+2103 (decimal 8451), which looks like the two character (°) and (C) without any spacing. When the value is displayed, there should be a space between the numeric value and the degree Celsius symbol. As a general rule, it is a good idea to store Celsius temperatures to two decimal places. This allows for precision in calculations, such as human body temperatures (36.1 to 37.8 °C).

When the United Kingdom went from Fahrenheit to Celsius, they used a simple rhyme in the public relations and teaching aids:

Zero is freezing, 10 is not.

20 is pleasant, 30 is hot.

This was also accompanied with a series of posters featuring an attractive model dressed in an artic parka at 0 °C, lighter clothes as you went up the poster and a bikini after 30 °C at the top.

32.2. FAHRENHEIT SCALE

Fahrenheit is named after the physicist Daniel Gabriel Fahrenheit (1686–1736), who proposed it in 1724. The freezing point of water is 32 °F and the boiling point is 212 °F at one standard atmosphere. The idea was to get them exactly 180 degrees apart to make it easier to mark thermometers.

The Fahrenheit Scale still exists simply because the United States is stubborn internally and will not convert to Celsius. Burma, Liberia, Belize, and Jamaica are the other holdouts, but that might have changed when you read this. The U.S. government keeps meteorological data and other official things in Celsius for compatibility with the rest of the world. But the weather reports, recipes, and other measurements are still given in Fahrenheit in daily use.

The Fahrenheit symbol has its own Unicode character (U+2109). But the use of this character is discouraged by the Unicode Consortium. The ordinary degree sign (U+00B0) followed by the Latin letter F ("°F") is the preferred way to display the symbol for degree Fahrenheit.

The conversion formulas between Fahrenheit (°F) and Celsius (°C) are:

°C = (5/9)*(°F−32)
°F = (9/5)*°C+32
−40 °F and −40 °C represent the same temperature.

32.3. KELVIN SCALE

The kelvin (symbol: K) is one of the seven SI base units. The Kelvin scale is a thermodynamic temperature scale where absolute zero, the theoretical absence of all thermal energy, is 0 K. The Kelvin scale was called "degrees Absolute" in the early days for this reason.

Notice that measurements are written without a degree symbol, the unit is "kelvin" in lowercase, but the symbol is an uppercase K. This is the convention for all of the basic SI units. Like all the other temperature scales, it is named after someone. In this case, that person is William Thomson, 1st Baron Kelvin (1824–1907), who first wrote of the need for an "absolute thermometric scale" when we had a better understanding of molecular movement and heat.

The kelvin is used in science and in engineering, because it expresses temperature intervals better than other scales which do not originate from Absolute Zero. Kelvin and Celsius are kept co-coordinated by ISO standards; That is, 1 K degree is also 1 °C. Conversion is a matter of addition.

Furthermore, we have the International Temperature Scale of 1990 (ITS-90), which defines an equipment calibration standard for making measurements on the Kelvin and Celsius temperature scales. This keeps everyone on the same page.

32.4. OTHER TEMPERATURE SCALES

There have been other temperature scales, but they are only of historical interest today. Some of them still have official symbols and definitions for conversion, but they are not actually used. This is not even a complete list, but it should give you a feel for the history.

32.4.1. Rankine Scale

Rankine is another thermodynamic temperature scale. It is named after the Scottish engineer and physicist William John Macquorn Rankine, who proposed it in 1859.

The symbol is R (or Ra if to distinguish it from the Rømer and Réaumur scales) without a degree symbol. The difference between the Kelvin scale and the Rankine scale is that a Rankine degree is defined as equal to one degree Fahrenheit, rather than one degree Celsius.

32.4.2. Delisle Scale

The Delisle scale (°D) was invented in 1732 by the French astronomer Joseph-Nicolas Delisle (1688–1768). Delisle reversed the usual order of things and the boiling point of water as his zero. In 1738 Josias Weitbrecht (1702–1747) recalibrated the

Delisle thermometer with 0 °D s the boiling point and 150 °D as the freezing point of water. The Delisle thermometer remained in use for almost 100 years in Russia, but was replaced with the Celsius scale.

32.4.3. Newton Scale

The Newton scale has nothing to do with the SI unit of force named after Isaac Newton. The Newton temperature scale was created by Isaac Newton to replace a descriptive temperature scale. By a descriptive scale, I mean one based on physical events like "hot as glowing coals in the kitchen fire" and other observations. Obviously, this is not too accurate! Newton built a thermometer with linseed oil and calibrated it starting at "melting snow" as zero and boiling water as 33 degrees. It is only of historical interest today, since we have Celsius.

32.4.4. Réaumur Scale

The Réaumur scale (°Ré, °Re, °R) sets the freezing and boiling points of water at 0 and 80 degrees respectively. The scale is named after René Antoine Ferchault de Réaumur, who first proposed it in 1730. This scale was popular in France, Germany, and Russia, but it was replaced by Celsius by the 1790s.

Its only modern use is in the measuring of milk temperature in cheese production. It is used in some Italian dairies making Parmigiano-Reggiano and Grana Padano cheeses and in Swiss Alp cheeses. See http://secondversion.blogspot.com/2007/07/hard-to-kill.html.

32.4.5. Rømer Scale

Rømer is named after the Danish astronomer Ole Christensen Rømer, who proposed it in 1701. The zero was set using freezing brine and the boiling point of water was defined as 60 degrees. It is no longer in use.

National Animal Identification System (NAIS)

The National Animal Identification System (NAIS) is a federally sponsored standard for tracking U.S. livestock, both domestic and imported. The U.S. Department of Agriculture (USDA) is currently implementing it thru the United States by means of federal grants, mandates, and state laws. It is not mandatory yet.

The purpose of NAIS is to track the movement of livestock from importation or production thru processing. The goal is to be able to identify all premises on which the livestock is located so all animals that have had contact with a "disease of concern" within 48 hours of discovery.

NAIS has three parts, but this book is more concerned with the encoding schemes involved. They are a good example of an emerging standard that is not yet in place.

33.1. PREMISES IDENTIFICATION NUMBER (PIN)

Premises Registration will assign a unique seven-character Premises Identification Number (PIN) to all the premises where the livestock is held within the state. The PIN is a seven-character alphanumeric code with an ISO-7064 MOD 37, 36 check digit. The PIN cannot contain the letters 'O' or 'I' to avoid confusion with the numerals zero and one.

There is a schema for the premises database that defines the data elements, which is keyed on the PIN. It includes the (longitude, latitude), phone numbers, contact names, and historical dates in ISO-8601 format (YYYY-MM-DD). I will not go into details here, but you can get a copy of "Program Standards and Technical Reference" as a PDF file from the USDA Web site. It includes a code for the type of premises.

Operation Type	
Code	Definition
B	Port of Entry
C	Clinic
E	Exhibition
L	Laboratory
M	Market/Collection Point
N	Nonproducer Participant
O	Boarding Facility
P	Production Unit
Q	Quarantine Facility
R	Rendering
S	Abattoir
T	Tagging Site

33.2. ANIMAL IDENTIFICATION NUMBER (AIN AND GIN)

There will be two levels of animal identification: individual animal and group or lot identification. Both levels use a unique 15-digit number on an implanted microchip or a radio frequency tag (RFID) or another physically readable device, like a metal ear tag. For some species, radiofrequency identification devices would be required.

Animal Identification Number (AIN)		
Position	Data Type	Comment
1–3	Numeric	ISO Country code
4–15	Numeric	Unique number >2,000,000

The AIN is concerned with the country of origin of the animals for tracking purposes.

Group or lot identification numbers (GIN) are used where groups of animals are managed together from birth to death as a group. In practice, only large confinement producers of poultry and swine would use these codes.

Group Identification Number		
Position	**Data Type**	**Comment**
1–7	Numeric	PIN
8–13	Numeric	Date in MMDDYY format
14–15	Numeric	Count of groups aggregated must be > zero

Several lots can be combined at market into one group for tracking purposes.

The ISO 11784 Standard stipulates that identification numbers can be "recycled" every 33 years. Since livestock such as cattle and pigs do not live that long (five to seven years would be long), duplicates should not be a serious problem.

The species codes is a three-letter abbreviation code based on a combination of common and biological names. They include the common livestock animals in the United States and not food animals from other cultures such as dogs, reptiles, insects, and so forth.

Species & Subgroup Codes		
Species	**Subgroup**	**Definition**
AQU	AQU	Aquaculture
	CLM	
	CRA	Clams
	CTF	
	MSL	Crayfish
	OYS	Catfish

(Continued)

Species & Subgroup Codes		
Species	**Subgroup**	**Definition**
	SAL	Mussels
	SBA	Oysters
	SHR	Salmon
	SLP	Striped Bass
	TIL	Shrimp
	TRO	Scallops
		Tilapia
		Trout
AVI	AVI	Avian
	CHI	Chickens
	DUC	Ducks
	GEE	Geese
	GUI	Guineas
	QUA	Quail
	RTT	Ratites (Emus, Ostriches, etc.)
	TUR	Turkeys
BOV	BOV	Bovine (Bison and Cattle)
	BIS	Bison
	BEF	Beef
	DAI	Dairy
CAM	CAM	Camelid (Alpacas, Llamas, etc.)
CAP	CAP	Caprine (Goats)
CER	CER	Cervids
	DEE	Deer
	ELK	Elk
EQU	EQU	Equine (Horses Mules, Donkeys, Burros)
OVI	OVI	Ovine (Sheep)
POR	POR	Porcine (Swine)

The animal gender and reproductive status codes are designed for livestock marketing rather than biology; compare these codes to the other sex codes in chapter 8. You do not buy a steer (castrated male cow) for breeding stock; capon (flesh of a castrated male chicken) sells at a higher price than regular chicken and so forth.

Animal Gender and Reproductive Status Codes	
Code	Description
M	Male
F	Female
C	Neutered/castrated male
S	Neutered/spayed female
X	Mixed (used only in groups)

33.3. ANIMAL TRACKING AND OTHER CONSIDERATIONS

Every time a tag is applied, a tag is lost or an animal needs to be retagged, an animal is killed, quarantined, missing, or dies, the event would have to be reported to the government database within 24 hours. There are also commingling events such as private and public livestock sales, regional shows, quarantine facilities, and exhibitions.

This database is going to be large, very expensive, and difficult to maintain. The first problem is the sheer size of the size of the livestock population. You can look at data from the USDA's National Agricultural Statistics Service (NASS), which conducts hundreds of surveys every year and prepares reports covering virtually every aspect of U.S. agriculture (http://www.nass.usda.gov/QuickStats). For example, as of 2008 June, there were 67,400,000 head of hogs and pigs. There are several producers that process over half million swine per year alone. Likewise, as of January 2009, there were 94,491,000 head of cattle.

Livestock has a life expectancy of two to perhaps five years, and each event has to be tracked. The exception is breeding stock which may be kept for 10 years or longer. The velocity of data updates is going to be huge. Such animal databases have already had problems in Australia.

This program can be very expensive. Costs for similar programs in other countries are estimated to range from $37 to $69 per head on average.

There are also technical problems with data collection. The type of microchip specifically recommended for horses and cattle, the ISO microchip, is designed to be reprogrammable, so anyone can easily change the numbers.

Most food-borne illnesses are from bacteria such as Salmonella, *E. coli,* and Campylobacter or Norwalk viruses after the livestock has been slaughtered. Japan tests every animal that enters their food chain, and England and the European Union also test significant numbers of cattle. In contrast, the USDA currently only tests about 1% of our cattle. Identifying the animals with electronic tags will not tell us if the animal is diseased or not.

The specific type of microchip recommended by the USDA and working groups, the ISO 11784/11785 chip, is designed to be programmed in the field before they are applied to the animals, and the same technology even allows them to be reprogrammed after they are in the animal. The Equine Species Working Group (ESWG) has recommended a specific type of microchip be used to identify horses. The ability to reprogram the chips was the basis for a television crime drama that involved a scam with a race horse.

Significantly, the ISO 11784/85 chip is not the type of microchip that has been generally used in horses, dogs, or cats in the United States for private purposes, and it emits on a different frequency, 134.2 kHz, rather than on the standard 125 KHz frequency.

ISO 11784 specifies the structure of the identification code. ISO 11785 specifies how a transponder is activated and how the stored information is transferred to a transceiver (the characteristics of the transmission protocols between transponder and transceiver). You can get an overview at http://www.rfidnews.com/iso_11784short.html.

34

ISO 216 Paper Sizes ("A," "B," and "C" Series)

ISO 216 paper sizes are used in most countries in the world except the United States. This is an old ISO standard that can trace its history back to German DIN standard 476 (DIN 476) in 1922 or even further back to the French. The best Web site for the history is http://www.cl.cam.ac.uk/~mgk25/iso-paper.html#history. The underlying ratio principle, like most mathematics, has been around for a while.

The size that most Americans have seen is the A4 (for example, A4 options on copiers and printers), because it is the most common commercial size. The underlying principle is that when rectangles with width/length ratio $(1/\sqrt{2})$ (approximately 0.707) are cut in half, the two new rectangles are still in that same ratio. This is also known as the "Silver ratio" to distinguish it from the "Golden ratio" (φ) which is a subject in itself.

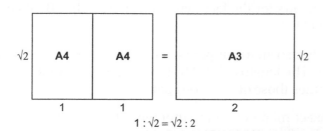

$$1 : \sqrt{2} = \sqrt{2} : 2$$

Doi: 10.1016/B978-0-12-374722-8.00034-7

Some of the formats were developed in 1798 during the French Revolution but were subsequently forgotten. The aspect ratio used by this standard has been known forever and it has competed with φ (phi), the golden ratio, for its mathematical properties.

Size A0 is defined so that it has an area of $\sim 1\,m^2$ (there are rounding rules). Successive paper sizes in the series (A1, A2, A3, etc.) are defined by halving the preceding paper size, cutting parallel to its shorter side (so that the long side of size "A"(n+1) is the same length as the short side of size An, again prior to rounding).

The A4 size ($210 \times 297\,mm$) is 6 mm narrower and 18 mm longer than the "Letter" paper size, $8\frac{1}{2} \times 11$ inches ($216 \times 279\,mm$), commonly used in the United States. That longer length is a problem for "Letter" size FAX transmissions. But the U.S. "Legal" ($8\frac{1}{2} \times 14\,in$) and the "Monarch" ($7 \times 10\,in$) paper size will work.

34.1. "B" SERIES

The "B" series formats are geometric means between the "A" series format with a particular number and the "A" series format with one lower number. For example, B1 is the geometric mean between A1 and A0. In the English-speaking print trade, the B series is for "bleed" printing. Bleed means that the color printing needs to go over the edge of the page so it can be trimmed to size in final product. The extra space allows for the fact that you will trim the "B" sheet to a smaller "A."

There is also an incompatible Japanese "B" series defined by the JIS. The lengths of JIS "B" series paper are approximately 1.22 times those of "A" series paper.

The exact millimeter measurement of the long side of Bn is given by (floor $(1000/(2^{\wedge}((n-1)/2)) + 0.2))$.

The RA and SRA series also specify the sizes of untrimmed paper used by printers.

34.2. "C" SERIES

The "C" series formats are used mainly for envelopes. An A4 page will fit into a C4 envelope and so forth. The "C" series envelopes follow the same ratio as the "A" series pages. For example, if an A4 page is folded in half so that it is A5 in size, it will fit into a C5 envelope (which will be the same size as a C4 envelope folded in half).

"A," "B," and "C" paper fit together as part of a geometric progression, with ratio of successive side lengths of $21/8$, though there is no size halfway between An and Bn+1: B4, C4, A4, D4, B5, and so on. There is a D series in the Swedish extensions to the system.

34.3. TOLERANCES

The tolerances specified in the standard are:

- ± 1.5 mm for dimensions up to 150 mm
- ± 2.0 mm for lengths in the range 150 to 600 mm
- ± 3.0 mm for any dimension above 600 mm

34.4. NON-ISO PAPER SIZES

Before ISO 216, there were a great many national or industry specific paper sizes that were a nightmare to use. The results were that the printing industry was constantly trimming paper to fit and throwing away literally tons of scrap. For example, IBM's internal print shop in the United Kingdom saved ~25% on paper costs when the country converted to ISO 216 as part of their metrification program.

The United States, Canada, and a few other countries are the non-ISO hold-outs, as usual. But Canada uses a P series of sizes, which are the U.S. paper sizes rounded to metric dimensions.

The U.S. and U.K. traditional paper sizes are a complete mess, so I will not spend a lot of time on them. Instead, I recommend that you download a copy of the book *Notes on the Standardization of Paper Sizes* by Arthur D. Dunn (http://www.cl.cam.ac.uk/~mgk25/volatile/dunn-papersizes.pdf).

Chapter

35

Compass Points

The compass was invented in China sometime before 200 BCE. The traditional universal agreement was that we have four cardinal directions (north, south, east, and west). After that, there were a lot of different ways to slice up the ordinal (i.e., noncardinal) directions.

But things are tricky. True north (i.e., the location of the Earth's North Pole) does not match the magnetic north (i.e., where a magnetic compass points). In fact, the magnetic force lines are not regular or stable. They vary over time. This is why Renaissance buildings in Europe that were set in position by a magnetic compass are oriented a few degrees off a true north-south alignment.

Today, we have all settled on a system that uses 360° in a clockwise direction with true north at 0°/360°. Decimal degrees are preferred over the degree-minute-second system in most navigation systems today. We also use global positioning system (GPS) satellites rather than magnetic compasses for serious work.

35.1. TRADITIONAL COMPASS POINTS

Before 1920, compasses were marked with a variable-length abbreviation code based on the English names of the cardinal points. This gave 32 angular divisions around the circle.

Doi: 10.1016/B978-0-12-374722-8.00035-9

For example, the northeast quadrant contains, in clockwise order, these directions:

Symbol	Name	Degrees
N	North	00.00°
NbE	North by east	11.25°
NNE	North-northeast	22.50°
NEbN	Northeast by north	33.75°
NE	Northeast	45.00°
NEbE	Northeast by east	56.25°
ENE	East-northeast	67.50°
EbN	East by north	78.75°
E	East	90.00°

The use of the "b" for "by" is a bit confusing. Alfred Hitchcock used the direction "north by northwest," even though it technically does not exist in this system. The extra "by" between the first and second cardinal direction letters was common slang among sailors, so NNW becomes north by northwest.

It would be more logical to continue the abbreviating pattern and use "NNNE" for "north by east," "NENN" for "northeast by north," and so forth. But it is hard to say strings of four letters fast, so the tradition serves a purpose.

35.2. OTHER COMPASS POINT SYSTEMS

Mathematicians like to use radians for trigonometry. A radian takes the radius of a circle and lays it along the circumference of a circle so that 0.5π radians = 90°, 1π radians = 180°, 2π radians = 360°, and so forth, with the ordinal directions expressed in term of π times a rational number. This is not very useful for navigation since π is irrational and the radius is hard to mark off on a circle.

Dividing a circle into multiples of four and six equal parts is both very simple and a precise geometric construction, so most compass systems use one or both of them, along with halving an angle.

The Chinese use a compass called a luopan, which has a 24-part division, for feng shui. Each division on a luopan approximates a terrestrial day. The device is marked with several different rings with various purposes. There are trigrams for Heaven, Fire, Thunder, Water, Mountain, Earth and other natural phenomena. An alignment thread is called the Dragon's Vein. Other rings contain "Kua Numbers" from a numerology system, the 9 stars, and 64 hexagrams each with its own name.

In the 19th century, some European nations adopted the "grad" (also called "grade" or "gon") system. In keeping with the metric system, a right angle has 100 grads, so a circle has 400 grads. You then divide grads into tenths to get a circle of 4000 decigrades. The bad news is that this used to sound too much like "centigrade" for temperature; it was one of the reasons for the change to Celsius and Kelvin for temperatures.

The military adopted the French "millieme" system. This has the compass dial divided into 6400 units (Sweden used 6300) or "mils" for additional precision when measuring angles. The value to the military is that one mil subtends approximately one meter at a distance of one kilometer. This is useful for dropping artillery shells on people.

Imperial Russia used a system derived from dividing the circumference of a circle into chords of the same length as the radius. This is the classic way you are taught to construct a hexagon in geometry. Each of these arcs was divided into 100 spaces, giving a circle of 600 units. Later, the Soviet Union divided these into tenths to get a circle of 6000 units, usually translated as "mils," something like the French millieme system.

The Qibla compass determines the direction of the Qiblah (Ka'bah) in Mecca. This Qibla compass is used by Muslims to determine the precise direction of Mecca for prayer. It is divided into 400 marks, like the grad system. You need to know what division your location is in (available on line or in annual books), find magnetic north, and then adjust the indicator for Mecca. Or you can buy a GPS system that never needs adjustment, from any company that stocks Muslim religious equipment.

36

Unicode

Unicode is a system intended to allow computer display of all the written languages on Earth. This is a very ambitious goal, but the Unicode Consortium (http://www.unicode.org) has been surprisingly successful. The work on this project began in 1987 as an extension of 8-bit ASCII to allow representation of the most common European languages that use Latin, Greek, and Cyrillic alphabets.

This quickly evolved into "Unicode 88" (http://www.unicode.org/history/unicode88.pdf), which uses a 16-bit encoding for European and Asian languages. When the first byte is all zeros, this matches to ASCII characters.

We are now on the Unicode 5.1 standard, which is available in print and on Web sites. The standard defines the abstract idea of a character, the encoding in binary or hexadecimal, and the display of the character. To make this a bit clearer, there is the abstraction of the Latin letter "X," the hexadecimal code for it, and thousands of type fonts and placements (subscript, superscript, underlined, circled, etc.) to display it in text.

The possible hexadecimal codes define a codespace of 1,114,112 code points in the range of 0000 to 10FFFF in hexadecimal. Theses are divided into "planes"—blocks of numbers that group related characters together. There are 17 planes, each comprising 65,536 code points or 256 rows of 256 code points. The standard notation for a character is to write "U+" followed by its hexadecimal number. For code points in the Basic Multilingual Plane (BMP), four digits are used (e.g., U+0058 for the character LATIN CAPITAL

LETTER X); for code points outside the BMP, five or six digits are used. The BMP is essentially Latin, Greek, and Cyrillic alphabets.

36.1. TYPES OF WRITTEN LANGUAGES

Writing systems that use a sequence of characters can be classified as an alphabet, alphasyllabary (abugida), syllabary, or logograms (hieroglyphics). In an alphabet, each character has a phonetic value and a sequence of symbols form a word. Consonant and vowels have separate characters—think of Latin. In an alphasyllabary, each symbol is built from a base symbol, usually a consonant, with vowel sound symbols added to it—think of Ethiopian (http://www.omniglot.com/writing/ethiopic.htm). About half of the writing systems in the world have an alphasyllabary. A syllabary uses symbols that represent syllables and consonant-vowel combinations with single symbols—think of Japanese. Logograms are unique symbols for concepts rather than phonetics—think of Chinese.

Latin, Greek, Cyrillic, and Arabic are the system with casing. Latin, Greek, and Cyrillic letters have an upper (majuscule) and a lower (minuscule) form. Arabic is a cursive, connected script whose letters have an initial form at the start of a word, a terminal form at the end of a word, an intermediate form in the middle, and a "standalone" form.

36.2. PRACTICAL AND POLITICAL PROBLEMS

If only written languages were easy! For just a little taste of what goes on, look at http://www.ibm.com/developerworks/library/u-secret.html.

Unicode assumes that a letter is a letter without regard to how it is displayed. But in mathematics there can be semantic differences among letters in different fonts. This is why we have TeX and LaTex (http://www.tug.org/twg/mfg/) for computer typesetting of mathematical text.

Collations really apply to only to alphabets. An alphasyllabary or syllabary is usually taught as an array with vowels on one dimension and consonants on the other. Ordering logograms is very difficult. Chinese dictionary systems are based on the number of strokes in the character and the concept of base radials. A radical is a character within another character that would have meaning by itself—for example, "bright" is made of the characters for "sun" and "moon" placed together.

But even within the same alphabet, there can be differences. In alphabets with casing, do the lowercase letters come after all the uppercase letters? Or do lowercase letters come after their corresponding uppercase version? Swedish puts accented letters after "Z," while Esperanto puts them immediately after the corresponding unaccented letter. German dictionary ordering was different in Germany, Austria, and IBM.

Languages that have no political power are often the easiest to get into Unicode. Academics who want to computerize research in dead languages do not get much opposition. This is why we have Egyptian hieroglyphs, Tolkein's invented alphabets in *Lord of the Rings,* and Klingon in *Star Trek.*

Politics among living languages can be interesting. One of the major conflicts is the Han Unification, which tries to coordinate Chinese, Japanese, Korean, and other uses of Han Dynasty Chinese characters in Asian languages. They drifted over the centuries so the same glyph is a little different in form and meaning.

The People's Republic of China simplified a lot of characters a few decades ago, but these are not universally accepted. For example, if you get a Chinese chess set (Xiangchi), the horse (pronounced "MA" and roughly equivalent to a knight in Western Chess) will have the traditional character but the instructions will use the simplified character.

36.3. NORMALIZATION

The predicate "<string> IS [NOT] NORMALIZED" in SQL-99 determines if a Unicode string is in one of four normal forms (D, C, KD, and KC). The use of the words "normal form" here are not the same as in a relational context. In the Unicode model, a single character can be built from more several other characters.

Accent marks can be put on basic Latin letters. When the order of the additional marks does not matter, the standard specifies a canonical ordering. Text searching would be prohibitive without this.

Certain combinations of characters can be displayed as single symbol. One example would be ligatures ("ae" becomes "æ"). But there are special symbols that can be constructed from parts. The Angstrom (non-SI unit of length equal to 0.1 nanometer, used to measure atoms) sign, Å, is also the "a-ring" letter in Swedish. The construction is used rather than having separate Unicode points for each one. But this is a matter of opinion and usage, as well as what the Unicode standard says.

Some languages, such as Hangul (Korean) and Vietnamese, build glyphs from concatenating symbols in two dimensions. Some languages have special forms of one letter that are determined by context, such as the terminal sigma in Greek or accented "ú" in Czech. In short, writing is more complex than putting one letter after another.

The Unicode standard defines the order of such constructions in their normal forms. You can still produce the same results with different orderings and sometimes with different combinations of symbols. But it is very handy when you are searching such text to know that it is normalized rather than trying to parse each glyph on the fly.

Normal Form	Description
Form D (NFD)	Canonical Decomposition
Form C (NFC)	Canonical Decomposition, followed by Canonical Composition
Form KD (NFKD)	Compatibility Decomposition
Form KC (NFKC)	Compatibility Decomposition, followed by Canonical Composition

37

Driver's Licenses

We have mentioned ISO, but there is also IEC, the International Electrotechnical Commission. The IEC is the organization that prepares and publishes International Standards for all electrical, electronic and related technologies (http://www.iec.ch), usually in coordination with ISO and national standards groups.

ISO/IEC 18013 standard defines the physical and data content of an ISO-compliant driving license (IDL). It includes the human-readable (visual) features and the placement of ISO machine-readable technologies on the card. It is a common basis for international use without restricting individual domestic or regional driver licensing authorities from incorporating their specific needs on the IDL. The idea is that ID-1 sized IDL will allow one card for both a domestic driving permit and an international driving permit (IDP). Countries that want to keep a domestic driving license (DDL) can issue a second card (with or without ISO machine-readable technologies). The IDL is supposed to replace the IDP paper document only. The IDL standard defines:

- minimum common mandatory data element set
- common layout for ease of recognition
- minimum set of security requirements

ISO/IEC 18013 allows domestic or regional driver licensing authorities to add more data elements and incorporate standard machine-readable technologies. They can also add physical document security elements over and above the mandatory ones.

Doi: 10.1016/B978-0-12-374722-8.00037-2

Those extra technologies include, but are not limited to, a magnetic stripe, integrated circuit with contacts, contactless integrated circuit, optical memory, ISO/IEC JTC1/SC31 one-dimensional or two-dimensional bar codes, biometrics, cryptography, and data compression. In short, just meet the minimal standards and then do whatever you want domestically.

37.1. ID-1 CARDS

As an aside, the ID-1 format is part of a series of card sizes defined by the ISO/IEC 7810 standard. This is the size of an ATM card, 85.60 mm by 53.98 mm. It is also a common size driver's licenses in the United States, Canada, Australia, New Zealand, Norway, and European Union countries. The U.S. passport card and many of the state driver's licenses also uses the ID-1 format.

Why is it so popular? It is so popular *because* it is the size of an ATM card. This means that we already have equipment for reading and handling it, that it will fit into wallets, and so forth.

The ID-2 format specifies a size of 105 mm by 74 mm, which is the A7 size in the ISO paper series. It was used for the German Personalausweis (identity document); this will change to ID-1 format cards in November 2010 to bring them up to the ISO 18013 rules.

ID-3 is 125 mm by 88 mm or the B7 ISO paper size. This format is used worldwide for passports and visas.

ID-000 specifies a size of 25 mm by 15 mm. This format is used for SIM cards in cell phones.

37.2. U.S. DRIVER'S LICENSES

In the United States, a driver's license is the most common form of personal identification for commercial and legal purposes. The DMV (Department of Motor Vehicles) in each state issues driver's licenses or a state ID for nondrivers independently of any national standards. Numbering, check digits, physical formats, and everything else could be different.

In the wake of 9/11, Congress passed the REAL ID Act of 2005 supposedly to prevent terrorism, reduce fraud, and improve the reliability and accuracy of identification documents that state governments issue.

The REAL ID Act mandates that each state issues driver's licenses or state ID cards only to people who can prove either U.S. citizenship or legal alien status by showing proper identification. These identification documents include a certified birth certificate, Social Security card, or passport. Furthermore, each state must digitize the verified ID documents and keep them on file for 7 to 10 years, along with digital photos of the document holders. Each state must keep an individual's personal information in a database that other motor vehicle departments across the country can access.

In addition, all American drivers would need to have a REAL ID–compliant license by December 1, 2014, or December 1, 2017, depending on the age of the driver. Those without the new document would need to show a passport or other federally approved identification to travel by airplane or enter a federal building.

Many states already have the required driver information on file to meet the proposed REAL ID regulations. Those states that do not keep this information will have to spend money to come up to spec. The only previous national automobile databases were at the National Criminal Information Center (NCIC) for stolen vehicles and vehicle recall information at the Federal Trade Commission (FTC).

Proponents see the act as a means to better verify identification, a method to improve communication between state agencies, and a move toward smart cards that can allow the government to deliver better services over the Internet.

37.3. ENHANCED DRIVER'S LICENSE (EDL)

The Canadian and U.S. governments developed the Enhanced Driver's License (EDL) as part of the Western Hemisphere Travel Initiative (WHTI). The United States and Canada have the longest common border on Earth and citizens of both countries have traveled freely across it for centuries. This is a major change in procedures. The EDL, passport, or other proof of identity and citizenship will be required for entry into the United States at land or water border crossings. A valid passport is still required to enter the United States by air.

According to the Department of Homeland Security, the government is aligning the REAL ID and EDL requirements. The main difference, though, is that obtaining a REAL ID requires proof of legal status in the United States (resident aliens, student visas, and so forth), whereas obtaining an EDL requires the applicant to be a U.S. citizen.

Furthermore, although the REAL ID will not necessarily include a radio-frequency identification (RFID) tag, the EDL will. This is because the EDL aims to expedite border crossing and identity verification by border patrols at a port of entry. If you have driven on toll roads in the United States, you have seen RFID tags that are read as vehicles pass under a reader at exit and entry points.

Several Trusted Traveler Programs are run by U.S. Customs and Border Protection (CBP). NEXUS is the system used between the United States and Canada, SENTRI is the same program between the United States and Mexico, and the FAST Driver program allows travel between the United States, Canada, and Mexico.

All of the cards are WHTI-compliant documents that provide expedited travel via land, air, or sea to approved members across the borders. The system uses RFID tags at border crossing and possible iris scanning (it is faster and more accurate than to do fingerprinting or other biometries) when a customs declaration is made.

The REAL ID Act actually took effect on May 11, 2008, but everyone got an extension until December 31, 2009. However, as long as a state verifies that it meets certain security and licensing standards by that point, another extension will automatically be granted that lasts until April 11, 2011. In the meantime, you can continue to use your driver's license or state ID card as official documents for entering a federal facility or boarding a plane.

Currency Units and Near Money

National currency systems have a base unit which may or may not be divided into subunits. Today, these subunits are usually in the ratio 1 base unit = 100 subunits or = 1000 subunits.

The only nondecimal currencies are Mauritania (1 ouguiya = 5 khoums) and Madagascar (1 ariary = 5 iraimbilanja). In both cases, the base unit has so little value that the subunit is not used, even in coins. As of June 12, 2009, the exchange rate was 1 U.S. dollar (USD) = 259.220 Mauritanian Ouguiya (MRO) and 1,895.90 Malagasy Ariary (MGA).

We like decimalized currencies because we use a decimal number system and accounting is much easier than handling fractions in a computer. But decimal currency is actually a "recent" invention. The Russian ruble was the first decimalized currency, when Peter the Great established the ratio 1 ruble = 100 kopecks in 1701.

The reason that decimalization took so long was that, for most of human history, trade was done with actual coins and not computerized math or even paper money. It is physically easier to split coins into piles that are multiples of two and three units. In the case of coins made of valuable metals, the coins were often cut into pieces—hence the term "pieces of eight" that you have heard in pirate movies all these years. You can cut a circle in eighths much easier than cutting them into tenths.

38.1. STOCK EXCHANGES AND NONDECIMAL UNITS

The last place that you might have seen a nondecimal unit is on the stock exchanges. U.S. stock exchanges used eighths or sixteenths of dollars until converting to decimals between 2000 and 2001.

The conversion triggered a reaction in 2003 from Wall Street firms. They were having steep drops in profits from stock trading. A good deal of the loss was supposed to be a result of the change of stocks trading in dollars and cents instead of fractions. And supposedly investors benefited from the switch to decimal currency units.

The Web site http://www.TheStreet.com joined other news organizations in switching entirely to decimal pricing in references to individual stocks in stories in 2000. But they explained the conversion problems in a short article:

> Our prices will be rounded to two decimal places. For example, in our old style we would say Philip Morris (MO Quote) lately was down 5/16 to 31 3/4. In our new style, we'd say it was down 31 cents to $31.75.

> Rounding may occasionally make the way we refer to a stock's price look a little counterintuitive. Here's a description borrowed from our colleagues at The New York Times: If a stock closes at $12.125 one day—and is thus listed as $12.13—and it rises $1.125 the next, the increase will be shown as $1.13, but the price will be $13.25, not $13.26.

38.2. DECIMALIZATION IN THE UNITED KINGDOM

The last significant holdout was the British pound sterling before decimalization in 1971. Until 1971, the pound sterling was divided into pence (1 shilling = 12 pence), shillings (1 pound = 20 shillings), and farthings (1 penny = 4 farthings). The farthing was dropped in 1960. A pound could be subdivided in 19 different ways into integral numbers of pence (for example, 1/4, 1/5, 1/6, 1/8, and 1/10 of a pound were respectively 60, 48, 40, 30, and 24 pence exactly) and in 8 additional ways into integral numbers of farthings (for example, 1/64 pound was 3 pence 3 farthings, written 3¾d).

This was particularly funny to computer people because this was when IBM was pushing PL/I, starting in the mid- and late 1960s. This was the first programming language that had pound sterling routines and data types built into it. This was not unexpected, since it was developed at IBM's Hursley Laboratories in the United Kingdom, as part of the development of System/360.

In those days, figuring out the complex U.K. currency system was a major programming effort. Many of the industries in the United Kingdom paid workers with a PHYSICAL pay envelope. This was a heavy paper sealed envelope with a printed form on the back that was filled out manually and had banknotes and coins inside. You had to order the right number of coins from the bank to fill the pay envelopes properly.

38.3. PHYSICAL CURRENCY CHOICES

"Of other worlds I dream and people not like me."

—Bob Mauris

Bob is both a *really good* artist and a wise man. This was the caption of a print he did of a little Centaur girl in thick woods watching a human knight riding toward a castle. Every database person ought to get out of the office and challenge their assumptions of every day life by traveling to a foreign country. Currency is a good place to start.

Remember that the name of a coin is not the value of the coin. A U.S. dime is a coin, which has the value of 10 cents.

Should paper money be different colors, so can easily tell them apart? But will this increase the cost of printing the currency?

U.S. currency is hard to differentiate in the dark and it is a serious problem for foreigners.

Should paper money be different sizes, so can easily tell them apart? But then you have storage problems in cash registers, and mechanical currency handling equipment.

Should paper money have Braille on it? Some countries already have Braille on their currency. But the raised dots are expensive to print and the dots can be compressed when the bills are packed into "bricks" for shipping. Using holes can weaken the bill and also increase printing costs.

This assumes that the bills are the same size, which is most likely these days. The traditional method has been that the blind fold various denominations of bills differently (http://www.afb.org/)

The rules are:

- Leave $1 bills unfolded
- Fold $5 bills lengthwise
- Fold $10 bills widthwise
- Fold $20 bills lengthwise and then by width. Or fold them just lengthwise and put them in a separate section in a wallet.

Alternately, you can have a sighted friend Braille your currency with a simple tool (http://www.lssproducts.com/product/6518/braille-writing).

Should the weight of coins be linked to their value? It is very handy if you can throw a bag of coins on a scale and convert its weight to its currency value. But then you have to use one metal for coinage; if you use multiple metals, then the value of one metal can exceed the currency value. This happened in the United States when silver prices increased and made it profitable to melt dimes for silver. Later, copper pennies became more valuable as metal than as coins.

The notches on the edge of coins were originally done to prevent people from filing or shaving the coins for the metal content. The hole in the center of some coins was originally for threading them on a string. Not all coins have been round—in fact, ancient China had coins in the shape of a knife blade! Nobody counterfeits coins today because it is not worth the effort, so these safety features are not so important.

However, we have vending machines that use coins. The U.S. government has done public service advertisements for each of the various attempts at making a $1 coin popular. For various reasons, these coins have not been, and most cash registers are not made with a coin tray that can handle the various sized coins that have been attempted over the years (http://en.wikipedia.org/wiki/Dollar_coin_%28United_States%29)

In what denominations should coins and bills be minted? There is a movement in the United States to stop making the copper pennies with a website at http://www.retirethe penny.org.

38.4. COUPONS

Coupons are third largest form of payment in the U.S. retail trade (cash and credit cards are the other two). As of 2008, over $350 billion of packaged goods coupons were offered yearly, as compared to $250 billion dollars in coupons in 2003. But the redemption rate varies with the economy. Consumers saved about $2.6 billion in 2008, for example. The recession of 2009 is probably the reason for reversal of the 15-year downward trend in coupon redemption.

About 90% of all coupons are distributed via Sunday newspaper inserts and usually have a lifetime of three months.

Retailers do not always submit the coupons for redemption directly to the manufacturers. Instead, they use a redemption service that aggregates the coupons, and then pays the retailers face value of each coupon, less the amount (if any) of charge-backs from the manufacturers. The charge-backs are usually expired, damaged, or counterfeit coupons.

The manufacturers pay a handling fee on each valid coupon to the redemption service; currently, this fee is about $0.08 per coupon. The rejected coupons are returned to the retailer so that they can try to get a manufacturer's sale representative to accept or exchange them.

Most of the physical processing for the United States is actually done in Mexico. Coupons are where banking was decades ago. There is still a lot of manual handling and industry standards are weak. Counterfeiting is a serious problem and has been used by terrorist groups as well as criminals.

It is not small money. On April 8, 2009, the U.S. Attorney's office in Milwaukee, the FBI, and the U.S. Postal Inspector's investigations led to guilty pleas by former International Outsourcing Services, LLC (IOS) plant managers Ovidio Enriquez and David J. Howard for their roles in an organized crime ring that, according to the government, defrauded coupon-issuing manufacturers of more than $250 million.

This coupon clearing house was laundering coupons through large retail accounts, including CVS, HEB Stores, Food Lion, Hannaford Brothers, Winn-Dixie, and Kash n' Karry Stores, without the knowledge of the retailers.

38.4.1. Types of Coupons

Coupons come in many forms, but their physical media has to contain a product code and an identifier for the offer at the manufacturer's side. A coupon is usually for one particular product, as printed on the document. This does not mean anything because all that counts is the bar codes. Manufacturer coupon bar codes can be for anything in a family of product or even for the manufacturer's entire product line.

1. Standard Manufacturer Coupons

   These are traditional newspaper coupons. While also printed in direct-mailers, magazines, and inserts, nearly 90% are distributed in Sunday newspapers.

2. Catalina Coupons

   These targeted coupons are usually printed at check-out, and contain offers or discounts on products related to the items the customer has just purchased. Originally, they were preprinted on the cash register receipt, but today they are created dynamically by the retailer's Point of Sale (POS) computer system.

   There are also POS systems that will scan coupons, physically shred the paper form, and electronically transmit the data for reimbursement. This gives the manufacturer a great of data that would be impossible to get from aggregating paper days or weeks later.

3. Special Coupons

   These coupons have complex offers, such as "buy one, get one free" or are deemed hard to handle because they are made of a sticky material, cardboard, plastic, are irregularly shaped, or are in poor condition.

   These coupons require a clerk to verify that the terms of the offer were met or to enter the data manually.

4. In-Ad Coupons

> Sponsored by the retailer or wholesaler, in-ad coupons usually appear in circulars or internal ads. They feature offers only redeemable within the sponsoring store, whose manufacturers typically absorb some of the cost. Although many often bear the words "Manufacturer Coupon," they are not the same as standard manufacturer coupons.

Coupons have been using UPC codes in the United States. Obviously, it would be nice if all the coupons had the same bar codes on them and that they agreed with the new EAN standards for retail.

Beginning in 2008 January, the bar codes on US manufacturer's coupons will begin a three step conversion from the old system, to a mixture of both old and new and finally to just the new system. The two dimensional bar codes will hold five times the data of the old UPC system.

Under the new system, GS1 will issue company prefix codes that are variable length with company codes as long as six digits.

An interim phase began in January 2008 that put both the UPC A and the GS1 DataBar on a coupon so that old equipment could still read it. The combined format had to be in place by the end of June 2008.

Beginning in 2010, all coupons are expected to use only the GS1 DataBar format. You can get a good overview in a downloadable document at http://www.gs1.org/docs/bar codes/databar/GS1_DataBar_Business_Case_Complete .pdf-2009-05-06

38.4.2. Trade Groups and References

The major trade groups are:

> Coupon Information Corporation, CIC (http://www.cents-off.com)

> Grocery Manufacturers Association, GMA (http://www.gmabrands.com)

> Food Marketing Institute FMI (http://www.fmi.org)

Association of Coupon Professionals, ACP (http://www.couponpros.org)

Although published in 1998 and dated now, "Coupons—A Complete Guide (Joint Industry Coupon Committee Coupon Guidelines)" is still a good place to learn how the U.S. grocery coupon industry works. It covers the old UCC/EAN-128 coupon extended code and the in-store and in-ad EAN-99 code. It also covers Internet coupons, coupon fraud electronic clearing.

Chapter 39

Recipes and Food Preparation

Home cooking in the United States is still done with traditional volumetric units. *The Boston Cooking-School Cook Book,* written by Fannie Farmer in 1896, was the first cookbook to use very specific and accurate measurements. Before that, cooks were given an ingredient list and a narrative description of the recipe. You were told to measure things by comparing them to common things: "a pat of butter the size of a walnut," "moose pie is made like caribou pie, but with less meat," and so forth.

Fannie Farmer's Cookbook, as it was later re-titled, was also one of the first cookbooks aimed at a housewife cooking for a smaller family. Many early cookbooks assumed that you were cooking for a family of 10 or for a church gathering.

39.1. WEIGHT VERSUS VOLUME

In European cooking, dry recipe ingredients tend to be measured by weight in grams rather than volume. A kitchen scale is common in European homes but not in the United States. Wet ingredients are measured in liters. Oven temperatures are given in Celsius instead of Fahrenheit, of course.

Weight is more accurate than volume. Thus, commercial food preparation is also done by weight in the United States today but with Imperial units.

But weight and volume do not have a simple relationship. Consider this short conversion list for one cup of dry ingredients to grams for a bakery:

All-Purpose Flour = 110 grams
Cake Flour = 95 grams

Confectioners' Sugar = 110 grams
Brown Sugar = 200 grams
Granulated Sugar = 225 grams
Butter or Margarine 225 grams
Cocoa = 125 grams
Flaked Coconut = 75 grams
Grated Coconut = 100 grams
Ground Almonds = 170 grams
Slivered Almonds = 80 grams

These conversions have to be done with a database that has both weights and volumes. These commercial databases will often have nutritional information so that content labels can be created without doing actual laboratory analysis.

39.2. SCALING A RECIPE

Institutional kitchens and commercial food producers often have to scale the number of servings of a basic recipe either up or down. SI units obviously make the math easier than the fractions and irregular units found in Imperial measurements.

But there is another problem. Some ingredients do not scale in a linear fashion. Simple examples are food coloring and strong flavoring agents; a few drops will do the job. Trying to scale it down to a single serving would require laboratory equipment, so strong ingredients are usually mixed into another bulkier ingredient, and that second ingredient is used as a carrier.

Scaling a recipe from one serving to 100 servings will not require that you cook the food 100 times longer. But extra or less mass can change the cooking and cooling times in a nonlinear fashion.

40

Portable Document Format (PDF)

The Portable Document Format (PDF) was invented by Adobe Systems Incorporated (http://www.adobe.com) in 1993 and it is the most widely used file format for general electronic documents. In fact, there is a good chance that if you bought an electronic copy of this book, it is in PDF.

The two advantages that PDF has over other electronic document formats are free viewing software for Windows, Mac, Linux, and other operating systems, and the ability to capture any print image in an electronic version as a PDF file.

PDF became a de facto standard because it was so widely used and because Adobe Systems did not put any restrictions on other organizations regarding developing software that use PDF files. All they did was retain ownership of the "PDF Reference Manual" that defined the standard.

Adobe Systems asked the Association for Information and Image Management (AIIM), also known as the enterprise content management (ECM) association, to work together with the American National Standards Institute (ANSI) to submit PDF to ISO, to make it from a de facto to a de jure international standard. This is similar to what IBM with SQL-86 when Phil Shaw submitted an IBM SQL manual as an ANSI document.

40.1. ISO 32000

In January 2008, the project was approved by ISO and the completed specification was published a few months' later

Doi: 10.1016/B978-0-12-374722-8.00040-3

as ISO 32000-1:2008, Document management—Portable document format—Part 1: PDF 1.7.

Although Adobe Systems has never tried to restrict the use of PDF, there are always nagging issues with proprietary standards. Will the owner make changes without warning? Will changes be drastic and affect existing code? Will the owner go out of business and leave us stuck?

As an example of such problems in the database world, Microsoft changed the semantics but not the syntax of their proprietary BIT between releases of SQL Server. It was originally a binary bit data type that could take on only the values {0, 1}; it then became a numeric data type that could take on the *numeric values* {0, 1} and was NULL-able. All data types in SQL are NULL-able. Older SQL Server programmers had never bothered with checking BIT data for NULLs. Their code assumed that if a BIT column was not equal to 1 then it was 0 and vice versa.

ISO standardization guarantees stability and openness in a way that proprietary standards, no mater how universal, cannot.

Adobe Systems is now just one company that builds PDF products based upon the ISO standard. Once published by ISO, the standard is stable for a fixed number of years. Small editorial mistakes may be corrected, but ISO 32000-1 as a whole cannot be changed without proper procedures for revisions and new editions of ISO standards.

Open contributions from the member countries are solicited. Draft standards are created and circulated for review (probably in PDF). The voting and decision process is transparent. If you are interested, you can contact relevant ISO technical committee—ISO/TC 171, Document management applications, subcommittee SC 2, Application issues—and take part in the project. But the document is over 750 pages long and fairly complex, so this is not a weekend hobby.

The ISO 32000-1 standard has references to 79 standards that are used in defining PDF, including standards such as JPEG, JPEG2000 and JBIG2 image formats, ICC Profile formats,

ASN.1 Abstract Syntax Notation, OpenType font format, XML, and Unicode.

40.2. THINGS THAT PAPER CANNOT DO

There are also ISO standards for constrained PDF subsets for special applications. These include:

- PDF/A for document archiving (ISO 19005-1:2005)
- PDF/X for professional publishing (ISO 15930 series)
- PDF/E for engineering documents (ISO 24517-1:2008)

Strangely, all of these standards actually predate ISO 32000-1. The Adobe Systems PDF was considered stable enough to use as a basis even before it was made official.

The original goal of PDF was to store an exact replica of documents as they would have printed on paper. But once a document is in an electronic format, you can search it, transmit it, and transform it in ways that paper cannot be handled. Think about the paper equivalent of hyperlinks—there really isn't one. It is not practical to run around an entire library, looking for references when you can click a mouse instead. Annotations can be made electronically for personal use or for shared for collaboration. The old method was lots of Post-it notes.

Video and sound can be embedded or hyperlinked to documents. Digital signatures and digital rights management fit in with forms management systems. Language translation is greatly helped by a digital format, but this is not perfect by any means.

Chapter 41

Temporal Data

Clifford Simak wrote a science fiction novel entitled *Time is the Simplest Thing* in 1977. He was wrong. And the problems did not start with the Y2K problems that we had in 2000, either. The calendar is irregular and the only standard unit of time is the second; years, months, weeks, hours, minutes, and so forth are not part of the metric system but are mentioned in the ISO standards as conventions.

SQL-92 added temporal data to the language, acknowledging what was already in most SQL products by that time. The problem is that each vendor made a trade-off internally and the syntax was proprietary. DB2 follows the ANSI/ISO syntax, SQL Server is just catching up in their 2008 version, and Oracle is still proprietary.

41.1. NOTES ON CALENDAR STANDARDS

Leap years did not exist in the Roman or Egyptian solar calendars before the year 708 AUC ("ab urbe condita," Latin for "from the founding of the City [Rome]").

Unfortunately, the solar year is not an even number of days; there are 365.2422 days in a year and the fraction adds up over time. The civil and religious solar calendars drifted with respect to the solar year by approximately 1 day every 4 years. For example, the Egyptian calendar drifted completely around approximately every 1,461 years. As a result, it was useless for agriculture, so the Egyptians relied on the stars to predict the flooding of the Nile. Sosigenes of Alexandria knew that the calendar had drifted completely around more than twice since it was first introduced.

Note: the abbreviations A.D. (Anno Domini-Latin for "in the year of Our Lord") and B.C. ("Before Christ") have been replaced by CE for "Common Era" and BCE for "Before Common Era" in ISO standards to avoid religious references.

41.1.1. The Julian and Gregorian Calendars

To realign the calendar with the seasons, Julius Caesar decreed that the year 708 (that is the year 46 BCE to us) would have 445 days. Caesar, on the advice of Sosigenes, also introduced leap years (known as bissextile years) at this time. Many Romans simply referred to 708 AUC as the "year of confusion" and thus began the Julian calendar, which was the standard for the world from that point forward.

The Julian calendar had a leap year day every 4 years and was reasonably accurate in the short or medium range, but it drifted by approximately 3 days every 400 years. This was a result of the 0.0022 fraction of a day adding up.

It was 10 days out of step with the seasons by 1582. (A calendar without a leap year would have drifted completely around slightly more than once between 708 AUC and 2335 AUC—that is, 1582 CE to us. The summer solstice, so important to planting crops, had no relationship to June 21. Scientists finally convinced Pope Gregory to realign the calendar by dropping almost 2 weeks from the month of October in 1582 CE. The years 800 CE and 1200 CE were leap years everywhere in the Christian world. But whether 1600 CE was a leap year depended on where you lived. European countries did not move to the new calendar at the same time or follow the same pattern of adoption.

The calendar corrections had economic and social ramifications. In Great Britain and its colonies, September 2, 1752, was followed by September 14, 1752. The calendar reform bill of 1751 was entitled "An Act for Regulating the Commencement of the Year and For Correcting the Calendar Now in Use." The bill included provisions to adjust the amount of money owed or collected from rents, leases, mortgages, and similar legal arrangements, so that rents and so forth were prorated by the number of actual elapsed days in the time period affected by the calendar change. Nobody had to pay the full monthly rate for the short month of September in 1752 and nobody had to pay the full yearly rate for the short year.

The serious, widespread, and persistent rioting was not caused by the commercial problems that resulted but by the common belief that each person's days were "numbered" and that everyone was preordained to be born and die at a divinely ordained time that no human agency could alter in any way.

Thus the removal of 11 days from the month of September shortened the lives of everyone on Earth by 11 days. And there was also the matter of the missing 83 days because of the change of the New Year's Day from March 25 to January 1, which was believed to have a similar effect.

If you think that this behavior is insane, consider the number of people today who get upset about the yearly 1-hour clock adjustments for Daylight Saving Time.

To complicate matters, the beginning of the year also varied from country to country. Great Britain preferred to begin the year on March 25, while other countries began at Easter, December 25, or perhaps March 1 and January 1—all important details for historians to keep in mind.

In Great Britain and its colonies, the calendar year 1750 began on March 25 and ended on March 25—that is, the day after March 24, 1750, was March 25, 1751. The leap year day was added to the end of the last full month in the year, which was then February. The extra leap year day comes at the end of February, since this part of the calendar structure was not changed.

In Latin, "septem" means seventh, from which we derived September. Likewise, "octem" means eighth, "novem" means ninth, and "decem" means tenth. Thus, September should be the seventh month, October should be the eighth, November should be the ninth, and December should be the tenth.

So, how come September is the ninth month? September was the seventh month until 1752 when the New Year was changed from March 25 to January 1.

41.1.2. Computerizing Calendars

Until fairly recently, nobody agreed on the proper display format for dates. Every nation seems to have its own commercial conventions. Most of us know that Americans put the month before the day and the British do the reverse, but do you know any other national conventions? National date formats may be confusing when used in an international environment. The date "12/16/95" in Boston was "16/12/95" in London, "16.12.95" in Berlin, and "95-12-16" in Stockholm. Then there are conventions within industries within each country that complicate matters further.

Faced with all of the possibilities, software vendors came up with various general ways of formatting dates for display. The usual ones are some mixtures of a two- or four-digit year, a three-letter or two-digit month, and a two-digit day within the month. Slashes, dashes, or spaces can separate the three fields.

At one time, the North Atlantic Treaty Organization (NATO) tried to use Roman numerals for the month to avoid language problems among treaty members. The U.S. Army did a study and found that the four-digit year, three-letter month, and two-digit day format was the least likely to be missorted, misread, or miswritten by English speakers. That is also the reason for "24-hour" or "military" time.

Today, you want to set up a program to convert your data to conform to ISO 8601 "Data Elements and Interchange Formats—Information Interchange—Representation of Dates and Times" as a corporate standard and EDIFACT for EDI messages. This is the "yyyy-mm-dd" format that is part of standard SQL and will become part of other standard programming languages as they add temporal data types.

The full ISO 8601 timestamp can be either a local time or UTC/ GMT time. UTC is the code for "Universal Coordinated Time," which replaced the older GMT, which meant "Greenwich

Mean Time." Because of the use of the letter "Z" to separate time from date in ISO 8601, it is also called "Zulu Time," after the radio and military naming system.

In 1970 the Coordinated Universal Time system was devised by an international advisory group of technical experts within the International Telecommunication Union (ITU). The ITU felt it was best to designate a single abbreviation for use in all languages in order to minimize confusion. The two alternative original abbreviation proposals for the "Universal Coordinated Time" were CUT (English: Coordinated Universal Time) and TUC (French: temps universel Coordinne). UTC was selected both as a compromise between the French and English proposals and because the "C" at the end looks more like an index in UT0, UT1, UT2, and a mathematical-style notation is always the most international approach.

Technically, Universal Coordinated Time is not quite the same thing as Greenwich Mean Time. GMT is a 24-hour astronomical time system based on the local time at Greenwich, England. GMT can be considered equivalent to Universal Coordinated Time when fractions of a second are not important. However, by international agreement, the term UTC is recommended for all general time keeping applications and use of the term GMT is discouraged. We will talk about leap seconds shortly.

Another problem in the United States is that in addition to having four time zones, we also have "lawful time" to worry about. This is the technical term for time required by law for commerce. Usually, this means whether or not you use Daylight Saving Time.

EDI and replicated databases must use UTC time to compare timestamps. A date without a time zone is ambiguous in a distributed system. A transaction created 1995-12-17 in London may be younger than a transaction created 1995-12-16 in Boston.

41.1.3. Leap Seconds

A leap second was added to 2008, just after midnight of New Year's Day. Originally this was done to keep astronomical time, based on the rotation of the Earth, in sync with atomic time. The Earth is actually slowing down because of the tug of the Sun and Moon, making the days slightly longer. However, atomic time, which is based on the oscillations of an atom, remains constant. These corrections have been made by the International Earth Rotation and Reference Systems Service since 1972.

Today, mobile phones, GPS systems, and computer operating systems synchronize their internal clocks against atomic clocks such as the signal provided by NIST. As of 2009, the international timekeepers have recommended abolishing the leap second and replacing it with a leap hour every ~600 years. Leap seconds would exist up to 2018, with a "leap hour" being added around the year 2600.

To hear the current time each minute in UTC, you can tune to radio stations WWV (Fort Collins, CO) and WWVH (Kauai, HI) on 2500, 5000, 10000, and 15000 kHz. If you live in the central or eastern United States or parts of Canada, you can tune to station CHU (Ottawa, Ontario) on 3330, 7850, and 14670 kHz. In the United States, you can also go to http://www.time.gov/ on the Internet.

The only opposition is from a few British Luddites, because it would mean that Greenwich Mean Time (GMT) would lose its status as the zone where local time is the same as the universal time.

41.1.4. Calendar Tables

The Common Era calendar is so irregular that the best way to work with it in a database is to create a calendar table with all your temporal data in it. The key is, obviously, the calendar date. You can pack 50 to 100 years into a relative small table that will be "read only" unless something exceptional happens. Do not try to calculate holidays in SQL—Easter alone requires too much math.

Here is a skeleton table:

```
CREATE TABLE Calendar
 (cal_date DATE NOT NULL PRIMARY KEY,
  fiscal_year INTEGER NOT NULL,
```

```
fiscal_month INTEGER NOT NULL,
week_in_year INTEGER NOT NULL, -- use ISO standard
holiday_type INTEGER NOT NULL
        CHECK(holiday_type IN ( ..), --
day_in_year INTEGER NOT NULL,
julian_business_day INTEGER NOT NULL,
 ...);
```

Derek Dongray came up with a classification of the public holidays and weekends he needed to work with in multiple countries. He had nine types of holiday:

1. Fixed date every year

2. Days relative to Easter

3. Fixed date but will slide to next Monday if on a weekend

4. Fixed date but slides to Monday if Saturday or Tuesday if Sunday (U.K. Boxing Day is the only one).

5. Specific day of week after a given date (usually first/last Monday in a month but can be other days, e.g., First Thursday after November 22 = U.S. Thanksgiving)

6. Days relative to Greek Orthodox Easter (not always the same as Western Easter)

7. Fixed date in Hijri (Muslim) Calendar—this turns out to only be approximate because of the way that the calendar works. An Imam has to see a full moon to begin the cycle and declare it

8. Days relative to previous winter solstice (Chinese holiday of Qing Ming Jie)

9. Civil holidays set by decree, such as a National Day of Mourning

As you can see, some of these are getting a bit esoteric and a bit fuzzy. A calendar table for U.S. secular holidays can be built from the data at this Web site, so you will get the three-day weekends:

http://www.smart.net/~mmontes/ushols.html

Time zones with fractional hour displacements:

http://www.timeanddate.com/worldclock/city.
   html?n=5
http://www.timeanddate.com/worldclock/city.
   html?n=54
http://www.timeanddate.com/worldclock/city.
   html?n=176
http://www.timeanddate.com/worldclock/city.
   html?n=246

But the strange ones are:

http://www.timeanddate.com/worldclock/city.
   html?n=5
http://www.timeanddate.com/worldclock/city.
   html?n=63

The Julian business day column is a good trick. Number the days from whenever your calendar starts and repeat a number for a weekend or company holiday.

```
CREATE TABLE Calendar
(cal_date DATE NOT NUL PRIMARY KEY,
 julian_business_nbr INTEGER NOT NULL,
 ...);
```

Let's assume that you take Good Friday thru Easter Sunday as a holiday.

```
INSERT INTO Calendar
VALUES ('2007-04-05', 42),
       ('2007-04-06', 43), -- Good Friday
       ('2007-04-07', 43),
       ('2007-04-08', 43), -- Easter Sunday
       ('2007-04-09', 44),
       ('2007-04-10', 45); -- Tuesday
```

To compute the business days between Thursday of this week and next Tuesday:

```
SELECT (C2.julian_business_nbr-C1.julian_business_
  nbr) AS bus_day_cnt
```

```
    FROM Calendar AS C1, Calendar AS C2
  WHERE C1.cal_date = '2007-04-05',
    AND C2.cal_date = '2007-04-10';
```

Notice that the answer is three business days; if I did not want to include Thursday, I would need to subtract one in the computation. Likewise, if I want to find the first business day (n) days from a given date, I add (n) or (n + 1) to the julian_business_nbr depending on my businesses rules. Weekends can be found with:

```
  SELECT MIN(cal_date), MAX(cal_date)
    FROM Calendar
  GROUP BY julian_business_nbr
HAVING COUNT(*) > 1;
```

41.2. SQL TEMPORAL DATA TYPES

Standard SQL has a very complete description of its temporal data types. There are rules for converting from numeric and character strings into these data types and there is a schema information table for global time zone information that is used to make sure that temporal data types are synchronized. As an international standard, Standard SQL has to handle time for the whole world and most of us work with only local time. If you have ever tried to figure out the time in a foreign city to place a telephone call, you have some idea of what is involved.

The common terms and conventions related to time are also confusing. We talk about "an hour" and use the term to mean a particular point within the cycle of a day ("The train arrives at 13:00 Hrs") or to mean an interval of time not connected to another unit of measurement ("The train takes three hours to get there"); the number of days in a month is not uniform; the number of days in a year is not uniform; weeks are not related to months; and so on.

All SQL implementations have a DATE data type; most have a separate TIME and a TIMESTAMP data type. These values are drawn from the system clock and are therefore local to the host machine. They are based on what is now called the Common Era calendar, which many people would still call the Gregorian or Christian calendar.

Standard SQL has a set of date and time (DATE, TIME, and TIMESTAMP) and INTERVALs (DAY, HOUR, MINUTE, and SECOND with decimal fraction) data types. Both of these groups are temporal data types, but datetimes represent points in the time line, while the interval data types are durations of time. Standard SQL also has a full set of operators for these data types.

41.2.1. Tips for Handling Dates, Timestamps, and Times

The syntax and power of date, timestamp, and time features vary so much from product to product that it is impossible to give anything but general advice. This chapter will assume that you have simple date arithmetic in your SQL, but you might find that some library functions would let you do a better job than what you see here. Please continue to check your manuals until the Standard SQL standards are implemented.

As a general statement, there are two ways of representing temporal data internally. The "Unix representation" is based on keeping a single long integer or a word of 64 or more bits that counts the computer clock ticks from a base starting date and time. The other representation I will call the "COBOL method," since it uses separate fields for the year, month, day, hours, minutes, and seconds.

The Unix method is very good for calculations, but the engine must convert from the external ISO-8601 format and the internal format and vice versa. The COBOL format is the opposite; good for display purposes, but weaker on calculations.

41.2.2. Date Format Standards

The ISO ordinal date formats are described in ISO-2711-1973. Their format is a four-digit year, followed by a three-digit day within the year (001-366). The year can be truncated to the year within the century. Standard SQL uses this all-numeric "yyyy-mm-dd" format to conform to ISO 8601, which had to avoid language-dependent abbreviations. It is fairly easy to write code to handle either format. The ordinal format is better for date arithmetic; the calendar format is better for display purposes.

Many programs still use a year-in-century date format of some kind. This was supposed to save space in the old days when that sort of thing mattered (i.e., when punch cards had only 80 columns). Programmers assumed that they would not need to tell the difference between the years 1900 and 2000 because they were too far apart. They were wrong and this caused the "Y2K" panic in that year.

Old COBOL programs that did date arithmetic on these formats returned erroneous negative results. If COBOL had a DATE data type, instead of making the programmers write their own routines, this would not have happened. Relational database users and 4GL programmers can gloat over this, since they have DATE data types built into their products.

41.2.3. Handling Timestamps

TIMESTAMP(n) is defined as a timestamp to (n) decimal places (e.g., TIMESTAMP(9) is nanosecond precision), where the precision is hardware-dependent. The FIPS-127 SQL Conformance test suite requires at least five decimal places after the second.

TIMESTAMPs usually serve two purposes. They can be used as a true timestamp to mark an event connected to the row in which they appear. Or they can be used as a sequential number for building a unique key that is not temporal in nature. Some DB2 programs use the microseconds component of a timestamp and invert the numbers to create "random" number for keys; of course, this method of generation does not preclude duplicates being generated, but it is a quick and dirty way to create a somewhat random number. It helps to use such a method when using the timestamp itself would generate data "hot spots" in the table space. For example, the date and time when a payment is made on an account are important and a true timestamp is required for legal reasons. The account number just has to be different from all other account numbers, so we need a unique number and TIMESTAMP is a quick way of getting one.

Remember that a TIMESTAMP will read the system clock once and use that same time on all the items involved in a transaction. It does not matter if the actual time it took to complete the transaction was days; a transaction in SQL is done as a whole unit or is not done at all. This is not usually a problem for small transactions, but it can be in large batched ones where very complex updates have to be done.

TIMESTAMP as a source of unique identifiers is fine in most single-user systems, since all transactions are serialized and of short enough duration that the clock will change between transactions-peripherals are slower than CPUs. But in a client/server system, two transactions can occur at the same time on different local workstations. Using the local client machine clock can create duplicates and adds the problem of coordinating all the clients. The coordination problem has two parts:

> How do you get the clocks to start at the same time? I do not mean just the technical problem of synchronizing multiple machines to the microsecond but also the one or two clients who forgot about Daylight Saving Time.

> How do you make sure the clocks stay the same? Using the server clock to send a timestamp back to the client increases network traffic yet does not always solve the problem.

Many operating systems, such as those made by Digital Equipment Corporation, represent the system time as a very long integer based on a count of machine cycles since a starting date. One trick is to pull off the least significant digits of this number and use them as a key. But this will not work as transaction volume increases. Adding more decimal places to the timestamp is not a solution either. The real problem lies in statistics.

Open a telephone book (white pages) at random. Mark the last two digits of any 13 consecutive numbers, which will give you a sample of numbers between 00 and 99. What are the odds that you will have a pair of identical numbers? It is not 1 in 100, as you might first think. Start with one number and add a second number to the set; the odds that the second number does not match the first are 99/100. Add a third number to the set; the odds that it matches neither the first nor the second number are 98/100. Continue this line of reasoning and compute (0.99 * 0.98 * ... * 0.88) = 0.4427 as the odds of not finding a pair. Therefore, the odds that you will find a pair are 0.5572, a bit better than even. By the time you get to 20 numbers, the odds of a match are about 87%; at 30 numbers, the odds exceed a 99% probability of one match. You might want to carry out this model for finding a pair in three-digit numbers and see when you pass the 50% mark.

A good key generator needs to eliminate (or at least minimize) identical keys and give a statistical distribution that is fairly uniform to avoid excessive index reorganization problems. Most key-generator algorithms are designed to use the system clock on particular hardware or a particular operating system and depend on features with a "near key" field, such as employee name, to create a unique identifier.

The mathematics of such algorithms is much like that of a hashing algorithm. Hashing algorithms also try to obtain a uniform distribution of unique values. The difference is that a hashing algorithm must ensure that a hash result is both unique (after collision resolution) and repeatable, so that it can find the stored data. A key generator needs only to ensure that the resulting key is unique in the database, which is why it can use the system clock and a hashing algorithm cannot.

You can often use a random-number generator in the host language to create pseudo-random numbers to insert into the database for these purposes. Most pseudo-random number generators will start with an initial value, called a seed, then use it to create a sequence of numbers. Each call will return the next value in the sequence to the calling program. The sequence will have some of the statistical properties of a real random sequence, but the same seed will produce the same sequence each time, which is why the numbers are called pseudo-random numbers. This also means that if the sequence ever repeats a number, it will begin to cycle. (This is not usually a problem, since the size of the cycle can be hundreds of thousands or even millions of numbers.)

41.2.4. Handling Times

Most databases live and work in one time zone. If you have a database that covers more than one time zone, you might consider storing time in UTC and adding a numeric column to hold the local time zone offset. The time zones start at UTC, which has an offset of zero. This is how the system-level time zone table in Standard SQL is defined. There are also ISO standard three-letter codes for the time zones of the world, such as EST for Eastern Standard Time, in the United States. The offset is usually a positive or negative number of hours, but there were some odd zones that differed by 15 minutes from the expected pattern, which were removed in 1998. On 2007 December 09, President Hugo Chavez of Venezuela decided to create his own unique time zone, putting the clock back half an hour on a permanent basis. This was unnecessary and done simply to put his country in a different time zone from the United States. Similar political crap has been done before, but it usually involves changing Daylight Saving Time (DST) at odd times in a year.

Now you have to factor in DST on top of that to get what is call "lawful time," which it is the basis for legal agreements. The U.S. government uses DST on federal lands inside of states that do not use DST. If the hardware clock in the computer in which the database resides is the source of the time-stamps, you can get a mix of gaps and duplicate times over a year. This is why Standard SQL uses UTC internally.

You should use a "24-hour" time format, which is less prone to errors than 12-hour (AM/PM) time, since it is less likely to be misread or miswritten. This format can be manually sorted more easily and is less prone to computational errors. Americans use a colon as a field separator between hours, minutes, and seconds; some Europeans use a period. This is not a problem for them, since they also use a comma for a decimal point.

One of the major problems with time is that there are three kinds: fixed events ("He arrives at 13:00 Hrs"), durations ("The trip takes three hours"), and intervals ("The train leaves at 10:00 Hrs and arrives at 13:00 Hrs") —which are all interrelated. Standard SQL introduces an INTERVAL data type. An INTERVAL is a unit of duration of time rather than a fixed point in time—days, hours, minutes, or seconds.

There are two classes of intervals. One class, called year-month intervals, has an express or implied precision that includes no fields other than YEAR and MONTH, although it is not necessary to use both. The other class, called day-time intervals, has an express or implied interval precision that can include any fields other than YEAR or MONTH—that is, DAY, HOUR, MINUTE, and SECOND (with decimal places).

41.3. EXPRESSIONS WITH DATE ARITHMETIC

Almost every SQL implementation has a DATE data type, but the functions available for them vary quite a bit. The most common ones are a constructor that builds a date from integers or strings; extractors to pull out the month, day, or year; and some display options to format output.

You can assume that your SQL implementation has simple date arithmetic functions, although with different syntax from product to product, such as:

```
A date plus or minus a number of days yields a new date.
A date minus a second date yields an interval of days.
```

Here is a table of the valid combinations of <datetime> and <interval> data types in the Standard SQL standard:

```
<datetime> - <datetime> = <interval>
<datetime> + <interval> = <datetime>
<interval> (* or/) <numeric> = <interval>
<interval> + <datetime> = <datetime>
<interval> + <interval> = <interval>
<numeric> * <interval> = <interval>
```

There are other rules, which deal with time zones and the relative precision of the two operands, which are intuitively obvious.

There should also be a function that returns the current date from the system clock. This function has a different name with each vendor: TODAY, SYSDATE, and getdate() are dialect for the correct CURRENT_DATE or CURRENT_TIME_STAMP. There may also be a function to return the day of the week from a date, which is sometimes called DOW() or

WEEKDAY(). Standard SQL provides for CURRENT_DATE, CURRENT_TIME [(<time precision>)] and CURRENT_TIMESTAMP [(<timestamp precision>)] functions, which are self-explanatory.

41.4. THE NATURE OF TEMPORAL DATA MODELS

Temporal data is pervasive. It has been estimated that 1 of every 50 lines of database application code involves a date or time value. Data warehouses are by definition time-varying: Ralph Kimball states that every data warehouse has a time dimension. Often the time-oriented nature of the data is what lends it value.

Integers, decimal numbers, strings, Boolean values, and most other data that we put into a computer are discrete. Time and real numbers are is a continuum. In a continuum, a value is not always known exactly. Consider the number pi (π); you can *approximate* it with a real number (3.141592653…) or a rational number (22/7), but you cannot express it *exactly*.

When we give a date, say "2009-12-31," it is really a duration that starts at exactly "2009-12-31 00:00:00" but it ends just before "2010-01-01 00:00:00." This is called a half-open interval in mathematics.

We are stuck with expressing the end of that day to whatever precision we have in my machine—say "2009-12-31 23:59:59.999999999" if we have nanoseconds in the hardware. Technically, we cannot use "2009-12-31 24:00:00" since that time does not exist in the ISO standards and in many SQL products it would "round" to "2010-01-01 00:00:00" anyway.

MySQL uses a proprietary notation for periods of years and year-months, so they can be expressed in a single column. They fill in the day or year field with "00" so that "2009-01-00" is the entire month of January 2009 and likewise "2009-00-00" is the entire year of 2009. Most other SQL products have to use {start_time, end_time} pairs that declare the end_time to be NULL-able so that an ongoing state of affairs can be modeled. You use the expression COALESCE (end_ time, CURRENT_TIMESTAMP) in VIEWS or queries for the current situation, or COALESCE (end_time, <<dead line timestamp>>) when there is a required ending time.

When you do math the floating point numbers, the other data type that models a continuum, you have better tools. The IEEE standard has the concept of floating point rounding errors; we know that values are not exact but the machine can try to keep errors to a minimum—not get rid of them but minimalize them.

Floating numbers are subject to mathematical operations that make no sense with dates. What is the square root of Christmas? What is February divided by pi? But equality is an operation that makes sense for all data types. Floating point numbers recognize the concept of epsilon (ε). We will treat two floating numbers as equal when they differ by some small number, ε.

Unfortunately, if you want to do this in most SQL products, you have to write the code yourself and use the CAST() or EXTRACT() function to round the temporal data to the same precision.

41.5. REFERENCES ON TEMPORAL DATA AND SQL

Richard T. Snodgrass is a professor at the University of Arizona (http://www.cs.arizona.edu/people/rts/) whose whole career is based on temporal databases. You can download a copy of his Morgan-Kaufmann book in PDF and get the SQL code at the university Web site.

Tom Johnston also wrote a series of articles on temporal SQL at http://www.dmreview.com, which will appear in a book in the near future.

42

Additive Congruential Generators

In many applications, we do not want to issue the numbers in sequence. This pattern can give information that we do not wish to expose. Instead, we want to issue generated values in random order. Do not get mixed up; we want known values that are supplied in random order and not random numbers. Most random-number generators can repeat values, which would defeat the purpose of this drill.

While I usually avoid mentioning physical implementations, one of the advantages of random-order keys is to improve the performance of tree indexes. Tree structured indexes, such as a B-Tree, that have sequential insertions become unbalanced and have to be reorganized frequently. However, if the same set of keys is presented in a random order, the tree tends to stay balanced and you get much better performance.

The generator shown here is an implementation of the additive congruential method of generating values in pseudo-random order and is due to Roy Hann of Rational Commerce Limited, a CA-Ingres consulting firm. It is based on a shift-register and an XOR-gate, and it has its origins in cryptography. While there are other ways to do this, this code is nice because:

1. The algorithm can be written in C or another low-level language as bit manipulations for speed. But math is fairly simple even in base 10.

2. The algorithm tends to generate successive values that are (usually) "far apart," which is handy for improving the performance of tree indexes. You will tend to put data on separate physical data pages in storage.

Doi: 10.1016/B978-0-12-374722-8.00042-6

3. The algorithm does not cycle until it has generated every possible value, so we don't have to worry about duplicates. Just count how many calls have been made to the generator.

4. The algorithm produces uniformly distributed values, which is a nice mathematical property to have. It also does not include 0.

Let's walk through all the iterations of the four-bit generator illustrated in figure 42-1:

```
iteration 1:  0001 (1)
iteration 2:  1000 (8)
iteration 3:  0100 (4)
iteration 4:  0010 (2)
iteration 5:  1001 (9)
iteration 6:  1100 (12)
iteration 7:  0110 (6)
iteration 8:  1011 (11)
iteration 9:  0101  (5)
iteration 10: 1010 (10)
iteration 11: 1101 (13)
iteration 12: 1110 (14)
iteration 13: 1111 (15)
iteration 14: 0111 (7)
iteration 15: 0011 (3)
iteration 16: 0001 (1) wrap-around!
```

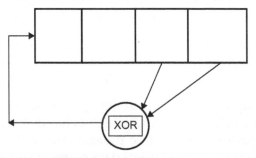

■ **FIGURE 42-1:** Initially the shift register contains the value 0001. The two rightmost bits are XOR-ed together, giving 1, and the result is fed into the leftmost bit position and the previous register contents shift one bit right. The iterations of the register are shown in this table, with their base 10 values.

It might not be obvious that successive values are far apart when we are looking at a tiny four-bit register. But it is clear that the values are generated in no obvious order, all possible values except 0 are eventually produced, and the termination condition is clear—the generator cycles back to 1 or whatever the starting value was.

Generalizing the algorithm to arbitrary binary word sizes, and therefore longer number sequences, is not as easy as you might think. Finding the "tap" positions where bits are extracted for feedback varies according to the word size in an extremely nonobvious way. Choosing incorrect tap positions results in an incomplete and usually very short cycle that is unusable. If you want the details and tap positions for words of one to 100 bits, see E. J. Watson, "Primitive Polynomials (Mod 2)," *Mathematics of Computation*, v.16, 1962, pp. 368–369.

The table given here shows the tap positions 8-, 16-, 31-, 32-, and 64-bit words. That should work with any computer hardware that you have. The 31-bit word is the one that is probably the most useful since it gives billions of numbers, uses only two tap positions to make the math easier, and matches most computer hardware. The 32-bit version is not easy to implement on a 32-bit machine because it will usually generate an overflow error.

Word Length
8 = {0, 2, 3, 4}
16 = {0, 2, 3, 5}
31 = {0, 3}
32 = {0, 1, 2, 3, 5, 7}
64 = {0 1, 3, 4}

Using this table, we can see that we need to tap bits 0 and 3 to construct the 31-bit random-order generated value generator (which is the one that most people would want to use in practice):

```
UPDATE Generator31
   SET keyval =
        keyval/2 + MOD(MOD(keyval,
            2) + MOD(keyval/8, 2), 2)*2^30;
```

Or if you prefer the algorithm in C:

```
int Generator31 ()
{static int n = 1;
 n = n >> 1 | ((n^n >> 3) & 1) << 30;
 return n;
}
```

43

Traditional and Metric Typographic Units

Typography has been around longer than the SI system. Printers in various countries invented many different measurement systems and a lot of them are still around. But they are mixed with computerized units as most typesetting is now computerized.

Truchet is an old French system that has not been used for centuries.

Didot is the name of a family of French printers, punch-cutters (punches are the hard metal tools used to make molds for metal type), and publishers. Their products became the basis for the measurement system used in Europe for centuries. This was based on the old French royal inch.

ATA is used in the United States and the United Kingdom, and is sometimes called the Anglo-Saxon point system. This what American type foundries have used.

l'Imprimerie Nationale (IN) is the national printing office for France. It succeeded the government office of "King's Printer for the Greek" created by François in 1538 to propagate the Belles-Lettres, the Royal Printing Office that founded in 1640 by Cardinal Richelieu under Louis XIII. After the French Revolution, it became the National Printing Office.

TeX and Postscript scales are a result of computerization of typography. Their sizes are based on computer displays. I will not go into the details of each of them.

Type sizes had traditional names such as Cicero, Pica, Ruby, Primer, Long Primer, and so on, which made things even more confusing to people outside the trade. If you want to get an idea of what this was like, get a copy of *The Colonial Printer* by Lawrence C. Wroth (http://store.doverpublications. com/0486282945.html).

The term "point" is the smallest basic unit of type height, but it has not been very exact:

- 1 point (Truchet) = 0.188 mm (obsolete today)
- 1 point (Didot) = 0.376 mm = 1/72 of a French royal inch (27.07 mm)
- 1 point (ATA) = 0.3514598 mm = 0.013837 inch
- 1 point (TeX) = 0.3514598035 mm = 1/72.27 inch
- 1 point (Postscript) = 0.3527777778 mm = 1/72 inch
- 1 point (IN) = 0.4 mm;
- 1 pica (ATA) = 4.2175176 mm = 12 points (ATA)
- 1 pica (TeX) = 4.217517642 mm = 12 points (TeX)
- 1 pica (Postscript) = 4.233333333 mm = 12 points (Postscript)
- 1 cicero = 4.531 mm = 12 points (Didot)

The printing and publishing software is dominated by American manufacturers (Apple, Adobe, Microsoft, Quark, etc.), which tends to handicap SI adoption.

The dominant unit of length today is the PostScript point (also called DTP-point system from DTP: Desktop Publishing), has with 25.4/72 = 0.352777... mm, which is very inconvenient relationship to the millimeter. Denoting a font size is therefore a problem. Consider the convention of an "em" in PostScript points. Historically, the "em" was the width of the widest metal type in a font, usually the uppercase letter "M". Today, the control points of digital font outlines are stored in terms of coordinates inside a unit square. This square is a vague equivalent of the maximum metal type size defined by the type mold and its side length has become the modern incarnation of the "em". As a result, no easily measurable dimension in a text matches the point length that designates a font size.

But the U.S. dominance in display hardware means that screens are still frequently specified in dpi (dots per inch), which equals the reciprocal of the pixel size multiplied by 25.4 mm.

Metric typographic units are already used in Japan and to some degree in Germany and other European countries. Japanese typesetters use the unit Q (quarter) for font sizes, where 1 Q = 0.25 mm, that is, the same modulus recommended by DIN 16507-2.

This measure coincides nicely with the most common pixel size on computer monitors. For example, a typical CRT screen has a display area of 320×240 mm, divided into 1280×1024 pixels, which makes each pixel 0.25 mm.

43.1. DIN 16507-2 FONT SIZES

This draft standard defines the following two font measures:

1. Font Size

    This is the baseline distance for which the font was designed. A font should normally be identified and selected by this size, because the intended base-line distance is much more relevant for practical layout work than the actual dimensions of certain characters.

2. Font height

    This is the height in millimeters of letters such as "k" or "H". In Latin and related alphabets, a let-ter has an "x-height" (height of letters such as "x" and others that sit on the base line upon which the type is set), ascenders (the parts of the letter that go above the x-height), and descanters (the part of the letters that go below the base line such as "g" or "y"). Kerning is the spacing between letters on a line; leading is the space between base lines. There are more terms such as mortising, rivers, tracking, and so forth that we will ignore. The traditional terms are based on metal type and how you had to physically shape them to print on a physical page. A mortise is cutting two pieces of metal type to fit closer together. A kern is a piece of metal type that has an extension that overlaps the piece of metal next to it. This is usually done in display type—usually for advertisements and display typography.

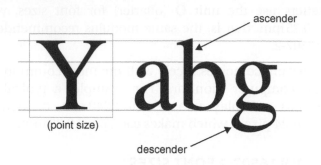

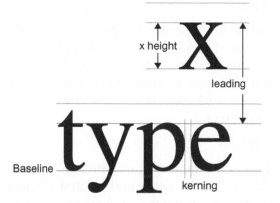

If we write "Helvetica 5.0," then this means tjatwe have a font that was designed for 5-mm line spacing. It will typically have an "H" that is 3.6 mm or 10.2 points tall (72% of 5 mm). Calculations become trivial: in a 60-mm high column, we can write exactly 60/5 mm = 12 lines. The baselines of text could be aligned with a millimeter grid.

DIN 16507-2 contains a list of preferred metric font sizes, together with the corresponding preferred 72% font heights in millimeters.

Overview of the Typographic Measurement				
Points	**Font-name (dimension)**	**mm (Didot)**	**mm (DTP)**	**Font line in Didot points**
1	Eighth Petit	0.376	0.353	
2	Quarter Petit	0.752	0.706	
2 ½	Microscopic	0.940	0.882	
3	Brilliant	1.128	1.058	
4	Diamond	1.504	1.411	less than 0.9
5	Pearl	1.880	1.764	less than 0.9
6	Nonpareil	2.256	2.117	less than 1.4
6 ½	Insertio	2.444	2.293	
7	Mignon Colonel Rough	2.632	2.469	less than 1.9 less than 1.4
8	Petit	3.008	2.822	less than 1.9
9	Bourgeois Rough Borgis	3.384	3.175	less than 2.4 less than 1.9
10	Corpus, Garmond	3.760	3.528	less than 2.4

The font size refers to the baseline distance for which the font was designed and is used to generally identify the font. The font height is the actual height of characters such as H or k. The font height is typically 72% of the font size as a preferred value, but this is of course depends on the font design.

Basing the font sizes on the x-height has advantages:

1. The x-height can easily be measured directly in a sample printout and is not an invisible dimension found only in font data. Whether two fonts appear to have the same height is primarily determined by whether their x-heights match.

2. The concept of x-height is also present in Greek and Cyrillic typography. Hebrew, Arabic, and Devanagari glyphs that do not have ascenders and descenders can be aligned quite nicely with a Roman x-height, too.

One idea floated in the international typographical community is to define a series of preferred font sizes. Unlike the values given in DIN 16507-2, this could be a geometric series in which the quotient of neighboring font sizes are based on the square root of two, so as to match the A-series paper sizes.

Instead of using pixel size in dpi, it would be much more convenient to use micrometers, as it is done in the semiconductor industry. So far, phototypesetters have traditionally used metric resolutions (with 10 micrometer = 2540 dpi being most common one), while laser and inkjet office printers currently still mostly have inch-based resolutions.

The DIN standards on metric typography are available only in German (use the Google translate option if you do not read German). ISO/TC130 will eventually set up a very similar international guideline for the use of metric font sizes.

Index

Note: Figures are indicated with an f.

Printed and bound by CPI Group (UK) Ltd, Croydon, CR0 4YY

03/10/2024

01040319-0008